PADDY THE NEXT BEST THII

BY

GERTRUDE PAGE

Chapter One.

Concerning Paddy's Blouse.

Paddy Adair, the "next-best-thing," as she was fond of calling herself, and the reason for which will appear hereafter, sat at the table, and spread all around her were little square books of "patterns for blouses," from which she was vainly endeavouring to make a selection. Meanwhile she kept up a running conversation with the only other occupant of the room, a girl with dreamy eyes of true Irish blue, who sat in the window, motionless, gazing across the Loch at the distant mountains. She heard no word of all her sister was saying, but that did not appear to trouble Paddy in the least, so doubtless it was not an unusual state of affairs.

"This one with green spots and pink roses would look the best with my blue skirt," Paddy said, holding one pattern at arm's length and surveying it critically, "but the blue one with the white border would look better with my grey. I wonder which you would choose, Eily? I wonder which would be the most becoming to my peculiar style of beauty, or," with a twinkle in her eyes, "I should say the most concealing to my unique lack of it. I think I'll risk the green spots and pink roses, because it doesn't really look half bad with the grey.

"Oh, but my hat!" with a comical exclamation of dismay, "there's my silly old hat has got pansies in it, and they'd look just awful with the green and pink, Eileen! What *am* I to do, with all my things different colours, that don't seem any of them to go together? I wonder if I'd better bring out my whole wardrobe and go through the hundred and one patterns again? Or shall I have a white-bordered thing, that is not particular and will go with just all of them? Only I'd have to start at the beginning to find it, and I'm so sick of the very sight of them. Here have I had these patterns three days, and I've already spent about five pounds' worth of brain-power upon a blouse that will cost five shillings. If only you'd help, Eileen!" looking up toward the figure in the window, "instead of staring at those silly old mountains like a stuffed goose!

"Eileen!"—as the dreamer took no notice—"Eileen! do you hear that I'm floundering in a sea of patterns! Your one and only sister, and you sit there like an Egyptian mummy stuffed with dried peas!

"I'll make you help—so there,"—and with a sudden movement she swept all the books of patterns into her arms and deposited them, helter-skelter, upon her sister's head, laughing gayly at the picture of solemn-faced Eileen with the little square books scattered all around and upon her.

"Now, Miss Sphinx," she said, "do you think you could come down from the clouds for five minutes and discuss anything so distressingly earthy as clothes?"

Eileen's face broke into a very sweet smile. She had not in the least intended to be indifferent, but long before Paddy commenced consulting her she had been in the middle of composing a lovely poem about mountains and streams and birds and things, and she had not really heard any of her remarks at all.

"What's the matter, Paddy?" she asked, eyeing the scattered patterns with amusement.

"Matter!" cried Paddy, "everything's the matter! How on earth am I to select a blouse that will go with a blue dress, a green dress, a grey dress, a hat with pansies in, and a scarlet tam-o'-shanter! I've been worrying with those stupid patterns for days, and instead of getting any nearer a decision, I keep on thinking of something fresh that nothing seems to go with. Now it's your turn to worry; you ought to, you know, because Charity begins at home."

"Why not have something in cream?" suggested Eileen; "it saves a lot of bother."

"Yes, and what do I look like in cream, with my sallow skin? It's all very well for you with your ivory and roses, you look well in anything. I don't think it was at all fair for you to have everything nice while I am burdened for life with a sallow skin and a snub nose. Cream flannel would be nearly as bad as brown holland for me, and when I wear brown holland you can't tell where the dress ends and I begin," and the corners of Paddy's mischievous mouth were momentarily drawn down in great disgust.

"You could wear bright-coloured ties," suggested Eileen, "and have one of every colour you wanted."

"Why so I could," brightening up, "and provided I don't always lose the colour I want at the moment of requiring it, it will save a lot of bother."

"But you always will, you know," said a gay masculine voice; "you'll keep every one waiting five minutes longer than usual hunting for the required colour, and then turn up in a red tie with a green hat," and before either of them could speak, Jack O'Hara, from the Parsonage, was coming through the window, head first, trailing his long legs after him. "I've just had a little practice at this sort of thing," he ran on. "I came from Newry, with the Burtons, a whole carriage full of them, and we had a great time. The train was just going to start when I arrived, and the station master had locked their compartment, and when I asked him to let me in, he tried to put me into a smoker next door. I said, 'No, thanks, not for Jack this journey.' He murmured something about the Burton's carriage being full up, and I couldn't go in it, so I said, 'You see if I can't,' and took a header through the window, right on to their laps."

"But you don't know them!" exclaimed Paddy, whose face at the same time expressed the greatest relish at the episode.

"I've been introduced," was the calm reply. "Fletcher introduced me in Hill Street a week ago."

"Whatever did they think of you?" asked Eileen, unable to resist smiling.

"Oh, we had a ripping time. They're awfully jolly girls, and they had that little imp Basil with them. He amused himself trying to throw everything he could get at out of the window as we went along. But touching this blouse," with a sudden change of voice, "why don't you ask my advice? You haven't either of you a grain of taste compared to mine."

"Yours!" exclaimed Paddy scornfully, "and there you sit with emerald green in your stockings, a yellow waistcoat, and a terra cotta tie."

"What's the matter with my stockings?" surveying his fine pair of legs with an air of pride. "That's the O'Hara tartan; I'm very proud of it. You're not supposed to look at me all at once. You should enjoy the stockings first, and then gradually work up to the waistcoat, and afterward to the tie."

"Get thoroughly seasoned and strengthened before reaching the face, I suppose you mean!" said Paddy, for which a well-aimed cushion brought her rippling red-brown hair half-way down her back.

Not that Jack had any occasion to feel insulted, because after twenty-four years' acquaintance with a looking glass, it was hardly likely he could be totally oblivious to the fact that Nature had been almost prodigal to him in her good gifts. One might go far to find a more sunny pair of blue eyes, a brighter smile, or a more handsome specimen of manhood generally. And to this was added a rare fineness of disposition, so full of sincerity and sweetness, that there was no room for anything small at all, not even the personal vanity that one would have felt obliged to forgive him. But, then, as a matter of fact, every one forgave Jack anything, and there was scarcely a house within a radius of twelve miles where he did not come in and out just as he pleased, finding an unfailing welcome when he entered, and leaving the same regret when he left. Yet he did things that would not have been suffered, by one in a thousand, in anyone else. He shot over every one's moors and covers uninvited, he fished every one's stream, he sailed every one's yacht, and rode most people's horses. He was, in fact, an arrant poacher, and yet neither gamekeeper nor owner could withstand his witty sallies, nor the laughter in his blue eyes when he was caught, and the young sinner himself used to say that though he was a poor clergyman's son with scarcely a penny to his name, he had some of the finest shooting and fishing in Ireland, and lived a life a prince might envy. Of course he ought to have been worrying about his future, and what would eventually become of him, but he was far too thoroughly Irish to do anything so foolish. "What's the use of worrying yet!" he would say. "Can't a fellow have a good time in peace, while he has the chance! I'll start worrying presently—if I don't forget"; then he would probably give his last sixpence to a beggar, and immediately afterward go into a shop to buy something for Aunt Jane that he thought would please her; and when he discovered, with surprise, that he was unable to pay for it, he would get the shopkeeper to put it down to his father and promise to call in another day with the money. But that would generally be the very last he would remember of it, and two or three months later the Rev. Patrick O'Hara would wonder when and why he had bought that copy of "The Eternal City," or that work-basket with red lining. It was no use asking Jack, because he had always forgotten; and though he would immediately empty his pockets into his father's lap, so to speak, there was never enough in them to make it worth while. It was quite the exception for Jack ever to remember anything. If he rowed across to Warrenpoint to buy the sausages for Sunday's breakfast, he would be quite as likely as not to return without them; and if he took a note, it was a hundred to one it came back in his pocket unopened, and remained there several days.

"Now I wonder what I came across for, Pat!" was a usual remark to the old boatman, when on the point of rowing himself back again.

"Faith! Ye've a head like a sieve, Mr Jack," Pat would reply. "Was it they sausages agen? or maybe something at the grocers? or some shoe laces for 'is riverence?"

"I don't know, I'm sure, Pat, but I'll just have to go and ask what I've forgotten. Begorra! if I'd no head at all to put these things into, they couldn't slip out again, could they! and then I shouldn't vex Aunt Jane's soul with my forgetfulness. If it was sausages, Pat, I'll fire my gun three times off the landing-stage, and you must just go up to the butcher yourself and bring them across;" with which he would whistle a merry tune and row leisurely back across the Loch. But long before he reached the other side, he would again have forgotten, and instead of going at once to the Parsonage, he would stroll into the garden of The Ghan House, which adjoined, to see if Paddy were available for the afternoon, or if by chance Eileen wandered dreamily under the trees gazing at the mountains.

One of the great problems of Jack's existence at that time, indeed, the only one that he ever took seriously, was whether he liked Paddy or Eileen the best. Ever since he was two years old, the Adairs had lived in The Ghan House, next door to the Parsonage, and he always declared he had distinct recollections of a long white bolster-like apparition in a nurse's arms, from the first day it appeared in the garden. He could just get about sufficiently well alone, then, to be always in mischief, and at his first opportunity, when the two nurses were deeply engaged in conversation, he got hold of the long clothes and tugged with all his might and main, to pull the baby on to the ground, a feat which he very nearly achieved. That was Eileen, and just as she had looked at him with big, calm, thoughtful eyes, then, not in the least disturbed by his vigorous attempts to unseat her, so she looked at him now in the first bloom of her beauty, quelling his over-exuberance of spirit, calming his boyish audacity, and making him sometimes feel as if he wanted to lie down and let her walk over him. But then on the other hand Paddy was such good fun! When the second bolster-like apparition appeared, he was four, and being somewhat weary of the solemn two-year-old Eileen he took rapidly to the ugly little brown-faced baby, whose eyes already began to dance with a suggestion of the mischievous tendency which only developed steadily year by year and claimed them kindred spirits from their earliest infancy. What the nurses at The Ghan House and the Parsonage suffered over those two imps of wickedness would fill a whole book; and why they were not drowned over and over again, or killed falling from trees, or run over on the railway that skirted the grounds, or suffocated in mountain bogs, remains forever one of the mysteries of their existence. And things were much the same still, though the nurses were no more and they had reached the mature ages of twenty-four and twenty, respectively. Where Jack went Paddy went, or very usually followed; and there was scarcely an act of daring even their busy brains could conceive, that they two had not achieved together—much to General Adair's delight and Mrs Adair's disquiet, for she felt that if her scapegrace daughter were ever to grow up at all she really ought to begin at once; and yet was quite at a loss by what procedure the change should commence. Boarding school had been tried, but there the girl had drooped and pined to such an extent that when the General went one day to see her, he had been so shocked and upset that he had had her trunk packed at once, and taken her straight back to Ireland without telling her mother anything about it, until they walked into the hall of The Ghan House.

"I can't help it," was all he had said, in reply to maternal remonstrances. "She wasn't meant for boarding school life. I expect when the Lord made her, He fashioned her for running wild by the mountains and Loch, and well just have to let her grow up in her own way." And an hour later he laughed till he nearly made himself ill over the spectacle of a small boat upside down in the bay, with Paddy clinging to it, while a coal barge waited alongside to pick her up and presently landed her close by the General's landing-stage, a mass of mud and water and coal dust.

"Better not let your mother see you," he managed to gasp. "Faith! I've wanted a boy all my life, but there's no doubt I've got the very next best thing." Then he went off to the Parsonage to tell Miss Jane and Miss Mary O'Hara, while Paddy slipped in the back way and was smuggled up to the bathroom by a faithful old housekeeper who worshipped any flesh and blood related to the General, whom she had known ever since he joined the Dublin Fusiliers, and embarked on the career that made his old regiment as proud and as fond of him, as he, to his last gasp, was of them.

But to return to the vexed question of the blouse, the three young people, having settled the difficulty concerning each other's taste to their satisfaction, though in a somewhat unflattering fashion, Jack and Paddy sat on the table swinging their feet and discussed the delicate question of what would best suit the latter's complexion.

Then suddenly Jack looked up with an innocent expression. "What's the good of wasting all this time about a body's complexion when they haven't got one!" he said.

"How dare you! I've a beautiful olive tinge!"

"Olive!" teasingly; "why you look as if you'd washed your face with my brown boot polish! It must be rather awful to be so ugly that you look much the same in anything," he finished.

"Oh, you scoundrel!—you long-legged kangaroo!—you big-footed elephant!—you—you—" and failing words altogether to express her feelings, Paddy commenced belabouring him over the head with a small sofa bolster, calling out to Eileen to "be a man and come and help her."

"No, no," gasped Jack, struggling to protect himself, "remain a woman, Eileen, and be ready to bandage my wounds when this vixen has worn herself out. Who would have dreamt I was letting myself in for this! Why I thought she knew she was ugly, it didn't seem possible she could help knowing it!—I—I—" but just then the door opened and in the midst of the racket Miss Jane and Miss Mary O'Hara stepped daintily into the room.

Chapter Two.

The Misses O'Hara.

In all the neighbourhood of the Mourne Mountains there was probably neither priest, nor peasant, nor layman so generally known and respected as the Rev. Patrick O'Hara's two maiden sisters. Miss Jane and Miss Mary they were known as generally, but among the young men and girls whom they loved, they were Aunt Jane and Aunt Mary always, and they were familiar figures at every gathering and every party for miles round! If anyone was in trouble, they went over to the Parsonage at Omeath as soon as they could; and if they could not manage this, it was practically a certainty that the two little ladies would very shortly look in upon them. The oldest inhabitants remembered them as two little girls, when their father was at the Parsonage before their brother; and later, as two very pretty, very charming young women, but why they were still at the Parsonage, and still the Misses O'Hara, was the one thing nobody did know. Certainly, they had been very much admired, and there had been some talk about Miss Mary and young Captain Quinn, of Omeath Park, but nothing had apparently come of it, for the Captain went away on active service, and came no more to Omeath. Several months after he left, both the sisters had gone abroad, and been away a year, but no one knew where they went to, and they never offered any enlightenment on the point. When they came back, however, they were very changed in many ways. Gaiety, which had been spontaneous before, seemed to have become an effort to both of them, and for some little time neither appeared to care to accept the invitations showered upon them as usual. Later on something of their old brightness came back, and they were once more the familiar figures everywhere that they had previously been. But though their joyousness came back, there was still an indefinable change and the suggestion of something hidden which none could solve, and to every one's surprise each "would-be" suitor was sent resolutely away. Finally, it became evident that the Misses O'Hara meant to remain the Misses O'Hara to their dying day, and live at the Parsonage as long as it was possible—the dearest little pair of old maids that ever gave their fellow-creatures cause to bless the Guiding Hand, that gave some women to one home and one family, and reserved others to belong to every one about them.

"My dear," they said to any of the myriad nieces who plied them with wondering questions why they had never married, and whether it was that they did not believe in matrimonial happiness, "there is no happiness in the world quite like that of a happy wife and mother, but it is not given to everyone to know it, and many come to a crossway in life, where they know they must mould their future without any hope of it. But for such, the Good Father has another happiness waiting, if they will take it and trust Him, and not repine because they might not choose. It is the happiness of a life filled with serving, and rich in the love of one's fellow-creatures of every sex and age and station. Our lives are filled to overflowing with, this happiness, and we are content to believe that what is lost to a woman in this life will be made up to her an hundredfold in some other life beyond."

"And then there is Jack!" one of them would add softly, and the other would reply with like softness, "Yes, sister, there is Jack."

By which one can easily gather, how, when the poor little baby at the Parsonage was left motherless at ten months old, he at once became the fortunate possessor of two new mothers, who would have gone through fire and water rather than let a hair of his sunny curls be hurt.

"We must not spoil him, sister," Jane, the elder, had said once, as they stood gazing rapturously at their new treasure.

"No, sister," Mary had replied, "it is only unkind mothers who spoil children, and so unfit them for the rough usage of the world and rob them of many a good friend they might afterward have won."

"That is exactly my view, sister; we will endeavour to act up to it, and yet make him as happy as the day is long."

Nevertheless, a more spoilt boy than little Jack O'Hara it would have been difficult to find, and, if Nature had not blessed him particularly with a nature proof against spoiling, he would probably have grown up the reverse of the adored young scamp he was. But then, possibly, it was just this that caused his aunts to swerve so widely from their fixed principle, for it would have required a heart of cast-iron to withstand such a boy as he. All his naughtiness was pure love of mischief, and he was always so genuinely sorry and penitent afterward, and so forlornly unhappy when he was in disgrace, that he made every one else in the house feel miserable until he was forgiven. No sooner was he undergoing a term of punishment than Aunt Mary would ask Aunt Jane to forgive him this once, or the cook would "make so bold" as to plead with Miss Jane, or the gardener would "mention it respectfully to 'is riverence."

"I think, perhaps, we might let him off just this time," one of the aunts would say, anxiously looking at her sister, and the other would reply gravely, "Yes, just this time, perhaps, but we must not do it again."

And if there happened to be anything he particularly wanted, much the same proceeding ensued.

"I'm afraid we mustn't let him have it sister!" Miss Mary would say wistfully. "We mustn't spoil him, must we?"

"No, sister, we mustn't spoil him," would be the reply with like wistfulness.

"Or, do you think, perhaps, just this once, sister?" half timidly.

"Well, perhaps, just this once," with a show of reluctance, "only it mustn't happen again, must it?"

"No, certainly not, sister, another time we will be firm for his good."

And so it went on for twenty-four years, and always "another time" was reserved for firmness on Jack's account, until "life" took the matter into her own hands, and threw an obstacle across his easy, flower-strewn path, that even his devoted aunts could not smooth away for him, and over which he must needs prove himself a man and fight his own battle. But of that anon.

"My dears, we have had some news!" began Miss Jane, "and we think you will be pleased, so we came across at once to tell you."

"Yes," murmured Miss Mary, nodding her small head gravely while her sister spoke, to show that the sentiment was equally hers, "we thought you would be pleased."

By this time, Jack and Paddy were again seated on the table, swinging their feet, in front of the two little ladies who sat side by side on the sofa looking rather like two little Dutch dolls. Eileen had returned to her window seat, where she could keep one eye and one half of her mind on the mountains, and the other eye and the other half for more mundane reflections.

"News!" exclaimed Paddy, clasping her hands ecstatically. "Oh! scrumptious; I just love news!" while Eileen and Jack looked up expectantly.

"We have heard from Mrs Blake this morning, and they are coming back to Mourne Lodge," continued Miss Jane, while Miss Mary, looking very pleased, murmured "Yes, coming back."

"Hurray!" cried Paddy, "Hurray! Hurray! Just think of the dances and picnics and things. Why don't you say you're glad, Jack—or do something to show it?"—and before he quite realised it, she had caught him by his coat and pulled him half round the room. Roused instantly, Jack proceeded to pick her up and deposit her in the corner behind the sofa, amid frantic struggles on his victim's part and a general flutter of the two little ladies to protect anything breakable in their vicinity. This, indeed, they did, partly from force of habit, for it was a standing joke in their circle that whenever Paddy and Jack were in the room together, Miss Jane kept her eye on one half of the room and Miss Mary on the other, and at the first symptoms of one of their customary "rough and tumbles," one little lady fluttered off collecting breakables from one side and standing guard over them, while the other little lady did likewise on the other side.

"It's all right!" said Jack, seeing their alert attitude, "I was only teaching her not to take liberties with my coat. Did you ever see such a scarecrow?" looking with delighted relish at Paddy's generally dishevelled appearance as she emerged from her corner. "You'd think she ought to make a fortune with a face like that as an artist's model for a comic paper, wouldn't you?"

"My dear, he's very rude," said little Miss Mary, patting the dishevelled one's hand.

"Yes, aunt, but he can't help it, and we have to be kind to people's failings, haven't we? It is something to be thankful for that you have been able to keep him out of an asylum so long, isn't it?" and then she ducked hastily to escape a shower of missiles, and the two little ladies flew off once more to the breakables.

Order being again restored, however, the news was further discussed, and the three young people learnt with varying degrees of eagerness that Mrs Blake intended both her girls to "come out" the next winter, and that Lawrence Blake, the only son, was going to remain at home for a time. This last piece of information contained in a measure the gist of the whole for the young people, but they each received it differently. Eileen turned her head, and with a slight flush in her cheeks gazed steadily across the Loch. Jack looked as near being annoyed as he felt at all warrantable, or as his insistently sunny face would permit, and Paddy, screwing an imaginary eyeglass into her eye, remarked in a drawl, "Remarkable! really remarkable! You are a credit to your charming sex."

"In whatever capacity was that?" asked Jack, as if he marvelled.

"Never mind," retorted Paddy; "because you have not the discernment to know a good thing when you see it, you need not suppose every one else is similarly afflicted. How delightful it will be to have a *man* among us again. One gets so tired of boys!"

"You don't mean to say you're going to uphold Lawrence Blake!" he exclaimed, apparently too disgusted to parry her thrust.

"Why not?" stoutly. "I'm sure he's a most superior young man."

"A pity he's such a conceited ass, then," muttered Jack, at which the two little ladies looked pained, and while one said gently, "My dear Jack, you must remember he is always extremely nice to us," the other echoed with like gentleness, "Yes, Jack, dear, remember he is always nice to us."

"Then I'll say he's a thundering good chap," was the ready response; "though that man or woman living could be other than nice to you passes my comprehension."

"Of course they couldn't," put in Paddy; "why I want to hug both of you every ten minutes whenever I am with you.

"Fancy if every one else did!" she ran on, "and our feelings got the better of us! How should you like it, aunties, if every one wanted to keep hugging you every time they saw you, and couldn't help themselves! You would never dare to wear your best bonnets at all, should you?—and I expect your caps would be everywhere but on your heads, or else would have a perpetually rakish tilt."

The two little ladies smiled without the least resentment, for they had long known that the varying angle of their caps was a source of great amusement to their large army of nephews and nieces, who stoutly maintained that when Aunt Jane's cap slipped awry, Aunt Mary's quickly did the same of its own accord, and *vice versa*, and therefore, it was more often the cap's fault than the owner's.

Jack, however, stood up promptly, and pulling himself to his full height, said, with a whimsical recollection of childhood, "Shall I be a man, aunties, and spank her?" This highly amused both little ladies, as it reminded them of a little mischievous girl who had pushed over her sister on purpose, and a sturdy, blue-eyed boy, who had promptly asked with a fiery resoluteness of purpose, "Shall I be a man, aunties, and spank her?" It was memorable also how disappointed he had been when told that "being a man" never meant spanking little girls at all, even when they were mischievous.

He would, doubtless, not have waited for any verdict on the present occasion, only just then the hearty old General entered the room, and Paddy, the father's darling, flew to him for protection. A general chattering and laughing ensued, and, presently seeing her opportunity, Eileen rose from her seat in the window, and with a curious subdued glow in her wonderful eyes glided silently from the room.

A few minutes later she was pulsing up the mountain with a free, eager step that not only proclaimed her an experienced climber, but bespoke a deep delight in thus climbing to the upland solitudes alone.

"I say, daddy," Paddy was saying, "isn't it ripping, we're going to have a man-about-town here! The real, genuine thing, you know, eyeglass and all, and as *blasé* as they're made. Won't Jack look like a countrified Irish lout with bats in his belfry!"

The General said afterward, it was nearly as good as a bit of Tipperary's extra-special, best Orangemen night.

Chapter Three.

Eileen the Dreamer.

There was one spot on the mountains near The Ghan House where, if you climbed high enough and were not afraid of an almost perpendicular path, you could get a glorious view, not only of the Loch and mountains, but of a wide stretch of sparkling silver, or dreaming turquoise, which was the sea.

It was here that Eileen Adair loved to sit and dream dreams and weave romances, such as only the true Celt knows how. What she put into them was known to none, and, indeed, probably never could be known, for they possessed that unfathomable, mysterious, yearning quality which is so present in Celtic blood, and were of those hidden thoughts and things which defy words to express them. Not that Eileen ever wanted to express them. She had not as yet met a kindred soul whom she felt could in any wise understand, and meanwhile, having the mountains, and the lake, and the sea, for companions, it did not seem that she needed a listener. She could talk to these in a rapturous silence as she could talk to no other, and feel that her spirit was one with their spirit, and that what men call "solitude" is in reality a wealth of deep companionship for those who have eyes to see and ears to hear. There was a good deal of the pagan about Eileen, for, though she always went to church, and tried to be earnest and attentive, it seemed so much easier to her to worship out in the open air among the upland solitudes of the mountain. And so real and intense to her in these solitudes was the consciousness of an All-pervading God-presence, that fear of any kind was impossible, and she was less lonely than under any other conditions.

It was doubtless these solitary climbs and silent musings, when she either thought deep, mysterious thoughts, or sitting motionless, absorbed into all her being the spirit of beauty around, that had deepened in her face year by year its dream-like loveliness. Eileen was rarely gay, but her smile was indescribably beautiful and impressed everyone who saw it. Paddy was her father's darling, and had been, in spite of his disappointment, ever since he learned that his second child was another girl and not the fondly longed-for boy. With a sense of vain regret he had looked dubiously at the small bundle with the cause of his regret somewhere inside it, and retired without further inspection. A few days later he got a full and uninterrupted view of an ugly little brown face, with a pair of particularly bright eyes, and a suggestion of roguishness that was entirely alluring. "Bedad!" he said, looking back into the bright eyes, "I badly wanted a boy, but you look as if you'd be the next best thing." And that was how Paddy got her self-chosen nickname.

The General was, however, very proud of Eileen, though half-unconsciously a little afraid of her. But what she missed in her father Eileen found amply in her mother, whose only fear was that she might worship this sweet-eyed, fair-faced daughter too much. Mrs Adair was a woman with whom few ever felt quite at home. Distinguished in bearing, and still with the remains of considerable beauty, she was in general an object of awe to her acquaintances. Those who once got to know her and were admitted into her friendship ever after loved her dearly—but these were few and far between. Foremost among them were the little ladies at the Parsonage, who had been waiting at The Ghan House to welcome their old friend's bride the day he brought her home from India. She had been just the same white-faced, reserved woman then, and for a little while they had been non-plussed; but one day a letter from India had told them her story, and soon afterward the three women had cemented a lifelong friendship in tears of common sympathy.

"I hear General Adair has married Miss Brindley and is taking her to your neighbourhood," the letter had run. "She was governess with a friend of ours in India, and we know her well and are very fond of her. Do all you can for her; she has had a very sad life, and lately, on the top of all the rest, saw her love killed before her eyes guarding her from a band of Afghans on the frontier. He was a cousin of General Adair's, and they were very devoted to each other, and the latter nearly lost his life also going to their assistance. Afterward he fell in love with Miss Brindley himself, and we helped to persuade her to marry him, because she was so friendless, and poor, and broken-hearted."

This, then, surely had something to do with the wistful expression in the little sad-eyed Eileen's face, and in later years so deeply entwined her round her mother's heart. Only Mrs Adair rarely showed it, for she was eminently a just woman, and in the peaceful waters of her after-life she put her sad past resolutely aside, and tried to live only for the husband who was so good to her, and for her harum-scarum tom-boy daughter, as much as for the child who would always possess the largest share of her heart.

But Eileen's eyes were not sad when she hurried up the mountain on the day the Misses O'Hara called with their piece of news. She carried a small packet of sandwiches and a flask which the cook had hastily prepared for her, and revelled inwardly at the prospect of at least five hours all to herself. She knew they would not be anxious at home, for both she and Paddy often took their lunch with them and vanished for a day, though it must be confessed nothing in the world would ever have induced the latter to waste an afternoon, as she would put it, mooning about on the mountains alone. No, Paddy would be off in the yacht, fishing or sailing, with or without Jack, or she would be away to Newry for tennis, or to Greenore for golf, or to Warrenpoint to see her great friend, Kitty Irvine, and listen to the Pierrots on the front; and in any case no one would dream of worrying about her, for had she not possessed a charmed life she must surely have ended her short career in some sudden fashion long ago.

But to-day it was not the five hours only that lit that glow in Eileen's eyes. It was something quite different—quite apart, indeed, from the whole tenor of her life, except for a few short months three years ago.

That was the summer when Lawrence Blake, instead of going off to foreign climes as usual, remained at his home, Mourne Lodge, a beautiful place in the mountains about two miles from The Ghan House. He kept his yacht that summer moored by the General's landing-stage, so each time he went out in it he passed through the grounds of The Ghan House, and one of his sisters usually ran in to fetch Paddy or Eileen if they chanced to be at home. Paddy, as it happened, much preferred the greater excitement, not to say danger, of taking her pleasures with Jack O'Hara, so it usually chanced that Eileen went in the Blakes' boat. In the middle of September Kathleen and Doreen Blake had to go back to Paris, where they were still finishing their educations, but somehow it had seemed perfectly natural for Lawrence still to go down to his yacht and for Eileen to keep him company. On the first occasion Jack and Paddy went with them, but an indefinable, strained feeling, owing doubtless to Jack's antipathy to the wealthy, polished University man, had caused the lively pair to come to the conclusion that it was too tame a proceeding altogether, and they could better amuse themselves elsewhere. In this decision Lawrence and Eileen were secretly glad to acquiesce, for there was never any peace for anybody when Paddy was on board. She would not sit still herself, nor let anybody else if she could help it, and was altogether a most dangerous young person to take on a small sailing yacht.

So sweet September glided into a sunny, warm October, and still Lawrence went through the grounds to the bay and Eileen met him at the water's edge.

To him she was a beautiful girl with poetical ideas, which he found rather amusing.

To her he was a revelation.

In all her nineteen years Eileen had never met any one so cultured as Lawrence Blake, except Jack's father, and he, since his wife's death, had grown so reserved and retiring that no one was able ever to bring him out of himself. There seemed to be nothing that Lawrence did not know and had not studied, and so eager was she to learn from him that she was blind altogether to the defects which made him an object of aversion to honest, outspoken Jack. It must be confessed, however, that Lawrence, when he liked, could be as charming a companion as any one need wish, and if it so pleased him, and he were not too lackadaisical, could make his way into almost any one's heart. It was generally said of him that he had the most disarming smile in the world, and from wearing a cynical, morose expression, could change in an instant to a polished courtier if he so wished, and turn an enemy into an ally after half an hour's conversation.

And it pleased him during that sunny October to stand well with Eileen. He liked her. She was not only beautiful to look at, but interesting to talk to, and a delightful listener, and for the rest— well, what harm in it?

So it chanced in the end that a certain subdued love-light drove much of the usual wistfulness from Eileen's eyes, and when unoccupied she would steal oftener to the mountains or sit longer in the starlight on her favourite seat by the Loch. Her mother watched her a little anxiously, but feared to do harm by speaking. Paddy treated it all as a great joke, and Jack, without in the least knowing why, felt a quite unaccountable longing to duck Lawrence in the bay whenever he heard him mentioned. Then suddenly Mr Blake died, and everything was changed. Lawrence, being very fond of his mother, rarely left her in her terrible grief. Finally, by the doctor's advice, he took her abroad, and the beautiful, hospitable house was closed, to the loss of the whole neighbourhood. That was three years ago, and now they were coming back once more, and it seemed likely that the old *régime* would recommence.

To Eileen it was simply "he" was coming back.

She told the birds about it as she hastened up to her beloved nook, and the little trickling streams, and the flowers, and the mountains that towered all round.

She was so sure he was coming back to her. Had he not lived in her thoughts and been the central figure of her dreams ever since he went away three years ago? Was it likely it could have been otherwise with him, after the way he had looked at her and sought her companionship?... And now he was to love her so much more than before, for had she not read and thought and studied, to make herself a fitter companion? She smiled to think what a little ignoramus she must have seemed to him three years ago. Of course she was that, compared to him, still, but she had at least tried to educate herself to a higher plane and knew that she had not tried altogether in vain. "Will he know it at once, I wonder?" she whispered to herself, sitting in her favourite attitude, with her elbows on her knees and her chin sunk deep in her hands, gazing at the deep blue of the distant sea. "Will he be glad? Is he feeling as I feel now?—as if Heaven had somehow come down to earth and shed a new loveliness over the mountains, and the valleys, and the sea?—as if one must always be good because of the joy in the world, and make everyone so happy that evil must eventually die out?"

Then she fell to dreaming golden dreams of love, and wonder, and tenderness, till her eyes shone, and losing all consciousness of time and space her soul carried her away into an unreal dreamland of ecstasy.

From this she was somewhat suddenly and forcibly awakened by the apparition of a stalwart form, not in the least ethereal or dream-like, with a gun on his shoulder and two brace of snipe in his hand. He had, moreover, emerald green on his stockings, a tan waistcoat, and a pale green tie instead of a terra cotta one that had raised such objections in the morning; and whatever Paddy or anyone else might like to say, he formed as pleasing a picture of a typical young Briton as any one need wish. He expressed surprise at seeing Eileen, but not being a good actor, any experienced ear would easily have detected that he had come to that spot with the express hope of finding her.

"Have you been up here long?" he asked, throwing down the gun and the birds in the heather and telling his spaniel to keep guard over them.

"About three hours, I should think," she replied, looking a little askance at the gun. "Is it unloaded?"

"Yes. You're not afraid of it, are you?"

"N-no," slowly. "Isn't it rather early to shoot snipe?"

"Yes, but there wasn't anything else."

"I thought you and Paddy were going across to Rostrevor this afternoon?"

"So we were, but we fell out."

"Has Paddy gone alone, then?"

"Yes. She said she'd rather swim across than have to go in the same boat with me." And he smiled at the recollection.

Eileen smiled vaguely also, but she was not listening very attentively, so she was not quite sure what she was smiling at. She had unconsciously slipped into her old attitude again, and, chin in hand, was gazing out to sea.

Jack, having thrown himself down beside her, pulled at the heather in silence, watching her secretly. "What do you think about when you sit here by yourself?" he asked suddenly. "It seems as if it must be so awfully slow."

"Oh, no, it isn't at all slow," she answered simply.

"But what do you think about?" he reiterated.

"I don't think I could explain," slowly, "except that it's just everything."

There was a short silence, then he said:

"You and Paddy are very different, aren't you?" And she smiled as she answered in the affirmative.

"I shouldn't think sisters are often so different," he went on. "Aunt Jane and Aunt Mary are almost exactly alike. There isn't much difference between Kathleen and Doreen Blake, either," he added, as if leading up to something, and then blurted out a little awkwardly, "I suppose you're very glad they're coming back?"

"Yes," Eileen replied simply; "aren't you?"

Jack did not reply, but remarked instead:

"I don't suppose Lawrence will stay at home long. This place is much too tame for him."

Eileen only gazed fixedly at the distant sea.

"I can't say I think it will be much loss to the neighbourhood," continued outspoken Jack. "He does fancy himself so."

"I don't think he does," she said. "It is only that the people about here do not appeal to him in some way, and so he stands aloof."

"We're not clever enough, I suppose; but we could give him points in a good many things, all the same," a little savagely, biting at a piece of string with his strong white teeth. "What has he ever done beyond taking a few degrees at Oxford?"

"You haven't even done that." And Eileen turned to him suddenly, with serious eyes. She was the only one of all about him who ever took him to task seriously about his idle life. His aunts were too fond and too indulgent, his father too wrapped up in his books and his loss, and Paddy, being as irresponsible and happy-go-lucky herself, only thought about the good time they were having in the present. Eileen, however, saw further, and sometimes tried to influence him.

He was silent now before the veiled reproach in her words, but presently, with an irresistible little smile, he said.

"You wouldn't have me go away and leave Aunt Jane and Aunt Mary weeping over my empty chair and old shoes and things, would you?"

"Perhaps you will have to go some day," she said.

"Yes, but why worry about it now? Sufficient unto the day—"

"Yes; only you are wasting your best years."

"Oh, I don't think so, and I'm not doing any harm to anyone."

"You may be harming yourself."

"How?"

Eileen gazed dreamily before her, and presently said:

"You see, I don't think life is altogether meant to be just a playtime for anyone. We have to make our five talents ten talents."

"But not all in a great hurry at the beginning."

"It is possible to put things off too long, though."

"That's what Paddy said because I kept her waiting nearly half an hour this afternoon. She was very uppish," and again he smiled at the recollection, and Eileen gave him up.

"You are quite incorrigible," she said. "I might as well try and inspire Kitty," and she patted the spaniel, now curled up beside them.

"Perhaps, but it really isn't worth while to worry now, it is? Everything's so jolly, it would be a pity to spoil it. You're so serious and solemn, Eileen. Paddy never bothers her head about any mortal thing—why do you?"

"I expect I'm made that way. It would not do for everyone to be the same. Shall we go home now? We shall be just in time for tea."

He got up at once and shouldered his gun, starting ahead of her to clear the brambles and stones out of her path, and turning to give her his hand where the descent became difficult. Had it been Paddy they would have scrambled down at a breakneck pace together, and he would have given no thought at all to her progress, for the simple reason that she would only have scorned it if he had.

But Eileen, somehow, was different. She was really quite as good a climber as Paddy, and probably a much surer one, but on the other hand she seemed more frail and dependent, and Jack liked helping her, even though he knew she would get along quite as well by herself.

At the lodge gates they met the two aunts, and Eileen was promptly carried off to the Parsonage to tea, the two little ladies at once commencing to pour into her sympathetic ears an account of the sad fate of one of their favourite cats as they went along.

"My dear, when we started out this afternoon," began Miss Jane, "we heard a most heartrending cry in the bushes, and after hunting about, we found such a pitiful object. It was scarcely recognisable even to us."

"Not even to us," echoed Miss Mary sadly.

"It was actually poor dear Lionel, one of Lady Dudley's last kittens," continued Miss Jane, "and what do you think had happened to him?"

"Was he caught in a trap!" asked Eileen.

"Oh, far worse," in a tearful voice. "Mary and I are feeling terribly upset about it."

"Yes; quite upset," came the sad echo.

"Has he singed the end of his tail?" asked Jack with due solemnity, "or has Lady Dudley been giving him a bad time because he stole her milk as usual?"

"Worse, my dear Jack, worse still," with a mournful shake of both heads. "He has fallen into a barrel of tar." And the two little ladies stood still suddenly, to further impress the terrible nature of the calamity.

"Oh, Christmas!" exclaimed Jack, unable to resist laughing, while Eileen asked most anxiously, "But he got out again?"

"Yes, my dear, but think of the poor darling's condition!"

"What a home-coming!" said Jack irrelevantly.

"He was coated all over with tar," went on Miss Jane, now addressing Eileen only, and ignoring Jack with contempt, "and he had tried to clean himself, and of course, in licking his fur, had swallowed a lot of tar."

"Actually swallowed it," put in Miss Mary on the point of tears.

"And of course he was in a dreadful state, and probably in great pain, so we put him in a basket and took his straight away to Dr Phillips."

"Tar must be very indigestible," murmured Jack.

"And did he cure him?" asked Eileen kindly.

"Alas, no: he said nothing could be done for him at all, and the kindest thing would be to poison him at once."

A big tear rolled down Miss Mary's cheek.

"Poor Lionel," she murmured tenderly.

"*We* buried him ourselves," finished Miss Jane, "under the cedar tree, as close to the churchyard gate as we could put him."

"Much better have put him by the rhubarb," said Jack, for which Eileen frowned at him over their heads, but instead of being in the least ashamed of himself, he looked up at the clouds and murmured feelingly: "Lady Dudley has still five living—let us be thankful for small mercies."

Chapter Four.

Paddy's Adventure.

Meanwhile in a very ruffled frame of mind, not only because Jack had kept her waiting half an hour, but also because she knew he had gone off quite contentedly up the mountain to look for Eileen, when he found he was in disgrace with her, Paddy trimmed her sail and sped across the Loch to Rostrevor. There was a fairly strong breeze, and the management of the boat kept her busy, but when she landed at Rostrevor alone, she had time to further anathematise Jack in her heart, and was in two minds about going up to the Hendersons at all. They had arranged to come over for tennis, but somehow Paddy did not think she wanted to play. She felt as if she wanted to work off her ill-humour by doing something daring, that would take her out of herself. So it happened that she stood on the quay irresolute and looked out to sea. Her quick eye was taking note of the wind and the tide, while her brain considered the advisability of taking a little trip toward Greenore. One half of her, the wise half, said, "Don't go; the wind is too choppy." The other half said coolly, "All the more fun! At the worst it would only mean a ducking, as you can keep near enough to the land to swim ashore." Then, however, came the thought that Jack would certainly find out she had given up the tennis because of him, and feel ever so pleased with himself. That, of course, would never do. Whatever she had to put up with in the way of tennis was better than giving Jack such a triumph after his behaviour.

"I guess I'll do both," she said, "and I'll tell Jack it was the finest tennis I ever had in my life."

Consequently she made fast the painter, reached her racquet, and made her way briskly to the Hendersons, meaning to play one set and then get back to the boat and have her sail.

Directly she appeared, she was hailed with a chorus of delight, and was instantly claimed for a partner by four or five different players, from whom she calmly made her choice like a young queen.

"I'm not going to play with you, Harry Armstrong," she said, "because you poach too much. Nor with you, Dick, because you're so slow—you always reach the ball a second too late, and it's bad for my nerves. And Basil Whitehead won't be serious enough. I guess I'll play with you, Bob," and she nodded to a shock-headed schoolboy of about fourteen, all arms and legs, and feet.

"How just jolly, thundering fine!" he exclaimed excitedly. "You are a brick, Paddy; we'll knock them into a cocked hat, won't we!"

"You know the other girls here are such awful sillies," he remarked to her confidentially, as they walked toward a vacant court. "A fellow can't have half a good time with a set like this. They're no better than a pack of schoolgirls," and he turned up his snub nose contemptuously.

"Oh, well, of course! when a 'man-about-town' like you comes along," said Paddy, "we all feel horribly countrified and shy and awkward. It's only natural, living away out here among the mountains."

"I suppose so," said Bob, hesitatingly, not quite sure whether she was laughing at him or not. "Still," brightening up, "they might be more like you if they tried. You know I think you're just an awfully jolly girl," he finished with great condescension.

Paddy made him a mock bow. "I'm sure I feel highly honoured," she said, "but you mustn't tell the other girls, or they'd be frightfully jealous, and hate me like anything."

"Well, you needn't mind that," he replied stoutly. "I'll look after you, and settle them pretty quick if they're cheeky."

"That's all right, then. Let's set to work and win this set, because I have an important engagement directly after tea."

Bob's face fell a little at this, but he quickly decided to make the best of the prevailing good, and not worry about what came next.

But Paddy did not get away quite so quickly as she had intended, as Kitty Irvine came and pulled her on one side to tell her an important piece of news in confidence.

"Have you seen him?" she exclaimed in an eager undertone. "Isn't he perfectly scrumptious?"

"Seen who!" asked Paddy in bewilderment—"Who's perfectly scrumptious?"

"Why, Colonel Masterman's nephew, of course. You must have heard about him?"

"The Mastermans at Carlingford?" still unenlightened.

"Yes, Colonel Masterman has a nephew come to stay with them, from London. Fancy you not knowing!"

"Well, I think I did hear Jack say something about it; but I had quite forgotten. When did he come?"

"Only yesterday, but he was in Newry this morning, and bought a picture post-card at the same time that I did."

"Ump!" expressively. "I loathe picture post-cards. He must be a nincompoop, if he actually buys them."

"Not at all," asserted Kitty. "He's probably going to send them home. He's not exactly handsome, but he has got the loveliest smile, and such a nice voice."

"Rubbish!" exclaimed Paddy, whose ill-humour was still not very far-off. "A man with a lovely smile and a sweet voice is always a silly ass. I expect he curls his hair, and wears patent-leather boots, and lavender kid gloves."

"You're very cross," from Kitty in an aggrieved tone; "I thought you'd be pleased to hear there was likely to be some one fresh at the tennis parties, to talk to."

"So I should be if they were jolly, but I'm sure this man isn't. He sounds just awful. I loathe him already."

Kitty was silent for a moment, then she asked suddenly, "Where's Jack?"

"I don't know," with a fine air of indifference. "He was so long getting ready, that I just came across without him. I must go back now, as I'm alone, and if the wind gets up, I mightn't be able to manage the boat. Say good-by to Mrs Henderson for me—she's just in the middle of a set," and without waiting for more, she slipped away unobserved, and hurried down to the water's edge.

Loosening her boat quickly, she sprang in and pushed off, the light of an adventure glowing in her eyes.

"Now to 'breast the waves,' as Eileen puts it in her poetry," she said gleefully, and headed for the open sea.

For about half an hour everything went well, in spite of the continued freshening of the breeze. Paddy trimmed her sail in a masterly fashion, and felt so elated that she quite forgot her grievance of the afternoon, and sang little "coon" songs to herself from joyousness.

Two or three times she met some old skipper who knew her well by sight, and shouted a word of warning, about the breeze being very stiff out beyond the bay—but she only called back a friendly good-day, and held on her way.

As she neared Greenore she met another boat, not much bigger than her own, which a young man was sailing, like herself, single-handed, and as they passed he watched her with no small wonder. He had himself started off at mid-day in spite of various warnings concerning the choppiness of the wind, but being a first-rate yachtsman he had no fear, and had even gone out into the open sea beyond Greenore. When, however, he met this other small skiff, handled only by a mere girl, he could hardly believe his own eyes, and could not help staring hard to make sure he was right.

"Upon my word!" he ejaculated mentally—"these Irish girls have some pluck,"—but he instinctively loosened his sail, and let it flap idly, while he turned with a half-anxious expression to watch her movements.

Paddy, already intoxicated with excitement, and what she had already achieved, was becoming more and more rash; and when a sudden strong gust caught her sail and nearly capsized her, the occupant of the other boat gave a muttered exclamation, and prepared at once to turn round, with a vague idea of hanging about in her vicinity.

He had scarcely got his bow toward her, when a second gust, a still stronger one, caught her before she had quite recovered from the last, and in less time than one can write, her boat was upside down, and she herself struggling in the water.

"Hold on to the boat," shouted a voice near at hand; "I'll be with you in a few seconds."

Paddy's first idea had been to swim for the shore, but at the sound of the voice, she was glad enough to turn and cling to her capsized boat, though with no small wonderment that anyone should be so near.

Then she recognised the little yacht bearing down on her, and saw that the occupant must have turned some minutes before, and probably been watching her. A moment later he was helping her up the side, and she stood before him, like a half-drowned rat—with the water pouring off her in all directions.

For one moment they looked at each other silently, not quite sure how to proceed, and then the humour of the situation became too much for Paddy, and she burst out laughing, he immediately following suit, quite unable to help himself.

"What in the name of wonder do I look like?" she said, glancing down at her dripping skirt, and the streams of water all round.

"A little damp!" he suggested, and they laughed again. "But you must be awfully plucky and awfully rash," he added, not without admiration.

"Oh, yes! I'm all that," asserted Paddy; "but I've got a charmed life, so it doesn't matter. I must look perfectly awful, though," and she laughed again.

"Not at all," gallantly; "but I'm afraid you'll take cold. Do you live near?"

"Only at Omeath, but we shall have to tack, so it will take rather a long time."

"I should think so," impressively. "We'll go into Carlingford, and I'll take you to my aunt's to get some dry clothes."

"Who is your aunt?" asked Paddy, inwardly admiring the skill with which he managed his boat; and not a little also his broad shoulders and frank, pleasant face.

"Mrs Masterman, at Dunluce."

"Goodness!" she exclaimed in surprise, without stopping to think. "Are you Colonel Masterman's nephew who came yesterday?"

"Yes, why?" looking up curiously.

Paddy found herself in a fix, and she flushed crimson, feeling ready to bite her tongue out for being so hasty.

"Why?" he asked again, in a way that made her feel she must answer.

"Only that I heard something about you this afternoon," she stammered.

"And what did you hear?"

His grey eyes had an amused twinkle in them now, and there was something so disarming about his smile; that with an answering twinkle in her own, Paddy looked at him slyly and said:

"Oh! nothing much—only that you bought picture post-cards."

Chapter Five.

Ted Masterman.

"Was that all?" asked Ted Masterman, reaching across to tuck his rain-proof coat, which he fortunately had with him, closer round her, and looking still more amused.

"Not quite, but it's all I'm going to tell you," said Paddy.

"Oh, no, it isn't," with a smile; "you're going to tell me the rest."

"How do you know I am?" archly.

"Because people always have to do what I want them to."

"How very odd!" in feigned surprise; "that is exactly how it is with me!"

"So I should imagine," looking into her laughing eyes with growing interest.

"That's pretty of you," she said, "so I'll go on. I was told you had a lovely smile."

"Someone was a kindly judge then. I wonder what you said."

The twinkle in Paddy's eyes literally shone.

"I said that if you bought picture post-cards and had a lovely smile you must be a nincompoop."

Ted threw his head back and shouted with laughter, exclaiming, "That's the best of all, and I quite agree with you!" Then they ran up against the landing-stage, and he hurried her out of the boat and along the road to his aunt's as fast as she would go.

"My dear child!" was all Mrs Masterman said, when she saw her, and without another word bustled her off upstairs, and flew to prepare a hot bath.

"It's nothing new," she explained in answer to Ted's queries later, shaking her head drolly. "She's just the wildest harum-scarum that ever breathed, and her father positively delights in it. I must take you to call. He'll laugh himself nearly ill over this escapade, but for my part, I think he would do better returning thanks for the multitudinous times she has been given back to him, from the very gates of death."

"But she wouldn't have been drowned to-day, aunt. She could have swum ashore."

"She might have had cramp, or caught her death of cold, or a hundred other things. It's dreadful, to my thinking, for a girl to be so absolutely a boy in everything. But there! she's young yet, and I daresay she'll improve by and by."

Ted, standing at the window with his hands in his pockets, staring across the Loch, had an odd, inward conviction that there was no room for improvement, but this he kept to himself, asking instead of her father and home.

A little later, he made their acquaintance, as his aunt decided to keep Paddy all night, and sent him to The Ghan House with a note of explanation. Jack and Eileen were just returning from the Parsonage as he arrived, and while Mrs Adair read the note aloud to the General, out on the lawn where they were sitting, the two young people sauntered up.

"Lord love us!" exclaimed the General gleefully; "was there ever such a girl before! Capsized, did she?—right out by Greenore!—managing the boat alone, too!—and out there a day like this —by my faith a good-plucked one! Here, Jack! you young scoundrel! why weren't you out with Paddy this afternoon? Here she's been getting capsized right out by Greenore and fished out of the water by this young man, while you were wasting cartridges trying to hit snipe.

"Here's my hand, sir," turning to Ted and giving him a hearty hand-shake, "and an old soldier's thanks and blessing, and if there's anything I can do for you at any time just name it. Lord! what a girl she is!" he finished, and held his sides and shook with laughter.

Meanwhile Mrs Adair added her thanks in a low, eager voice, asking anxiously after Paddy's welfare; and Jack took stock of the stranger generally.

When he had finished reassuring Mrs Adair concerning her daughter, and reasserting that he had really done nothing at all deserving of thanks, Ted returned Jack's scrutiny with almost as great interest, wondering if this handsome young Irishman were Paddy's brother.

"Let me introduce you to *my* eldest daughter," said Mrs Adair. "Eileen, this is Mr Masterman from Dunluce."

Eileen shook hands with her usual charming smile, and then Mrs Adair introduced Jack, who, after a little further scrutiny, started on his favourite topics of shooting and sailing, and finding Ted as interested as himself, they quickly became good friends.

"Your daughter called out something about returning in the morning," Ted said to Mrs Adair, as he prepared to leave. "Some fishermen have been out for the boat this afternoon, so very likely she will return in it."

"Perhaps you will accompany her," said Mrs Adair at once. "*We* shall be delighted to see you to lunch if you will."

Ted thanked her and accepted the invitation gladly, then hurried back with various portions of Paddy's belongings to Carlingford, hoping vaguely that she might have insisted upon getting up and coming down to dinner. Manlike, he had quite forgotten she could hardly appear without a dress, and he felt quite unreasonably disappointed when he found the table only laid for three, and he and his uncle and aunt sat down together.

"I took the precaution of locking Paddy's door," Mrs Masterman remarked, as they sat down. "I know what a terror she is to manage, and after such a wetting it is most important that she should remain in bed for the rest of the day."

She had scarcely finished speaking when an apparition in the doorway, clothed in an assortment of odds and ends of borrowed garments, and with a face wreathed in smiles, remarked: "I wish roses hadn't thorns. Coming down the spout was child's play, but the beastly thorns on the rose creeper have quite spoilt my elegant hands."

Mrs Masterman's arms went up in horror, but the depressed rescuer was instantly all smiles likewise, while he made room for her in his seat.

"If you'd known me as well as my own father does," Paddy replied to her hostess' expostulations, "you'd as soon have thought of putting me down the well, as locking me in a 'common or garden' bedroom. There's always a spout, or a coping, or a bow-window with leads, or something. How do you do, Colonel Masterman?" extending her hand graciously. "I couldn't be expected to stay upstairs, with such delicious odours coming from the kitchen, could I now?"

"Why, of course not, of course not," exclaimed her host, who vied with her father in enjoying all her adventures; "you must be very hungry after such an adventure."

"I should just think I am—*ravenous*!"

"But my dear, there is a tray all ready for you, and I was just going to send your dinner upstairs."

"I know you were, and you are very sweet and kind, but I've got an odd failing about meals. I simply can't eat, however hungry I am, if I'm alone. It's quite terrible, you know," looking abnormally serious. "I might be ready to eat myself with hunger, and if I'm all alone I couldn't take one single bite."

"A lucky thing for yourself," laughed Colonel Masterman, "though not, perhaps, for anyone who chanced to be with you—for you'd be quite certain to begin on them first."

"It would depend upon who it was, and if they were nice and plump."

"Oh, my dear," exclaimed Mrs Masterman in a shocked voice; "what a dreadful idea!"

"Then we'll change the subject," said Paddy, adding roguishly, "Do you like picture post-cards, Mr Masterman?"

"I think people are very wanting in taste and very out-of-date who don't," he answered promptly; "but perhaps in an out-of-the-way place like this you have not yet seen many?"

"On the contrary," sweetly, "we have seen so many that we are positively sick of the very sight of them. I'm thinking of starting a society, like the one in New York, for suppressing the tune called 'Hiawatha,' only mine will be directed against the post-card craze."

"But I think they are so beautiful," said Mrs Masterman, looking up from her plate with a puzzled expression. "Really! sometimes I can hardly tear myself away from Linton's, they have such beautiful specimens."

"No? Well, you must take Mr Masterman with you to-morrow. He'll simply love it, and he won't know how to tear himself away either. Colonel Masterman will have to come by the next train to try and lure you both home again."

Ted Masterman's expression had a "wait-till-I-catch-you" air, but she only went off into an airy description of her youthful admirer on the tennis court, which lasted until the two elder ones retired to their books, leaving her and Ted to amuse each other over their coffee in the conservatory. Paddy at once opened fire with a cross-examination.

"So you live in London?" she remarked; "seems to me one might as well live in a coal mine."

"Oh, come! that's rather strong; London is a grand place."

"It's a good thing you think so, since you live there. I loathe the very name of it."

"But why?"

"Why? Everything's why. Look at the dirt, and the smoke, and the smuts," in a tone of unutterable disgust. "On a fine day the poor sun struggles to shine through the atmosphere, and only succeeds in giving a pale, sickly glow, and on a wet day the clouds appear to literally rest on the house-tops and rain-smuts. If you look up, you see nothing but roofs and chimneys, and if you look down, you see nothing but paving-stones and basements, and if you look round generally, you see little else but pale, sickly, tired people all trampling on each other to live."

"Didn't you ever look in the shops?"

"Yes, and I got so sick of them, I just longed to go inside the windows and jumble everything up into a heap anyhow, and then write a big 1 shilling 11 pence farthing over the whole lot.

"The only thing I really enjoyed," running on, "was the front seat on the top of an omnibus, with a talkative driver. That was always funny, whether he discoursed on politics, or religion, or the aristocracy; or expressed himself forcibly on motor-cars and the 'Twopenny Tube.' Do you use the Tube much?"

"Nearly every day of my life."

"Goodness!—and you still live! Don't you think Dante must wish he had thought of a Tube for his Inferno? It must be like Heaven to come here and sniff our lovely mountain air all day long. I wonder you don't go about with your nose in the air too busy sniffing to speak."

"It reminds one of what one might imagine Heaven, in various ways," he said, with smiling innuendo.

"Eileen and mother might stand for the angels," she ran on, "and Jack for the prodigal son or penitent sinner."

"And where would you be?"

"Well, I guess I'd be most useful helping Saint Peter keep the door," looking wicked, "but perhaps I shouldn't be admitted at all.

"Not but that I'd stand as good a chance as Jack," she finished with a decisive air.

"Is Jack Mr O'Hara?"

"Yes. He lives at the Parsonage next door to us."

"And you've known him all your life?"

"Every single bit of it. I can remember hitting him in the face, and kicking at him generally, as soon as I can remember anything."

"Then I suppose you've made up for it all since."

"Oh, dear no! except to hit harder as I grew stronger."

"He's very handsome," said Ted a little thoughtfully. "He's Irish," replied Paddy promptly.

"Ah, yes! I forgot," slyly; "it covers a multitude of sins, doesn't it, to be Irish?"

"We usually call them virtues!" she rapped out, quick as lightning, and then they both laughed, and a moment later the Colonel was heard calling to them to come and play Bridge with him.

The following morning they sailed back together, and Ted was made to remain, much to his delight, for the rest of the day. They played tennis all the afternoon, and then, after having tea on the lawn, rowed across the Loch to Warrenpoint to listen to the Pierrots. When they came to sit quietly, however, everything did not continue quite so smoothly. Jack had been playing tennis with Paddy most of the afternoon, because it made more even games, but now he manifested a marked desire to talk to Eileen, just as Ted, who had been playing with Eileen, wanted now to talk to Paddy. With the usual contrariness of events, Eileen was perfectly indifferent which of the two she talked to, but Paddy, a little upset by her old playfellow's growing predilection for her quiet sister, wanted to talk to Jack.

The time had hardly come yet for Paddy to realise just why she was upset. She only knew that Jack somehow stood alone in her little world, and felt vaguely that no future could be happy without him.

For a little while she succeeded in keeping the conversation general, but as Eileen grew more and more dreamy, and Jack silent, she finally tossed her head, told them they were the dullest pair she had ever the misfortune to be out with, and went for a walk along the front with Ted.

Meanwhile, left to themselves, Jack again introduced a certain topic constantly in his mind.

"The Blakes came back to-day," he said suddenly; "they crossed last night."

Eileen gave a little start, and was silent a moment.

"How do you know?" she asked at last.

"Barrett, at the station, told me they were in the boat train."

"How many of them?" trying to speak naturally.

"All, Mrs Blake, Kathleen, Doreen, and Lawrence."

There was a pause, then he added, "I suppose Lawrence has just come to settle them in."

Eileen remained silent. The news had taken her by surprise, as she had not expected them for a week or two, and she felt her pulses throbbing oddly.

Then an unaccountable presentiment that Lawrence was somewhere near took possession of her, and, making some excuse about feeling cold, she got up to follow Paddy and Ted Masterman along the front. Jack, wishing very much to remain as they were, was obliged to get up also, and they walked briskly in the direction of Rostrevor.

They had not gone far before Eileen caught her breath a little, at the sight of two figures coming toward them.

Nearer they came and nearer, the girl chatting merrily, and the man listening with languid amusement. Eileen felt herself watching—watching—for the upward glance, the recognition, the pleased greeting.

They were almost together now—he looked up—the recognition came instantly, but a second later, Lawrence Blake had raised his hat and passed on with a bow.

Chapter Six.

Lawrence Blake.

While Paddy and Jack were sitting on the table a week previously, swinging their feet and discussing the news of the Blakes' home-coming, just brought by Aunt Mary and Aunt Jane, Lawrence Blake, in his own special sanctum in Cadogan Place, lounged in a big arm-chair, and considered the interesting subject of his own boredom. He was particularly bored with his mother and his two sisters. Having seen a good deal of them in the last three years, he was anxious for a spell of existence without them.

And now his mother wanted him to go across to Ireland with them before his projected tour to India. And it was so beastly damp and dull in Ireland—so altogether unpleasant. Then there would be this tiresome "coming-out" dance of the girls; such a fatuously idiotic idea to have a preliminary "coming-out" at home, and then repeat it in grander measure in London. He didn't mind going out of his way occasionally to please his mother, but to be bothered with Doreen and Kathleen was too much to expect. To his august personality they were so young, and crude, and foolish. He told himself he was bored to death with their aimless vapourings, and this time he must really follow his own inclinations, and let them go to Ireland without him—at which decision he got up leisurely, and prepared to stroll round to the club.

But almost at the same moment, the door opened, and a soft voice said, "Are you here, Lawrence?"

An antique Egyptian screen of beautiful workmanship hid the interior of the room from the door, and it was not until an intruder had passed it, he could tell if the room were occupied or not.

"I am," replied Lawrence casually; "but I am just going out."

Mrs Blake closed the door and advanced into the room, seating herself in the big chair he had vacated.

"I want you to come to Ireland with us," she began at once, with a note of persuasion in her voice. "There is so much you ought to see to on the estate, before you start off again travelling."

Lawrence remained standing on the hearthrug.

"May I smoke!" he asked, with a mixture of indifference and courtesy that was entirely typical of him.

His mother inclined her head, and looked anxiously into his face.

It was, perhaps, noticeable that, in spite of his non-responsive manner, she in no wise appeared abashed, merely reiterating her request.

But then who should know a man better than his mother, if she happen to have been blessed with discernment? With Lawrence and Mrs Blake this was emphatically the case, hence the direct opening of the subject, without any preliminary leading up. Mrs Blake knew when she came to the smoke-room that he had made up his mind not to go; she knew that he would be politely unresponsive and calmly difficult. As a matter of fact, he almost always was, but she had found that directness was better than any amount of circumvention, and, though he could not be driven, he could just occasionally be led.

"Why do you want me to go?" he asked. "It only causes dissension, and you know more about the estate than I do."

"Perhaps. But I ought not. Do you never intend to take it in hand?"

"I did not think of doing so, until most other things had failed."

She was a clever woman, who had won through a good deal of stress and difficulty, with a husband she adored and a son she worshipped, both of whom had been what is generally described as "peculiar tempered." If she had cared for either of them less, the home would have been pandemonium. Fortunately for all concerned, her love had stood every test, and her natural cleverness had been content to expend itself on tactfully managing her male belongings. The people who had only a superficial insight, and were at considerable pains to pity her, might have saved their sympathy. Mrs Blake was eminently no object for condolence. A clever woman must have some outlet for her cleverness, and why not direct it toward managing two interesting, if difficult, specimens of the male sex? If she truly loves them, what could be more engrossing, and what reward more enthralling, than the intervals of devotion and tenderness won by consummate tact? Certainly, these had never been missing; both men, below the surface awkwardness and obstinacy, unswervingly returned her devotion.

It was the other members of the household who suffered generally, and felt aggrieved at the male belongings with which they had been saddled. It was in allusion to this that Mrs Blake now remarked:

"Kathleen and Doreen would not quarrel with you, if you spared them your sarcasms."

"Kathleen and Doreen are silly little fools," coldly.

"It is only that they don't understand you," she told him, "and you must remember they are very young. Of course you often aggravate them purposely, when you are not pointedly indifferent to their very existence, and they are quite justified in resenting it."

"Then why not let well alone, and go to Ireland without me?"

"This dance is to be a sort of family affair, and I want you to be present."

He shrugged his shoulders, and his thin, clever face broke into a half-satirical smile; "You don't want me to aggravate the girls with my presence, but you want me to be there. Couldn't I please you best by promising to be there in spirit?"

"Why don't you want to come?" ignoring his flippant air.

"Why do you want to go?" he retaliated.

"We have been absent so long and I must bring the girls back to town for the winter. It is a good opportunity to put in two months there."

"My dear mother, Mourne Lodge has got on so nicely without us for three years, it will quite safely manage to exist until July. I dislike rushing about needlessly. In an age of exclamation stops and interrogation marks, couldn't you support me in trying to be a semicolon for a little while?"

She smiled, but refused to humour him.

"You are to come, Lawrie," she said, getting up, "and you are to try and be nice to the girls. Perhaps if you were to forget they were sisters?" significantly.

"They will not allow me to. No one but sisters would go out of their way to be so persistently aggravating."

"Except a brother," with a little smile.

"Perhaps; but the brother, you must remember, is not always there from choice."

"Well, you won't see much of each other in Ireland, as they will be out all day with their own friends. Come, Lawrence—put up with us for a few weeks longer; your companionship will mean so much to me."

And it was then one of those swift and sudden changes transformed his face, as it had done the face of his father, and made everything worth while. He bent down with a look of fond amusement, and kissed her forehead.

"I don't know why in the world I went to the trouble of making up my mind not to come," he said; "I should have saved my energy, realising that a wilful woman always has her way."

Mrs Blake smiled a little wistfully, and moved toward the door, which he hastened to open for her. She was thinking if only she could conjure up that lightning smile, with its extraordinary charm, a little oftener, or if only he would—

But what was the use of expecting Lawrence to be rational and considerate. Had he ever been? He was tired of gaiety, yet he hated monotony. Tired of idleness, yet indifferent to his estate. Tired of flirting, yet averse to considering marriage. Full of latent possibilities of achieving, that he was too indolent to develop. She hoped someone, or something, would sting him alive some day, but at present he persisted in adopting the *rôle* of the *blasé* looker-on, and no one appeared to have any influence over him whatever.

For his part, left alone, Lawrence once more sank into the roomy, inviting-looking chair, instead of going out, and watched his cigarette smoke with a cogitating air.

He was thinking of Eileen Adair.

She had probably grown prettier than ever since he last saw her, and he had an artist's appreciation of beauty. He was glad that she would be there. Her high-flown idealistic sentiments would probably be somewhat boring, but, on the other hand, she was simple and natural, with a simpleness and naturalness that were decidedly refreshing for a change. And then there was that young fool, Jack O'Hara, at the rectory, who could look such outspoken dislike, and seemed to develop rather a sudden fancy for Eileen whenever Lawrence was winning her smiles, and he, himself, overlooked. It would be rather amusing to annoy him.

Yes, since he must go to humour his mother, he was glad Eileen would be there. They would go on where they left off for a little while. He was not quite sure at what stage that was, but it involved many very sweet, serious upward glances from a pair of exceedingly beautiful eyes, and some enlightening on his part that was entertaining, because so surprising. Of course he would be circumspect, and not intentionally mislead her. He would, in fact, make a point of shocking her, partly for her own sake, and partly, because, when a girl became fond of him, she usually bored him to extinction at once. After which, he once more got up and prepared to go to the club.

"I shall not be in to dinner," he told the butler as he went out, having forgotten to mention the fact to his mother, and half an hour later he was making a fourth at bridge at a table called the Monte Carlo table, because the players always played for specially high stakes; and, except with an interval for dinner, would continue until the early hours of the morning.

And on the mountain side, Eileen was dreaming, and Jack was trying to fathom her, and both were alike in vain.

Chapter Seven.

Lawrence Finds Eileen on the Shingles.

For several paces after the encounter at Warrenpoint, neither Jack nor Eileen spoke, and though he tried hard to see her face, she kept it resolutely turned from him toward the Loch.

"Is Mr Blake's friend someone staying with them?" she asked at last.

"I expect so," he answered. "I don't remember ever seeing her before."

Eileen was feeling a little sick and dazed, so when they met Paddy and Ted Masterman, she suggested at once that they should return home, and Paddy, feeling irritated with things in general, agreed with alacrity.

"Oh, by the way," she remarked later, as they were going up to bed, "Mr Masterman and I met Lawrence Blake with that Harcourt girl, who used to stay with them. She's a cousin or something, don't you remember? Lawrence used to say she could talk as fast as three ordinary women in one, but that as she never expected to be answered, it was rather a rest, because you needn't listen. That's how he looked to-night; as if he were taking a rest."

"Are you sure it was Miss Harcourt? I didn't recognise her."

"Quite sure. She looks very different with her hair up, that's all. I should have stopped them, but I heard her say they were very late, and they seemed in a hurry, so I didn't."

Eileen turned away in silence, but a weight was lifted off her mind.

The following day, as she was sitting reading by the water, while Jack and Paddy were out fishing, a firm step on the shingle suddenly roused her, and Lawrence himself approached.

"How do you do?" he said, with a pleasant smile. "I came down here before going up to the house, rather expecting to find some of you such a beautiful afternoon."

Eileen shook hands simply, with the usual greetings, but a lovely flood of colour, that she could not control, spread over her face, and was noted with a certain amount of gratification by Lawrence's experienced eye.

"It's pleasant to be seeing old friends again," he said. "May I sit down?"

She moved to make more room for him, and asked at once after his mother and sisters.

"Mother is very well," he said, "and the girls are full of frocks and hair-dressing. There's to be a big dance next month, and I suppose I shall have to stay for it."

"Were you going away again, then?"

"I rarely stay long anywhere," a little ambiguously.

"Have you decided where to go?"

"Not quite. I shall not decide until a few days before starting, I expect. But how is everybody at The Ghan House? Does his lordship of the rectory hate me as cordially as ever? I see Paddy has not yet managed to get herself transported to a better clime."

While Eileen replied to his questions, her slender white hands played a little nervously with a flower, and her deep eyes fluttered between the distant mountains and her companion's face. She felt he was studying her, and knew there was admiration in his eyes, and her heart felt foolishly glad.

"Have we been away three whole years?" he said presently. "How strange! It seems like three months now I am back. Shall I find everyone as unchanged as you, Eileen?"

"I am three years older," she said, with a little smile.

"Yes, but there are some people to whom the years make very little difference. I think you are one of them."

"Yet I feel different."

"How?" looking at her keenly.

"It wouldn't be easy to describe. It is just different, that's all," and she gazed a little wistfully toward the mountains.

"I expect you are getting too thoughtful," he said.

"You ought to go away somewhere, and see something of the world outside these mountains."

"I am very fond of the mountains," she told him simply. "I don't want to go away. I do not think any place could be as lovely as this."

"That is where you are wrong. I acknowledge the scenery among these mountains is very beautiful, but there are heaps of equally and indeed more beautiful places in the world.

"The only thing is one gets tired," relapsing into a languid manner, that Eileen could not but see had gained upon him during his absence. "I'd give something not to have seen, nor heard, nor learned, more than you have. To have it all before me, instead of all behind."

"But surely,"—leaning forward with ill-concealed eagerness—"the future is just brimming over with interest and possibilities for you."

"Why for me particularly?"

"I was thinking of your brains, and your money, and your position—why you have everything to make life interesting."

He shrugged his shoulders, and the expression on his thin cynical mouth was not pleasant.

"Oh, I don't know about that. It's too much bother altogether. I've seen behind the scenes too much to care; it's all rather rotten at the core, you know—everything is."

Eileen looked pained, and gazed away to her beloved mountains. "I am sorry you feel like that," she said simply; "it is all so beautiful to me."

"Just at present perhaps—but by and by—"

"I hope it will be, by and by also. Anyhow, I shall still have my mountains."

"And after all they're nothing in the world but indentations and corrosions on the crust of a planet, that is one in millions."

There was a pause, then she asked slowly: "Is that how you look upon human beings?"

"Yes, more or less. You can't deny we are only like midges, coming from nowhere, and vanishing nowhere; or at best, ants hurrying and scurrying over an ant-hill. 'Life is a tale, told by an idiot, full of sound and fury, signifying nothing.'"

"Ah, no! no!" she cried, turning to him with a beseeching look in her eyes. "If that were so, where would be the use of all its sacrifices, and conquests, and nobleness?"

"Where is the use of them?" in callous tones.

She looked at him blankly a moment, then got up and walked to the water's edge, feeling almost as if he had struck her.

After a moment he followed, and stood beside her, idly tossing pebbles into the water.

"Take my advice, Eileen," he said, "and don't get into the way of caring too much about things. It's a mistake. Later on, your feelings will only turn, and hit you in the face."

"And what is it your favourite poet, Browning, says?" she repeated half to herself—

"One who never turned his back, but marched breast forward,
    Never doubted clouds would break,
Never dreamed though right were worsted, wrong would triumph,
    Held we fall to rise, are baffled to fight better,
    Sleep to wake."

"It sounded well," he sneered. "No doubt if I were to write a novel it would be full of beautiful sentiments that sounded well—and I should care that for them in my heart," and he snapped his fingers carelessly.

She looked up and descried Jack and Paddy coming over the Loch toward them.

"Here are the others," she said, almost with an air of relief. "They have just seen us and are coming in."

"Hullo!" cried Paddy, as they came within earshot. "I hope your Serene Highness is well."

"Very well, thank you," replied Lawrence, giving her his hand as the boat reached the landing-stage. "I was just remarking to your sister, that you had not succeeded in getting yourself transported to a better clime yet!"

"No, the old proverb seems to be reversed in my case, I am not too good to live, but too good to die."

"Or else too bad, and so you are always getting another chance given you," remarked Jack.

"Be quiet, Jack O'Hara, for the pot to call the kettle black is the height of meanness. Come out of that boat and say 'how do you do' prettily to this great man from abroad," and her brown eyes shone bewitchingly.

Everybody in the neighbourhood teased Paddy, and Lawrence was no exception.

"'Pon my soul!" he exclaimed with feigned surprise, "I believe you're growing pretty, Paddy."

"Nothing so commonplace," tossing her small head jauntily. "What you take for mere prettiness is really *soul*. I am developing a high-minded, noble, sanctified expression; as I consider it very becoming to my general style of conversation. Father thinks it is 'liver,' but that unfortunately is his lack of appreciation, and also his saving grace for all peculiarities."

"I should call it pique," said Jack, "if by any chance I was ever treated to a glimpse of anything so utterly foreign in the way of expressions, on your physiognomy."

"Oh, *you* wouldn't recognise it," was the quick retort. "'Like to like' they say; and I never find it is any use employing anything but my silliest and most idiotic manner and expression with you.

"But with Lawrence, of course," running on mischievously, "it is only the high-souled and the deeply intellectual that he is in the least at home with. Witness his companion last night, with whom he was so engrossed he could not even stop and shake hands with old friends from cradlehood."

"To tell you the honest truth," said Lawrence, "my cousin, Miss Harcourt, had got so thoroughly into the swing of some extraordinary harangue, which required nothing but an ejaculation every five minutes from me, and seemed to go delightfully on without any further attention whatever, that it would have been downright cruelty to interrupt such a happy state of affairs. I knew I should be seeing you all to-day, and at the last moment my heart failed me. I might add that the harangue lasted until we got home, and a final ejaculation on the door-step, with a fervent 'by Jove,' satisfied, her beyond my best expectations. If my life had depended upon it, I could not have told anyone what she had been talking about."

"It must simplify life tremendously, to have such a perfect indifference to good manners," said Paddy, who could never resist a possible dig at Lawrence.

To her, he was the essence of self-satisfied superiority, and she apparently considered it one of her missions in life to bring him down to earth as much as possible. Lawrence found it on the whole amusing, and was not above sparring with her.

"You are improving," he remarked, with a condescension he knew would annoy her; "that is a really passable retort for you."

"I am glad that you saw the point. I was a little afraid you might have grown more dense than ever, after being absent from Ireland so long."

"Ah! Lawrence Blake!" exclaimed a voice close at hand, as the General and Mrs Adair joined them from a side walk. "How are you? I'm very glad to see you back again. We all are, I'm sure," and he bowed with old-world courtliness.

Lawrence thanked him, and walked on a few paces with Mrs Adair to answer her warm inquiries for his mother and sisters.

Afterward he told them about the dance to take place shortly, for his sisters' "coming out" and left Paddy doing a sort of Highland Fling with Jack round the tennis court to let off her excitement. She tried to make her sister join in, but Eileen only smiled a little wistfully, and when no one was looking, stole off by herself to the seat down by the water, where Lawrence had found her in the afternoon.

There she sat down and leaned her chin on her hand, and gazed silently at the whispering Loch.

Was she glad or sad?

She hardly knew.

She could not forget the unmistakable admiration in his eyes, and yet—and yet—

"Like midges coming from nowhere and vanishing nowhere, or wits hurrying and scurrying over an ant-hill," she repeated vaguely. "Ah! he could not have meant that—surely—surely he could not... For if so, what could one ant be to him more than another?"

For a moment her heart was heavy, then she remembered his fondness for his mother and took comfort again.

"It is only that someone or something has disappointed him," she told herself, "and it has made him bitter and cynical, but it is only a passing mood. By and by he will change again, and perhaps I can help him.

"Yes," her eyes glowed softly, "perhaps I can help him to find faith again, and to be happy instead of hard and indifferent."

The stars came out and a crescent moon hung over the mountains.

The night was gloriously beautiful—gloriously still—and a deep restfulness stole over her spirit. In the deep, silent depths of her Celtic imagination, in which dwelt ever paramount, before all, that divine love of beauty which imbues a too often prosaic world with a vague wonder of loveliness, and fair promise, she saw only the heights to which men might rise, and the power of goodness, and held to her ideals in the face of all destroying.

She was aroused at last by a step approaching over the shingle that was so like the step of the afternoon that she started and held her breath in wondering expectation.

But it was only Jack, seeking for her with anxious qualms about the damp night air, and a certain glow in his eyes when he found her, which might have told her many things, had she had leisure to observe it.

"You had better come in, Eileen," he said simply. "It is too damp to sit by the water. I have been looking for you everywhere; I was so afraid you would take cold."

She got up at once, and with a murmured word of thanks, followed him silently to the house, still lost in a far-off dream of happiness.

Chapter Eight.

Paddy's Pigs.

A spell of beautiful autumn weather brought Lawrence often to the beach as of old to get his boat, but Kathleen and Doreen no longer accompanied him. They were not asked, and had they been would have declined the honour. A nameless feud was waging between the *dilettante* brother and the two lively Irish girls, scarcely less wild than Paddy, who resented his cool superiority and cutting sarcasms to their inmost core.

It did not interfere with anyone's pleasure, however, as they had hosts of friends all over the countryside, and Lawrence preferred having Eileen to himself. It was hardly realised by the elders that with so many young folks about two should have much opportunity of being alone, or a little more discretion might have been shown. They were all supposed to be out together, and probably were at the start-off, but a moment's thought might have suggested Paddy and Jack most unlikely occupants of Lawrence's trim yacht.

However, they were mellow, dreaming days, and an atmosphere of peaceful dreaminess seemed to pervade them all—like the calm before a storm.

To do Lawrence justice, he did not go out of his way to win Eileen's love. On the contrary, he did go a little out of his way to shock her, but since she possessed divination enough to realise something of this, it had the opposite effect. She was so simple and natural herself that she was incapable of understanding deception. She believed Lawrence wanted her to know him at his worst—to know all the thoughts he harboured so directly opposed to her dearest beliefs—and so let her love him as he was instead of as she would have him.

And the mere idea only stimulated her love. Pained she inevitably was, but the offered up her pain at the shrine of Love, and went deeper into the maze.

If Lawrence dimly perceived this, he blinded himself to it. To him love-making was a very different process to this calm interchange of ideas, and he certainly refrained from much that he would not have thought twice about with any other pretty girl who interested and pleased him. Could any more be expected? No one could ever say he made love to Eileen. He did not make love to her, but he sought her companionship beyond all other, and looked his admiration of her quiet loveliness, regardless that to such as she these delicate attentions were almost a declaration. For the rest, a man must have something to amuse him, and her *naïveté* really was rather refreshing, and of course it wouldn't hurt her to learn a little more about the world generally from a less narrowed horizon. So he sought her day by day, and made no further allusion to that projected Eastern tour, till Eileen forgot all about it, and waited in a dreaming ecstasy for her joy to take actual shape.

The only two who seemed at first to scent danger were the harum-scarums, Paddy and Jack. Such glorious days could not, of course, be wasted in a piffling little sail on the Loch or mooning on the beach, but there was time occasionally for a passing thought of the two who sailed and mooned so contentedly.

"I can't think why Eileen doesn't pack him off," Paddy said once. "He makes me want to stamp, with his calm superiority. Fancy spending hours listening to the drivel he talks when she might be ratting with us,"—which somewhat remarkable comparison would no doubt have rather astonished the Oxford B.A.

As a matter of fact, he was enlightened with it the following day, for while leaving The Ghan House to go home, he was suddenly knocked nearly silly by a flying, furious apparition, who charged into him round a sharp corner, carrying a blackthorn in one hand and a ferret in the other.

For one second Paddy regarded him with unmistakable disgust for staying her progress, then her face suddenly grew excited again, as she exclaimed: "There! there, see, there it goes. Come on— we'll have him yet," and dragging the astonished Lawrence after her, charged on down the hill. "Here! you take the ferret," she gasped, "but mind how you hold him. He bites like old Nick," and she thrust the offensive little beast into his hand. Lawrence took it with as good a grace as he could! command, and when they ran the rat to earth exhibited a momentary enthusiasm nearly equal to hers.

"There!" said Paddy, holding up the slaughtered vermin, with shining eyes. "Wasn't that a good catch?"

"Very. What shall I do with this!" and Lawrence held up the ferret, with which he had again been unceremoniously saddled, with a comical air of martyrdom.

"Put it in your pocket for the present," promptly "or are you afraid of spoiling the shape of your coat?" with a scornful inflection, as he looked vaguely disgusted.

"You can put it so, if you like," he retorted, "though. I have many other coats."

"What's the matter with Peter?" eyeing the ferret affectionately. "He's a beauty—if only he didn't bite so. I'll take him, if you like. Come along back to the barn and I'll find you another blackthorn. You can't think what sport it is. Fancy sitting in a spick and span little yacht, that could hardly turn over if it tried, and talking about stuffy, uninteresting people like Browning and Carlyle, when you might be *ratting*!" Leading the way up the hill again.

"Fancy!" ejaculated Lawrence. "You must really take me in hand. I'm afraid my education has been guided into foolish and worthless channels."

"You needn't bother to be sarcastic," hurrying on, with her eyes eagerly on the barn. "It's all wasted on me. I know what's life and fun. You only know a lot of useless stuff that someone thought about life a long time ago, I don't know how Eileen has the patience to listen to you. Come on,"—growing more excited—"Jack and Mr Masterman have evidently unearthed some more!"

"I bow to your superior wisdom," with a little smile that made his face suddenly almost winsome, and straightway threw himself heart and soul into the ethics of ratting, noting with a slight amusement, the big, cheery Ted Masterman's evident predilection for the fair ratter.

But it was over Paddy's adventure with the pigs that he won his first real spark of approval from her.

Paddy and Jack had a great friend near by in the person of one Patrick O'Grady, who farmed a small farm with an Irishman's dilatoriness, helped therein by the two playmates. Paddy had sown seed for him, ploughed, harrowed, and dug potatoes—Jack likewise—both considering it their due, in return, to be consulted on all matters pertaining to the farm. This was how it came about that Paddy was mixed up in the sale of the pigs. She was at the farm when the disposal of those forty-five young pigs was discussed, and naturally took an active part in the impending decision. It was finally decided they should be sold by auction at the next market, and Paddy should mingle with the crowd—Jack also, if procurable,—to run up the prices. She also undertook to turn up the previous afternoon, bringing Jack with her, to help to catch the forty-five little pigs and put them in a wagon. When they arrived on the day in question they were first of all regaled with tea by Patrick O'Grady's housekeeper, who was commonly called Dan'el, though whether from her transparent fearlessness of all things living, or because her enormous bulk was supported on feet that could only, under ordinary circumstances, belong to a big man, remains a mystery. Paddy had once remarked that if you were out in a storm with Dan'el it didn't matter about having no umbrella, because if you got to the leeward side you were sheltered same as if you were up against a house, but that, of course, was a little of Paddy's Irish exaggeration. Howbeit, having finished tea, the farmer piloted them all to the big barn into which he had driven the pigs ready for catching.

"I thought we'd have 'em all together here," he remarked, "but 'tis a pity there's no door to close the entrance."

"Never mind," said Paddy slyly, "Perhaps if there had been you couldn't have got them in." At which Patrick scratched his head and looked thoughtful a moment before he replied:

"Why, no, begorra! I'd never thought o' that; but how's we goin' to keep 'em in whiles we catches 'em?"

"We must have Dan'el," said Paddy promptly. "She shall be Horatio and keep the bridge," whereupon poor Dan'el was duly installed to fill up the doorway with her accommodating bulk. Then began a rare scrimmage. Bound, and over, and through dashed those young pigs, with Paddy and Jack and Patrick after them—shrieking with laughter—till Paddy finally leaned up against the wall on the verge of hysterics and begged for a halt.

"Don't let me see Dan'el for a few minutes," she prayed Jack. "Come and stand in front of me. When I see Dan'el rolling about in that doorway, like a German sausage on a pivot, it makes me feel as if I should burst."

By this time half the pigs were safely installed in the wagon, but this, instead of lightening their labour, considerably increased it, for the remaining half had more room to escape their pursuers. Finally a farm youth was called in to help, and the work progressed until only a dozen remained. A brief halt was again called, and then they all returned to the fray feeling refreshed. Unfortunately the pigs were refreshed also, and had apparently taken advantage of the halt to concoct some plan of concerted action. They slipped and scuttled between legs with a lightning speed that suggested a reinforcement of the devils of old time, until the moment came for the grand coup. This consisted in a dash at Paddy's legs, which took her entirely by surprise and tripped her up, she emitting a shriek that made everyone pause a second to see if she was getting killed. In that same second, while the moment of unguarded surprise still held their captors, another concerted rush was made for the mountainous apparition in the doorway. The breach was carried gloriously. Dan'el came down like an avalanche, and in the pandemonium that followed it was discovered she had entrapped one small pig under her person, and its shrill screams were mingled stridently with the helpless laughter of the outwitted captors. Paddy lay on the floor, buried her face, and gave it up. Tears poured down her cheeks, and for very exhaustion she could not look on while the two men, nearly as helpless as she, tried to hoist poor Dan'el on to her feet and release the screaming little pig. They got her to a sitting posture, and then they had to take a rest while Jack leant up against the wall of the barn, hid his face on his arm, and shook with convulsive laughter. The pigs meanwhile, in a distant corner of the yard, held another council of war, squeaked and grunted their glee and awaited developments. When Jack was moderately calm again, and Paddy recovering, Dan'el was finally hoisted to her feet and prevailed upon to do a little more entry blocking while the pigs were chased round the yard, and after a terrific hunt they were all safely collected in the wagon, ready to start for market at daybreak.

So far all was well, but the next day Paddy's praiseworthy intentions of getting her farmer friend good prices did not have quite the result she had anticipated. Again and again the clear young voice rang out with a higher bid, to be outdone satisfactorily by some pig-desiring Pat; but occasionally there was no higher bid, and then the pig was surreptitiously replaced among the rest, to be re-offered presently. How long, in consequence, the sale of pigs might have proceeded, it is impossible to say. Jack, who was having a little fun on his own, sometimes mingled with the buyers, and disguising his voice, made careful bids after solemnly advising Paddy to go one higher, till a system of buying in and re-offering was in progress that seemed likely to last until doomsday.

At last Jack came up to Paddy with an inquiring air.

"What in the world are you going to do with fifteen pigs, Paddy?" he asked. "I shouldn't buy any more if I were you."

"I—buy—fifteen—pigs!" she exclaimed. "What in the world—"

"Well, of course, you have," he urged. "They're all in the wagon waiting for you. Patrick just asked me if you were going to drive them home yourself," omitting, however, to mention that he had previously impressed upon the doubtful Patrick that the pigs belonged to the fair buyer. "After robbing him of purchasers, you can't very well leave them on his hands. I don't suppose he'll want you to pay in a hurry, but you must take charge of them."

Paddy regarded him with a haughty stare, and then turned to encounter the visibly perturbed Patrick.

"They fifteen pigs, miss," he began hesitatingly. "Are they to go to The Ghan House?"

"They're not mine," she declared stoutly. "I bought them for you."

"Very good of you, miss; but what would I be wanting with 'em, when I be selling 'em?"

Paddy looked perplexed. "Whose in the world are they?" she asked doubtfully. "They're not mine—and they're not yours—I give it up."

"Begorra! I'm shure I dunno, miss," and Patrick fell to scratching his head in great perplexity; "but it seems as if, seeing I sold 'em and you bought 'em—"

"But I bought them for you."

"But if I was selling 'em, how could I want for to buy 'em?"

"If Patrick doesn't want them," put in Jack, "of course you must take them home, Paddy. I'll help you drive them."

"Oh! don't be an idiot!" stamping her foot. "They don't belong to me."

"But you've just said you bought them."

"I didn't."

"You did; you said you had bought them for Patrick."

Paddy stamped her foot more impatiently still and grew more perplexed.

"Share, and it's beyond me," and Patrick fell again to his head-scratching. "If you bought 'em it seems as if they ought to be yours, don't it?"

Paddy looked round with a worried air, and at that dreadful moment descried Lawrence, in the very act of dodging two small pigs that had escaped their owner and were making tracks back to the wagon as fast as they could go. She signalled to him, and he came up at once.

"I don't know what's happened to Newry," he said, "but every third person seems to have acquired a small pig. I've been dodging them for the last half-hour. They're all over everywhere."

Jack began to chuckle in a most annoying manner.

"Paddy's bought fifteen," he said.

"I haven't. Be quiet, you—you—great, silly clown."

"Now, don't get cross, Paddy," soothingly; "and you've said so many times that you did buy them that it sounds dreadfully like a fib."

Paddy looked as if she were not quite sure whether to laugh or cry, and Lawrence asked:

"What's the matter, Paddy? Why does he say you've bought fifteen pigs?"

"It's just this way—" began poor Paddy.

"The real trouble," put in Jack, "is that Patrick O'Grady doesn't know whether he's been *selling* pigs or, buying them, and Paddy doesn't know whether she's been *buying* pigs or selling them. For the last two hours they've been doing both in a sort of cycle, and now they're left with fifteen on their hands, and we want a Solomon to say who they belong to," and he exploded again.

"If you don't shut up, Jack—I'll—I'll throw a pig at your head," said Paddy furiously.

"And I offered to help you drive them home," in an aggrieved voice.

"I'll help instead," volunteered Lawrence. "I'm a positive genius at pig-driving."

"Or I could take them to The Ghan House on my way back," said Patrick cheerfully.

"But they're not mine, I tell you. I don't want the things. What in the world could I do with fifteen pigs?"

"They certainly wouldn't be very nice in your bedroom, and I don't see where else you could hide them," put in Jack.

"Come, what's it all about?—don't mind him," as Paddy again looked furiously at her tormentor. "Perhaps I can help?"

Wherewith, turning her back on the delinquent, who continued to chuckle audibly, Paddy related the history of the fifteen pigs, and the Gordian knot she and Patrick had managed to tie between them.

Lawrence had a good laugh—not the least at Paddy's mystified air as to whether she had bought the pigs or not—and then he nobly offered to solve the difficulty by taking them off her hands.

"You can take them to the Mourne Lodge farm," he told the no less bewildered Patrick, "and call for the money in the morning."

Paddy was instantly all smiles. "And don't forget my commission, Pat!" she cried.

"Your commission was for *selling*," was Jack's parting shot. "You *bought* these, so you can't claim it."

"Let's all go and have coffee at the café," suggested Lawrence. And ten minutes later Paddy and Jack were again chuckling uproariously over the relation of the whole episode from first to last.

And it was then that Paddy, under the spell of a certain sense of gratitude, decided Lawrence was very nice when he liked, and, of course, if Eileen was growing to care for him, and thought she would be happy with him, it was no use worrying about things. It was, of course, too much to expect that Lawrence could do other than love Eileen if she would let him.

Chapter Nine.

Concerning a Supper-Dance.

As the date fixed for the great dance drew near, no other topic of conversation was of any real interest. Even the two little ladies at the Parsonage got quite excited over it, and confided to Paddy and Eileen one afternoon, that they were each having new dresses on purpose.

"Oh! how splendid!" Paddy cried ecstatically; "do tell us what they are like."

"Black silk," said Miss Jane. "And Honiton lace," added Miss Mary.

"Lovely!" cried Paddy. "I am certain you will be the belles of the ball. No one will look at Eileen and me."

"Nonsense, my dear," shaking her head; "two old things like Mary and myself belles of the ball indeed! No, no; you and Eileen will be that, and we shall rejoice to see it."

"Now you are sarcastic, auntie," shaking a threatening finger at her; "as if any belle of a ball ever had a sallow skin and snub nose like mine. No, if I am a belle at all it will have to be from a back view only. I really do think my hair is prettier than Eileen's, so with the front of her and the back of me, we ought to carry off the palm."

"What about Kathleen and Doreen?" put in Eileen, "they have improved wonderfully."

"Yes, and their dresses were bought in Paris. It's not fair," and Paddy pulled a face. "We all ought to have started equally with dresses made in Ireland."

"My dear, dress makes very little difference," said little Miss Mary; "expression and manner are everything, and Kathleen and Doreen, though charming girls, are both a little stiff at present. I haven't a doubt your programmes will be full almost before you are in the ball-room."

"I guess so," said Paddy mischievously. "I've promised twice the number of dances there are already, but as I've forgotten who they were all to, it doesn't matter. I am thinking of arriving with two boards like a sandwich man, and on one side I shall have in large letters 'Please note all previous engagements cancelled,' and on the other 'Book early as a great rush is anticipated.'"

The two little ladies laughed merrily, and then suddenly grew serious and looked at each other, as if preparing for some pre-arranged announcement.

"My dears!" began Miss Jane, the spokeswoman, while Miss Mary nodded her head in solemn agreement.

"Mary and I have each been looking through certain of our old treasures to see if we could find anything suitable to give you for this happy occasion, and we have decided upon the two fans our uncle, General Alvers, gave to us for our first ball in Dublin. They are old-fashioned, perhaps, but they are very good and we hope you will value them for our sakes."

"Yes, that is it, sister," murmured Miss Mary; "we hope you will value them for our sakes."

"How good of you!" cried Paddy and Eileen together, and then Paddy flew straight at each little lady and hugged them both in turn. When she had released them, Miss Jane rose and went to a drawer, and took from it two parcels which she slowly began to unfold. At last, from enough tissue paper to have kept half a dozen fans in, she drew two beautiful hand-painted ivory ones, and presented them to the two girls.

"Oh! lovely! lovely!" and Paddy was almost beside herself. "But how can you bear to part with them!"

"Are you sure you would not rather lend them?" asked Eileen gently.

"No, my dear, Mary and I have thought it over, and we have decided it is folly to hoard up pretty things that might be giving pleasure to someone we love. We had our time when we were young, and we were very happy, and loved pretty things as you do. Now it is your turn, and we must sit and look on."

"You seem to have been doing that always," exclaimed Paddy with a sudden burst, "just sitting and looking on at other people's happiness," while Eileen slipped a hand into little Miss Mary's with her slow sweet smile.

"Oh, no, my dear," Aunt Jane answered at once, "we had just as gay a time as you and Eileen when we were your age."

She paused.

"And then!" said Paddy, with half-veiled eagerness.

The two sisters looked at each other a moment, and then Miss Mary said a little nervously:

"Not just yet, sister. Some day, if they still care to know we will tell them, but not just yet."

Eileen pressed the hand in hers with silent sympathy, while warm-hearted Paddy took the opportunity to administer two more hugs in the middle of which Jack entered and claimed that it was his turn next.

"Look what aunties have given us," cried Paddy, ignoring his request. "Their own beautiful fans that they had for their first ball."

Jack duly admired, and then asked what they were going to give him that they had worn at their first ball.

"Hadn't you two sashes!" asked Paddy of the little ladies; "he could wear one round his waist, and one for a tie, and just think how pleased he would be, and how he would strut about in the ball-room, like a dog with two tails."

"I'll strut you about in a few minutes," remarked the maligned one, "speaking of your elders and betters in that light fashion."

"Betters!" echoed Paddy scornfully. "Did you say *betters*?"

"I did, Madam. Do you mean to dispute it!"

"It is so utterly silly, it is hardly worth while," and then she ducked hastily to avoid the missile aimed at her head, and a second later they were flying round the room after each other.

Instantly there was a flutter of skirts, and the two little ladies were collecting breakables, while Miss Jane gasped to Eileen in a horror-struck voice:

"The fans, my dear! The fans!"

Eileen rescued the two heaps of tissue paper with their precious contents, and then held the door open for Paddy to fly out. The next moment they saw her scrambling over the wall between the two gardens, with Jack at her heels.

Eileen remained with the two little ladies, and presently they all went down to the beach together. Here they sat and worked, while Eileen read aloud to them, until they were disturbed by a footstep on the shingle and looked up to see Lawrence Blake approaching.

Instantly, in spite of herself, a crimson flush dyed Eileen's cheeks, and an anxious look passed between the two little ladies.

Lawrence came up with his pleasantest smile, and greeted all alike with his polished charm, and though the two little ladies had long felt an instinctive mistrust of him, they could not but be impressed, and received him graciously. A boat was pulled up on the beach, beside where they were sitting, and with the same perfect ease, he seated himself upon it, and drew them into conversation. For one moment they made an effort to maintain a formal atmosphere; but since it pleased Lawrence to be gracious, they could no more resist him than anyone else, and almost before they knew it, they were deep in an eager discussion on the picture galleries of Europe.

At the most interesting part a maid from the Parsonage came to say they were wanted, and with real reluctance they rose to go.

Nevertheless, as they walked across the garden their faces grew serious.

"He talks wonderfully well," said Miss Mary at last, anxious to know what was in her sister's mind.

"Yes; wonderfully. He is no doubt an extremely cultured young man. And yet—" she paused.

"And yet?" asked Miss Mary.

"I cannot help it," answered Miss Jane gravely, "but there is something in his face that makes me distrust him. I—I think I wish he had never come back to Omeath."

"I wish so, too, sister," said Miss Mary, with like gravity. "I wish it very much;" then they passed into the house.

Meanwhile Eileen sat on, and Lawrence leaned against the boat and looked into her beautiful eyes. He had a way of doing this that was vaguely a caress in itself, and that made poor Eileen's heart flutter almost fearfully, at the mere thought of all it, perhaps, involved. When he looked at her like that, it made no difference that he might be seated some little distance away, and their conversation of the most matter-of-fact order; the whole atmosphere was electric to her young ingenuousness. Lawrence might tell himself he meant no harm; and console himself at occasional uneasy moments with the reflection that he had uttered no word of love, nor drawn any nearer to her than was entirely circumspect; yet he, of all others, could not fail to know just what power of magnetism he was able to throw into a glance, and what inflection of unnamed tenderness could delicately colour his voice, though he spoke of only the most commonplace things. Had he not practiced the fine art half over the world; and quietly walked in to conquest, over the heads of far better looking and more attractive men. Yet he remained unattached: a circumstance sufficiently dangerous in itself. Never in all these years had he gone one inch too far; never become more than lightly entangled; yet always a conqueror. The personality that imbued him to his finger-tips, coupled with a certain indifference, against which women who loved him flung themselves in vain, yet could not break away, had undoubtedly worked far more harm and misery than the honest, gay flirtations of many a more censured man. Yet he had good points and could be lovable. Was it, perhaps, the age he lived in? the *blasé*, free-thinking, free-living set he had become identified with, tipping the delicately adjusted balance to the wrong side. However, that might be, the hour had gone by when anyone could save Eileen; it must now be either radiant joy or heart-broken misery. And meanwhile, into her beautiful eyes, noting also the delicately moulded form and exquisite skin, Lawrence looked that vague caress, with a willfully blind indifference to the future. He only knew that she was entrancingly fair to gaze upon; and he had not by any means suffered from the boredom he had anticipated, before yielding to his mother's persuasions.

He chatted on a little while casually now, and then suddenly brought the colour flaming to her cheeks by saying, with a charming air of persuasion:

"If I am not too premature, Eileen, will you promise me the first dance, and the supper-dance on Thursday? I feel it's rather cheek asking you so soon; but I shall get so bored doing the host all the evening; I wanted to make quite sure of the two dances that matter the most."

Under the lowered lids her eyes shone. She had so hoped he would ask her for the supper-dance; the event of the evening at their merry dances, and yet had hardly dared to hope. Still, with an exquisite flush, she bantered him a little. "But you may change your mind by Thursday! It seems a long way off yet, and it would be so awkward for you if you did."

He laughed lightly. "I'll promise to tell you if I do, I'll go down on my knees and implore your pity and clemency, and your permission to ask someone else."

She laughed with him, and then he added, "Mind, I don't say I shall be content with those two only, but I daren't claim another now. Perhaps, if my duties as host allow me another opportunity, you will again be kind?"

She said nothing, but glanced away from him, feeling deliriously happy; and at the same moment Paddy emerged from the garden, with Jack and Ted Masterman, one on either side of her.

Lawrence got up at once. "Here comes your sister," he remarked, "with her usual train of admirers. If you will not mind making excuses for me, I will say good-by, as I have to ride on to Carlingford;" and he hurried away.

"Where's his august majesty off to, in such a hurry?" asked Paddy, as she came up. "I was just going to ask him to reserve the supper-dance for me, as I always like a supper-partner who thinks it is too much trouble to talk, and so leaves more time for eating."

"He had to ride on to Carlingford," said Eileen, rising, "so he asked me to excuse him to you. How do you do, Mr Masterman? I am glad to hear you are going to remain for the ball after all."

"Thank you," Ted answered heartily. "I wouldn't have missed it for anything, if I could possibly help it."

"Mr Masterman has just saved my life, or at any rate my beauty," remarked Paddy. "What do you think I ought to do?"

"How?" questioned Eileen.

"Well, you see, I caught my foot on the top of the wall, when I somewhat hastily left the Parsonage just now, and he happened to be on the other side, in just the right spot to catch me."

"I expect the poor chap was nearly crushed to death," remarked Jack. "He'll go home with a nice opinion of wild Irish girls."

"I shall, indeed," was the fervent rejoinder, looking hard at Paddy; but as usual she was already attending to something quite different, and the remark, with its double meaning was entirely lost upon her.

Later on, they all four strolled down to the water after dinner, and Jack managed to detain Eileen a little behind the others.

He was a trifle awkward and shy as if he had something on his mind, and at last, without much preliminary, he blurted out, "You'll give me the supper-dance, won't you, Eileen? I wanted to ask you before, but I thought you'd think I was so silly to be asking so soon."

"Oh! I'm sorry, Jack," with genuine regret for his sake; "I've promised it."

"You've promised it!" he echoed in astonishment.

"Yes, this afternoon."

"To whom?" looking hard into her face.

"To Lawrence Blake," and she did not meet his eyes.

Jack stood still suddenly, without quite knowing it, and stared across to the mountains. It seemed to him all in a moment as if some grim phantom had suddenly risen, and menaced him for the first time in his life, with a vision of striving and failure.

He ground his teeth together angrily.

"Curse Lawrence Blake," he muttered, and kicking some pebbles angrily into the lake, strode forward.

Chapter Ten.

A Letter from Calcutta.

Paddy sat on the morning-room table swinging her feet, and Jack leaned against the mantelpiece with his hands in his pockets, biting at the end of an empty pipe fitfully, as was his wont when all did not fall out as he wished.

"There was a little girl
And she had a little curl
Right in the middle of her forehead,"

sang Paddy.

"And   when   she   was   good
She   was   very,   very   good;
And when she was naughty, she was 'orrid."

"Are you going to save me the supper-dance, Paddy!" he asked, without moving.

Paddy put her head on one side like a little bird, and eyed him quizzically a moment in silence.

"How many people have you already asked!" she said suddenly.

He coloured a little under his sunburn.

"Why should you suppose I have asked anyone!"

"I only wanted to know if you had. You have got a very tell-tale face, and now I can see for myself. Was it Eileen!"

"Are you going through this cross-examination with all your partners?" with a touch of sarcasm.

"It wouldn't be necessary. You are the only one likely to use me as a makeshift."

"You are in a beastly temper this morning."

"Oh no, I'm not," good-naturedly. "I only had reasons of my own for wanting to know. I suppose Eileen was already promised to Lawrence Blake!"

"It was like his impudence," savagely.

"I don't see that. 'First come, first served,' is a perfectly fair rule. You should have been sharper and got there before him. You see you're too late in this quarter also."

"What! Have you promised too?"

"Yes; yesterday."

Jack bit his lip and felt furious with himself and all the world.

"What in the name of fortune am I to do?" he asked. "With neither you nor Eileen for the supper-dance, I shan't know myself."

"You must ask Kathleen Blake, of course. It is what you ought to have done all along," and then suddenly Paddy swung herself half across the room and stepped out of the French window into the garden, and vanished in the direction of the shore. It was unpleasantly present in her mind that Jack had not been sufficiently interested to ask to whom she had promised the dance; and it left her in that mood when the only relief is occupation. So she untied the boat, stepped in, and proceeded to take a steady row. If Jack continued blind, she wondered vaguely, what would become of them all?

"Heigho!" she murmured, resting on her oars. "It seems to me we're all changing. Jack's getting serious, and Eileen is getting serious, and if I don't mind I shall get serious too. What a pity we can't stay children another ten years." She looked a little dreamily to the horizon. "I wonder if something's going to happen," she mused. "I've an odd feeling somewhere, either in my head, or in my boots—I don't quite know which—that there's something in the air; an 'Ides of March'— sort of feeling that makes me inclined to be quite tragic and Julius Caesarish. Well! well!"— gripping her oars again—"if it comes, it comes, Paddy Adair, and you'll just have to make the best of it. Meanwhile you had better make hay while the sun shines, and go out with the boys shooting as you promised," and she turned homeward again.

Eileen, from far up in the mountain, watched her a little wonderingly, recognising the boat and Paddy's vigorous strokes, even from that distance. But she was too engrossed with her own thoughts to wonder long, and presently gained her own favourite nook, in which the October sun was shining warmly. Here, sitting down in her favourite attitude, she leant her chin in her hands and gazed at the turquoise sea on the horizon. But the old soft dreaminess was changed to-day for that wistful, troubled look that had grown of late, and in the depths of the deep blue eyes there was a new sadness.

"I cannot help it," she said at last. "Whether he is a good man or not; whether it is right or wrong, I love him, I love him."

Then, raising her eyes to the deep vault of the blue above, she breathed softly, "Oh God! help me to help him; teach me, teach me, that if the time comes that he should want me, I may be ready and strong to lead him back to love, and faith, and happiness. For the rest, if there must be suffering, I will try to be brave and content."

Then she got up and started down the mountain, and when she was about half-way home she turned a boulder and came suddenly upon Lawrence Blake with his gun and his dogs.

Instantly his thin face lit up with a smile.

"I saw your sister with Masterman and O'Hara about fifteen minutes ago," he said, "and I wondered where you were. Your sister shot a rabbit running in fine style."

"She is a splendid shot," replied Eileen warmly. "She killed her first snipe this summer."

"Did she, indeed! That's excellent for a girl. But then she ought to have been a boy, really, oughtn't she? One can't help feeling there's good material wasted."

"Why wasted?" she asked.

"Well, to be rather rudely candid, I am not an admirer of your sex at all."

"Isn't it rather poor to judge the many by a few who may have disappointed you?"

"It would be more correct to say the 'few' by the many who have disgusted me."

"I am sorry," she said simply: "I wish it had not been so."

"If you knew the world as I do, you would see that it could hardly be otherwise."

"Still, I am sorry," she reiterated; "dreadfully sorry."

He watched her a moment covertly.

She was looking her best, with the freshness of the mountain air glowing in her eyes and cheeks. He was thinking she looked as well in her tam-o'-shanter, short skirt, and blouse, with linen collar and cuffs, as anything he had ever seen her in. Compared with some of the resplendent beauties he had admired, she was as the cosy fireside is to the marble palace, or the fragrant violet is to the dazzling poppies. And then for a moment on the mountain side, with the fresh blowing winds, and the fragrance, and the loveliness of the lake and mountains, an unusually soft mood seemed to take possession of him, and something apart from her beauty to stir his pulses and rest his senses. As they moved on, he dropped the bitter, sneering tone so habitual to him, and chatted to her frankly and charmingly with unmistakably an assumption of some special link between them.

Later on, Eileen went in home with shining eyes and light footsteps, feeling as if already her prayer had been answered; and Lawrence's mother glanced at him across the luncheon table, wondering to what good angel they were indebted for his amiability, instead of his more usual taciturn moodiness.

In the afternoon he drove her out himself to pay a call some miles distant, chatting pleasantly all the way; and at dinner, he condescended to discuss various matters connected with the dance, instead of preserving his customary silence.

Then he went into his den for a smoke, and so preoccupied was he for a few moments that he did not notice a large, flat piece of pasteboard lying on the table, which had evidently arrived by the evening post. Instead, he glanced with a casual air of appreciation round his beloved bachelor domain, wondering, half-unconsciously, if perhaps the time were coming for him to settle down and give up his wanderings.

His eye roved dreamily over his fine collection of foreign swords, picked up in all quarters of the globe, and many other strange weapons of warfare, arranged fantastically upon the walls—his sporting prints, worth large sums of money as originals—his guns and riding stocks—his trophies of big game shooting.

Lastly, his books, of which he had also a fine collection, though it could not altogether be said to be a credit to his taste; and his prints and photographs strewn in all directions.

"I wonder what Eileen would think of them?" was the involuntary thought in his mind, and his thin lips parted in a slight smile.

Then he caught sight of the carefully tied pasteboard, and stepping forward picked it up with a curious expression.

"By Jove!—Queenie," he muttered, seeing the writing, and proceeded to cut the string.

Then he drew from its wrappers the full-length portrait of a beautiful girl in fancy dress.

For a long time he stood perfectly still looking at it, then he held it at arm's length, trying it in different lights, and surveying it with keenly criticising eyes.

"Superb," was his final verdict, muttered under his breath; then he leaned it up against another photograph in the place of honour on his writing desk, and turned his attention to a little scented note that had accompanied it. A printed slip of newspaper was enclosed in the letter, but first he read, in a bold, girlish handwriting:

"Dear Old Lawrie,—

"Read the enclosed slip and bow down—even your cynical old head owes homage to such a paragon, and foreseeing my victory, in gracious acceptance of the same homage, I send you the latest portrait of this Queen of Beauty.

"When shall we prepare your den for you, and duly banish your favourite enemies? You said you would come again in the autumn—and consequently Calcutta waits.

"Earl Selloyd haunts our door-step, and mamma has a fancy for a peer as son-in-law. *Comprenez*?

"Queenie."

On the slip of newspaper he read:

"At the fancy dress ball last night, given in honour of Lord Kitchener, one of the most striking among the younger women was the beautiful Miss Gwendoline Grant-Carew, only daughter of the Hon. and Mrs Jack Grant-Carew. She is undoubtedly one of the reigning queens of English beauty, and as charming and vivacious as she is fair to look upon."

Holding the letter in his hand, Lawrence again gazed critically at the portrait on his desk, and the suggestion of a pleased expression dawned on his face.

"So Selloyd's trying to get in the running there, is he?" he mused. "Beastly cad! I owe him one or two since our college days. It will be almost as good sport as tiger shooting to spoil his game for him. I think I'll start for India next month."

Then he put the little note carefully into his pocket-book, and, lighting a cigar, sank into a deep arm-chair and stared into the fire, dreaming of Gwendoline Grant-Carew.

Chapter Eleven.

The Scrimmage Party.

Yet the very next morning he was again at Eileen's side, again looking that unspoken homage into her eyes.

It was the occasion of what was generally known as a Scrimmage Party at The Ghan House, to which he has been inveigled partly on false pretences.

"Are you coming to my birthday party?" Paddy had shouted to him as he was riding past in the morning, from the top of a hen-house where she was busily endeavouring to mend leakages in the roof.

He reined in his horse, and came as near as he could get.

"What in the name of fortune are you doing up there?"

"I'm fixing on a few odd slates to keep out the rain. Don't you admire my handiwork?"

"Why don't you let your man do it? Lord!" with amusement, "I never saw such a position."

Paddy glanced at her somewhat generous display of ankle, and her feet trying to hang on to the roof.

"To tell you the honest truth, Jack was supposed to be going to do it, while I handed up the slates, but we quarrelled."

"You seem to enjoy quarrelling with your friends beyond anything. I wonder you have any left."

Now that he had come near, he was in no violent hurry to go on, for Paddy, perched on her hen-house roof, had a roguish, dare-devil look that was distinctly alluring.

"Oh! they come round again," airily. "It would often be more fun if they didn't. That's why I like quarrelling with you. Your thunder-clouds last longer."

"Then in future I shall suppress them altogether."

"Not you. You wouldn't know yourself amiable too long."

"Am I so very bad-tempered?"

Paddy glanced up from her work.

"You're the most detestable person I know, as a rule," she informed him.

Lawrence could not help laughing, though she was evidently quite serious.

"I suppose the few intervals when I bask in the sunlight of your favour, are when I buy pigs to oblige you, and that kind of thing! I shouldn't have taken you for a time-server, Paddy—only liking people for what you can get out of them."

"Daddy was ill over the pigs," she remarked, ignoring his thrust. "I told him while we were at tea, and he choked, and got dreadfully ill, because every time he was just calming down, he remembered about Dan'el on the floor, or about you having to buy my fifteen. I daren't even mention such a thing as a pig in his hearing now. He isn't strong enough for it. You see he hadn't quite got over my charging into you when I was after that rat, and then making you carry the little beast of a ferret and join in," and her eyes shone bewitchingly.

"If you think I'm detestable, what do you suppose I think of you?" he asked.

"Oh, no one thinks at all when it's me," with a funny little pursing up of her lips, and a sweeping disregard of grammar. "You see, I can't be judged after any ordinary standard, as I'm not ordinary. I'm not a girl, and I'm not a boy—I'm Paddy—'Paddy-the-next-best-thing.'"

He laughed again. "Oh no! you're not ordinary," he agreed, "and I'm rather sorry there are not some more Paddys—I like the breed."

"Jack doesn't," calmly going on with her tinkering. "He started helping me to do this job, and then he got wild, and when I suggested he took the slates off the good part to mend the bad, he went off in a huff. He implied that he could do with me when I was funny, but not when I was silly," and she chuckled to herself with a remembering relish.

"He has very bad taste. He should like you in any mood."

"His taste is apparently much the same as yours." Paddy looked up with a queer expression in her eyes, before which he glanced away. He knew she was alluding to Eileen. "Unfortunately for him," she finished calmly.

Lawrence glanced at her again, and when he did so he blew that she had spoken with intent. She had given him either a hint or a warning; he could not quite say which; but he understood at once, that in her eyes he was already her sister's recognised suitor. He touched up his horse to ride on. "Well, good-by," lightly. "May I bring you a birthday present this evening?"

"No," she laughed back, "bring a few thunder-clouds to entertain me."

It was not until the evening began, that he discovered what kind of a party he had accepted an invitation for.

Paddy enlightened him.

"You've got to begin by sitting on the floor, and playing, 'Brother, I'm bobbed!'" she announced. "You'll find it rather hot work, but you can cool down afterward, while someone takes your place."

"I've a great admiration for you, Paddy," he answered calmly. "But not for all the Paddys in the world will I sit on the floor and play, 'Brother, I'm bobbed!'"

"Tut tut!" mimicked, Paddy, screwing up an imaginary eyeglass. "Your—your—shoe a little too tight—did you say!—or was it your—ahem—divided skirt...?"

"I said I should not play 'Brother, I'm bobbed,'" repeated Lawrence, laughing; "but if a score has to be kept of the bobbing—whatever process that may be—I am at your service."

"You can go and sit with Daddy, and the old people," scathingly. "You might have guessed my birthday party wasn't very likely to be reclining in arm-chairs, and conversing politely."

"May I, as a special favour, be allowed first to mention a package in the hall, intended for your Serene Highness—?"

"A package!—in the hall!—Oh! go and sit where you like, and do what you like," and she flew off to look for it, returning triumphantly with the finest production in confectionery that Newry could boast.

After that Lawrence was left in peace, to sit by the delighted old soldier, who laughed till he was again ill, at the wild scenes which ensued; until the climax of Paddy on the floor, with a small table of bric-à-brac, and the coal box on top of her, with the coals flying in all directions, proved too much for him. When she at last scrambled to her feet, with a face Jack and Doreen Blake had surreptitiously smudged with coal dust, he had to be led away to his own den for a smoke, whither Lawrence accompanied him. "These Scrimmage Parties are too much for me now-a-days," said the fine old warrior, sinking back into his big chair. "Lord! what a girl she is!—what a girl she is!" and there was a ring of delight and pride in his voice, which his gentle, beautiful daughter never inspired.

"She informed me this morning she was not a girl," remarked Lawrence. "She said she was neither a girl, nor a boy, she was Paddy!"

The father chuckled in delight. "It's about true, for there's not her like anywhere. Begorra, lad! —if she'd been a boy—there'd not have been a soldier in the British army to touch her. But she'll go far yet," nodding his head sagely. "I'll give any beautiful woman points in another two or three years, and back Paddy against her. While the other woman's doing her hair, and arranging her dress, and thinking what to say, Paddy'll be getting there. She won't need to stop and think. She'll be just herself, and if I'm not much mistaken, the men'll go down before her like ninepins. O Lord!—and she'll snap her fingers in their faces, and go rampaging on, like a real, thoroughbred Irish Fusilier.

"But I shall not be there to see," dropping his voice suddenly to a note of sadness. "Take my advice, Lawrence, and marry young. I married too late, and when everything is just at its best, I shall get my summons to go." He shook his head mournfully, and sank for a moment into a reverie, seeing his heart's darling, his boy that was a girl, queening it over an admiring throng, and he no longer at hand to rejoice. Lawrence commenced to chat with him of his travelling adventures, in his most engaging manner, to cheer him up; smiling inwardly a little at his estimate of the tom-boy, whom he could hardly conceive as yet, compelling anything but the indulgent fondness for an amusing child.

A little later she broke in upon them herself, to say they were all going for a row on the Loch by starlight, to finish up with an impromptu open-air concert, with Ted Masterman's banjo, and Kathleen's guitar. They rose to follow her, and soon after the whole night seemed to ring with merry choruses from the two boats; a rowdy one containing Jack and Paddy, and a few other kindred spirits; and a quiet one with Lawrence and Eileen, little Miss Mary, and one or two other less boisterous members of the party.

Eileen was very quiet. Owing to the number in the boat, she and Lawrence, he rowing and she in the bow, were nearer than they had ever been before, and only the alluring darkness around them. The rowers shipped their oars for a little to listen to the others, and Lawrence turned round to the silent figure, half-sitting, half-reclining, beside him.

It was an entrancing night, warm and luscious and still, but for the lapping of the water against the boat, and the merry sounds from the other party. Overhead gleamed and glittered a million stars. All round, mysteriously grand, mysteriously lovely, towered the Mourne Mountains. Eileen felt herself breathing fitfully, under the spell of some ravishing, dream-like ecstasy. He was so close to her that his coat brushed against her arm, and the touch thrilled through all her being. Yet she never moved nor spoke, looking out into the fathomless, mystical depths of the night, one little hand resting lightly on the edge of the boat, unconsciously near to her companion.

And something in the enervating atmosphere, and the dream-like charm, again had that dangerously soothing effect upon Lawrence. Look where he would, think as he would, he could not turn his consciousness from the sense of that little soft hand so temptingly close to him in the darkness. What would she do if he followed his impulse, and clasped his own over it.

He tried to think of other things and forget it. If it had been any other girl—but not Eileen—no, he dare not trifle with Eileen. Yet it was such a little thing, and he wanted desperately at the moment to feel the touch of the little warm fingers in his. One more effort to forget—one more failure—and in the shadows his thin, artistic fingers closed over those others.

Eileen did not move nor speak. For the moment she was too much taken aback, and then she was only aware of a swiftly beating heart, and a heavenly sense of delight. But in a few moments, out of the shadows, shot the other boat straight toward them, with Paddy leaning over the side. She reached out her hand, and grasping at the bow that held Lawrence and Eileen. Her grasp closed over a dim white object, two hands—a man and a woman's—clasped together.

"Ah!" said Paddy to the darkness, with rather startling suddenness, and then subsided into silence.

Chapter Twelve.

The Ball.

Paddy was dressed first, because Eileen did her hair for her, and when she was ready she surveyed herself with critical eyes in the long pier glass.

"I rather think Paddy will surprise them to-night," she remarked. "They'll be coming round and asking her where her snub nose and sallow skin are. I shall say, 'They are still there, good people, but don't you observe that her hair has entirely effaced everything but itself?'"

In truth she was right, for it would be hard to find lovelier hair than Paddy's, and under Eileen's skillful handling it had, indeed, overshadowed everything else.

It was of a rich auburn tint, as fine as silk, and had a way of waving and curling in thick masses, with a beautiful natural wave, when given sufficient freedom. Paddy, in her perpetual haste, usually spoilt it by twisting it too tightly, but to-night Eileen had given the rich coils full play, and they curled themselves lovingly round Paddy's pretty forehead and slender neck in a way that somehow concealed her failings by drawing all attention to themselves. And then, too, she had the fine eyes of her country, and to-night they sparkled and danced in a way that was wholly bewitching. "Daddy," she called through into her father's room, "you just won't know me I look so beautiful. You never thought I could look even pretty, did you?—but just wait till you see!"

Then she danced into his dressing-room, and swept him a low courtesy.

"Begorra!" exclaimed the old General delightedly, "you'll take 'em all by storm yet. Get out your scouts, young men, and lay your plan of action, for there's a prize to be captured and carried off to-night, and no mistake."

"No, there isn't, then, daddy, for I don't mean to be captured nor carried off, nor anything else, as long as I can just stay here at The Ghan House with you and the motherkins," and she threw her arms round the old soldier's neck and hugged him until he cried out that he would be suffocated.

Then she smilingly surveyed her crumpled lace.

"I guess we'll get into trouble if we don't mind!" she remarked. "See what you've done to my lace!"

"What *I've* done, indeed! I should like to know who had a finger in that pie beside yourself."

Paddy smoothed her lace and went downstairs a little thoughtfully, to see if Jack had come across yet from the rectory.

She found him standing in the hall, and when he saw her he exclaimed, "Is that you, Paddy?—is that really you?"

"Yes," with a little nod, "it's really me. You've always been at great pains to impress upon me that I'm hopelessly plain, Jack. Perhaps, now, you'll have the politeness to own you were wrong," and she looked up at him with her brilliant smile.

"I don't somehow feel sure that it's you yet, though," he answered. "Where did you get all that hair from?"

"It's been there all along, but I couldn't be bothered to do it properly, so to-night Eileen did it."

"Isn't she dressed yet?"

"No; so I took the opportunity of coming down to be admired before I am outshone." She tripped across the hall and stood where the full light of the lamps shone upon her, throwing back her small head triumphantly, and unconsciously striking an attitude full of grace and piquancy.

There was a dark wainscoting round the hall, and Jack saw with no small surprise that, thrown into relief by the dark background, her dainty dress becoming her perfectly, she formed a really lovely picture. His admiration showed in his eyes, and suddenly a beautiful flush spread over her somewhat colourless cheeks.

"That's the first time you've ever seen anything in me but a harum-scarum tom-boy, isn't it, Jack?" she said, and there was an unaccountable note of wistfulness in her tone. "Look again—Eileen will be here directly, and then you will forget."

A light footstep sounded at the top of the stairs, and instantly she dashed her hand across her eyes as if to drive away some unwelcome recollection, and laughing gayly, called:

"Come along, Eileen; I've been playing your *rôle* of family beauty for nearly ten minutes, just to see how it felt, but 'harum-scarum Paddy' suits me best, and you've come just at the right time to save me from a total collapse."

Jack took a step forward to the staircase, with all his soul in his eyes, as Eileen came slowly down, saying:

"Don't be silly, Paddy. I'm sure the first place is yours to-night."

Jack said nothing, but he thought he had never in all his life seen anything so beautiful as Eileen Adair. She wore white only, and the fluffy, lacy style that was so becoming to Paddy was replaced in her dress by an almost severe simplicity, that suited perfectly her Madonna-like sweetness, and deep, calm, wonderful eyes.

"Well, we won't let Jack be a second Paris, anyhow," laughed Paddy, "because he would not give a perfectly unbiased judgment, being already prejudiced. But where are the aunties?" turning to the drawing-room, from which came a sound of voices; "are they here yet?"

"Rather!" exclaimed Jack impressively. "You just see! I tell you, you and Eileen are not in it," and they all crossed the hall together.

Paddy threw open the drawing-room door with a flourish, and, as they entered, exclaimed, "Behold!—not the meeting of the two great monarchs of old, but the meeting of the reigning beauties of Omeath to-day."

Then she darted forward toward the two little ladies, crying, "Oh, you look just lovely!—lovely! I really must hug you."

"Oh! my dear! my dear!" they both gasped, and Miss Jane got quickly behind her chair, while Miss Mary fluttered across the room and ensconced herself behind the sofa.

"What's the matter!" cried Paddy. "I won't touch you—I promise I won't. Do come out and let us have a full view."

After thoroughly reassuring themselves that she really meant it, Miss Jane stepped forward, and Miss Mary timidly followed suit, and then began a general criticising and admiring all round, in which Jack joined in his usual lively fashion.

"Aunties, don't you think Cinderella's Fairy Godmother must have been here with her magic wand!" he exclaimed, "and turned Paddy into as much of a beauty as she could possibly get her? I shall take care not to be dancing with her at twelve o'clock, because I feel quite certain on the first stroke of the hour she will become herself again, and her hair will be coming down, her dress torn, and she will look just like she does in ordinary life."

"Then we shall only be better paired than we were before," retorted Paddy, "because you do not look in the least like a prince. Aunt Mary, you are lovely!" running on with eager warmth. "Oh! I should like to know what you looked like at my age."

"She was very beautiful, my dear," said Aunt Jane proudly. "I always dressed her for balls myself."

"Oh; no, not quite that, sister," murmured Miss Mary, in anxious self-deprecation; "just pretty, perhaps, sister, but that was all."

"No; beautiful," asserted Miss Jane again, in a voice that allowed no contradiction.

"And you the same, Aunt Jane, I expect!" said Eileen, smiling.

"No, I was more like Paddy here. I knew that my chief charm lay in my expression and spirits, and so I did not worry any more than she about my appearance and clothes."

"Do I understand you to say you didn't bother to wear clothes, Aunt Jane?" asked Jack in solemn surprise, at which the two little ladies looked horrified and Paddy and Eileen laughed, and just then the General, who had at last managed to get into his extra-special best dress suit, bustled into the room.

"Jack, my boy," he said, taking the younger man's arm, "take my advice and don't let yourself get stout. If you only knew what I have gone through, trying to get into these clothes!—I wonder

I didn't have a fit of apoplexy! There! I do indeed! And five years ago they fitted me perfectly. Bedad! I'm not sure now the coat won't split all up the back before the evening is half over, and I'm afraid to see if I can sit down for fear it might result in my not being able to go to the ball at all."

"We wouldn't go without you, daddy, anyhow," exclaimed Paddy. "Don't the aunties look lovely? Aren't you just dreadfully in love with both of them? I'm sure mother will be jealous before the evening is over."

"Certainly I am; I always have been! Didn't you know that, you minx! If they hadn't both been so obdurate long ago all sorts of things might have happened, eh, Jane?" and the old man laughed heartily. "Do you remember boxing my ears under the mulberry tree one Sunday afternoon? Faith! you were a vixen," and he laughed so heartily that Mrs Adair hurried forward with anxious reminders concerning his clothes.

"They weren't made to laugh in, daddy," cried Paddy delightedly, "and I feel a little like that about mine, so we'd better keep together, and remind each other occasionally, hadn't we?"

Carriage wheels were heard then, and the roomy omnibus engaged to carry them all to the Lodge drove up to the door.

The two little ladies got in first, holding their new silk dresses very high above their ankles, and carefully folding shawls all round them before they ventured to sit down, in case there was a speck of dirt on the seats. Then Mrs Adair and Eileen, whose eyes were shining already with a new happiness; and lastly Paddy and Jack hoisted the General up between them, so that there was the least possible strain upon his clothes.

Then they set off amid the usual sparring between Jack and Paddy, a gentle sort of purring from the two little ladies, and sundry loud guffaws from the General. Only Eileen and her mother were silent—the one lost in a dear dreamland of delicious anticipation, and the other anxiously, watching with vague misgivings in her heart.

There were no misgivings for Eileen that night. The last week had held so many dear moments, her mind was only too ready to be blinded to all else and wait dreamily for her joy.

But a mother's eyes see so much, and Mrs Adair knew her world—likewise little Miss Mary, who, in the midst of her soft purring, now and then threw wistful glances toward Eileen's shining eyes and beautiful face.

Mrs Blake and Lawrence received their guests in the large billiard-room, which had been cleared for dancing, and by the time the party from The Ghan House arrived quite a large number had already collected. When General Adair led Miss Jane into the room with old-fashioned courtly grace, followed closely by Mrs Adair and Miss Mary, and the young folks at their heels, there was quite a little stir among the chatting groups. For though they did not entertain in a big way themselves, General and Mrs Adair were known and respected throughout the county, while the two girls were favourites wherever they went; and, as has already been said, the little ladies from the rectory were almost an institution.

When Mrs Blake and Lawrence had shaken hands with them, others clustered round eagerly, but Lawrence had time to look hard into Eileen's eyes, and murmur, "Don't forget the first dance is mine," before she was carried off by other friends. Paddy and Jack were almost immediately seized upon by Kathleen and Doreen, who were in great glee over their own coming-out.

"How does it feel?" asked Jack. "Anything like a snail squeezing out of a shell, or like falling out of a tree?"

"Neither," they exclaimed; "more like being crowned queen."

"And expecting everyone to bow down to you," added Doreen gayly. "I hope you are prepared to be finely ordered about?"

"That won't be anything new. It seems to me I have been at yours and Kathleen's beck and call ever since I can remember—to say nothing of Paddy and Eileen, who treat me as if I was only created to wait on them. I suppose I shall be expected to lead off the ball with one of you!" feigning disgust.

"What impudence!" they cried together. "Here are we impressing upon you that in future you are to treat us with great respect, and you start off by coolly claiming one of the greatest favours we can confer."

"Not at all," quoth Jack. "I merely await your orders. I know that one of you will expect me to have the first dance with you, and all I ask is, which?"

"Then you are just wrong," said Doreen, tossing her head. "I wouldn't lead the dance off with you—if—if—my kingdom depended upon it."

"Well, I never asked you to," wickedly. "You shouldn't be in such a hurry to decline before you're asked."

"You wretch," with a laugh. "Well, I'll just take you to pay you out. There—write 'Jack' on the first line at once," and she handed him her programme.

Jack took it readily, for of the two he preferred Doreen, the younger, and he calmly proceeded to write his name faintly the whole way down the cardboard.

"Goodness!" she cried, when he gave it back to her. "Look at this, Paddy! Did you ever see such cool impudence?"

"They're nearly all promised to me," said Paddy calmly, "so it's of no consequence, and now we can both treat him as we like. He'll be very useful if we get partners we don't like, and, of course, he can't dance with anyone else."

"No of course not—what fun," and Doreen and Paddy went of gayly, while Jack sought Eileen.

"He's put the supper-dance very black, so he means that," said Doreen. "Why isn't he having it with you as usual?"

"I guess he thought he'd like a change," Paddy replied loyally, "and quite time," and Doreen was satisfied.

The next moment a voice in Paddy's ear, with a ring in it that she could not well mistake, said quietly:

"I've been looking everywhere for you, Miss Adair."

"Then you must be very blind," she answered brightly, "for in my own estimation I've been very much *en évidence* all the time so far. But perhaps you did not recognise me?"

"Perhaps," with a little smile, and Ted Masterman surveyed her in that quiet, masterly way of his, that always made Paddy feel rebellious, with the most unmistakable admiration written on his face.

"You look like the Great Mogul," she exclaimed, "criticising me in that calmly superior way. It's all my own hair; don't be alarmed."

"It's the most beautiful hair I have ever seen," he said, in a quiet way that could not possibly offend her. "I always thought it was a pity you did not treat it better."

"Then you had no business to think about it at all, or to criticise me."

"A cat may look at a queen. How many dances are you going to give me, now I have risked losing my berth to be here!"

"Perhaps two," hiding a twinkle in her eyes.

"More," he answered.

"No," resolutely.

"I say *more*."

"I don't care what you say."

"I am going to have my dances all the same," and he gained possession of her programme.

"I've a great mind to cancel the supper-dance, and not have any with you," trying to look annoyed.

"Now you look angry," he said; "but don't be cross to-night. After to-morrow I shall not trouble you again for a long time, so you can well afford to be magnanimous."

Paddy evidently agreed, for she took back her programme and only feigned a slight frown when she saw his name on four different lines.

Without meaning to be unkind, the thought, "perhaps it will vex Jack," entered into her mind and stayed there.

And so the game at cross-purposes went on.

Chapter Thirteen.

Paddy's Views on Sentimentality.

When the music for the first dance commenced, General Adair led out Mrs Blake, and almost simultaneously Kathleen and Doreen with their partners, and Lawrence with Eileen followed suit. Paddy, however, waited breathless, to watch her father.

"I'm all on thorns," she explained to her partner. "I simply can't dance for a minute or two. Daddy's clothes are too tight for him to laugh in with any safety, so goodness knows what will happen if he dances long!—I must warn him."

She succeeded in getting within earshot, and at a loss for an appropriate warning, remarked in an audible whisper, with feigned anxiety: "Daddy—remember Lot's wife," which so tickled the old soldier that he nearly come to grief through her, instead of being saved from it.

"How well she looks to-night!" Mrs Blake said warmly, following Paddy with admiring eyes. "You must be very proud of your girls, General. One is beautiful, and the other full of originality and charm."

"I am, Madam," he said. "I am, indeed. There's not an officer in the British Army knows less about fear than Paddy—she'd storm any stronghold in the face of any guns, and never turn a hair. If she'd been a man, she'd have written her name in English History. I used to fret about it a little, but Lord! I wouldn't change her now for all the fame in Europe. I'm thinking there's just as much need in the world for brave women as brave men, and none too many of them."

"Indeed, you are right, General. Paddy will find her vocation yet, and perhaps write her name in history too."

Meanwhile, Lawrence and Eileen glided round almost in silence. Both were perfect dancers, and content while the music continued to leave all conversation alone. Afterward they rested in a small alcove, and Lawrence took the opportunity to feast his eyes on his partner's loveliness.

"You are looking splendid, Eileen," he said, with unwonted warmth for him, "that dress suits you perfectly. Did you choose it yourself?"

"Yes," lowering her eyes, that they might not tell too plainly their tale of gladness.

He hatched her a moment, thinking of her perfect naturalness, and then across his mind floated the picture and remembrance of Gwendoline Carew. How different they were, these two girls, who, for the present at any rate, held sway in his fickle affections.

Against Eileen's simplicity, he could not help a little inward smile at the thought of Gwendoline's past-masterdom in the art of attracting, and holding, and queening it generally over the opposite sex. He thought he would like to see them together, and supposing Gwendoline should take it into her head to be jealous, he smiled inwardly at the notion of what her summing up of her rival might be.

Then Eileen looked up into his face, and somehow again his defences grew weak.

"Out of sight, out of mind," had ever been his motto, and while the image of Gwendoline faded, a recklessness took possession of him to enjoy the evening to the full. It was so seldom he found anything to enjoy now, and he easily persuaded himself Eileen was too sensible to jump to rash conclusions.

And for the rest! well! he was going to India directly, and things would easily smooth themselves out again.

So he leaned forward and talked to her just in the way she liked best, and the way that brought the colour quickest to her cheeks, and the changing lights to her eyes that were so good to look upon.

"Now I must go and give myself up to duty," he finished with a sigh, when the second dance was about to commence. "It feels rather like journeying through a sandy desert, with an occasional oasis when I dance with you."

"Oh, no!" she said quickly. "There are such a lot fit nice people here, you will enjoy it all ever so much."

"Opinions differ," with a slight shrug of his shoulders. "But I shall certainly get half an hour's amusement out of Paddy."

The supper-dance at all private dances in the neighbourhood of Newry was looked upon as the dance of the evening, because it was the one in which any two young people who had a special preference for each other could be quite sure of a *tête-à-tête*. Things were arranged very leisurely, as it was customary for the hand to follow to supper after the guests, and meanwhile the young folks amused themselves.

On this particular occasion, however, there chanced to be several young folks to whom circumstances had not been kind, and consequently, contrary to all precedent, the time hung heavily.

Of these, Jack perhaps was the greatest sufferer. If he could have been with Eileen he would have been in a seventh heaven, but not only was he debarred of this, but he saw with raging heart two vanishing forms in the direction of one of the conservatories, unmistakably those of Eileen and Lawrence Blake. At supper he had been near them, and in one or two brief passages, his honest outspoken antipathy to Lawrence has been neatly turned upon himself by the accomplished society man, and there had at the same time been a half-tolerant, amused expression in his eyes that made Jack feel like a caged wild beast. This naturally had only given his enemy the greater secret satisfaction.

Then if only he had had Paddy, he thought he might have relieved his feelings a little; but having Lawrence's own sister for a partner, there was nothing for it but to try and hide his chagrin under a show of hilarity. In this he at least entertained such of those who remained chatting in groups by the fire.

He little dreamed, however, that poor Paddy was in scarcely better plight. Not that she disliked Ted Masterman in any way, indeed she liked him immensely, but when he was lover-like it fidgeted her, feeling just that soreness over Eileen, that made any other man's attentions unwelcome and irritating.

Nevertheless, she found herself sitting in the little alcove half-way up the big staircase with him, where the moonlight came through the stained-glass window and made a pattern on the floor, shaded by the heavy curtains from the glare of the lights.

Below them in the bright comfortable hall near a large log fire, they could see the little groups, that laughed and applauded, while Jack in company with a youth as lively and irresponsible as himself, feigned a merriment he was far from feeling. Paddy watched, and in her own quaint way, rebelled against a Fate that made puppets of herself and her friends, for she understood exactly what was passing in Jack's mind.

Indeed, she was so engrossed that she gave quite a start when her companion, after watching her in silence for some minutes, remarked quietly:

"I'd give something to know what you are thinking of, Miss Adair."

"Why! the group down there, of course," she answered. "They look so pretty, don't they, in evening dress, with the big old hall for background and the firelight on their faces?"

"Yes," quietly, "but personally I can find a still more pleasing picture close at hand."

"Oh, the moonlight!" with a gesture of impatience. "It's making you look quite sentimental. Please don't give way to it, though, because if so, I shall be obliged, to give up this comfortable chair and go to the hall. I can't bear sentimental people; they irritate me frightfully."

The man smiled a little in the shadow, and the look of innate strength and resoluteness of purpose deepened on his face. There was that in Ted Masterman's eyes to-night, as from the vantage ground of shadow, they jested unceasingly on Paddy's face, which suggested a preparation for a struggle in which he meant to win.

How long or how short seemed a matter of little importance just then; for one instinctively saw in him the steady perseverance of the man who knows how to wait.

And it is generally to such the victory is given; for greater than the power of riches, or learning, is the power of knowing how to wait.

Ever since Ted Masterman helped a drenched, dripping figure of a girl into his little sailing yacht, and met that frank face that ended in laughter, in spite of her sorry plight, he had known himself her slave, and that henceforth the purpose of his life would be to win her. If the winning was to be hard, and suffering entailed, he was prepared to face it, because he knew that Paddy was worth the cost, whatever it proved, from the first time that he saw her in her own home.

His keen eyes noted instantly that the charm and brightness, which made her so popular abroad, were just as freely lavished upon her own circle, and that if she were beloved by her outside friends, she was yet more beloved and idolised there.

Then, when he found her perfectly indifferent to his attentions, the spirit of conquest was roused within him tenfold, and he loved her yet more for her airy independence.

He half guessed her feeling for Jack O'Hara; but Jack's devotion to Eileen had recently become so plaint to all except Eileen herself, that he did not let it trouble him. In this he was wrong, for Paddy was, before all thing, staunch, and having given her affections, she would not easily change.

"I'm not getting sentimental at all," he replied. "I know better, for I don't want to have my head bitten off my last evening."

Paddy smiled, and was mollified.

"It's awfully silly, isn't it?" she said. "I hate anything sentimental. I like people who call a spade a spade."

"And I wonder what you like them to call love?" he suggested.

"Oh, 'love,' I suppose, only they needn't look like sick sheep over it, and prefix half a dozen idiotic adjectives."

"I thought perhaps the mere word was too sentimental," with a little smile, "and you would prefer to invent some term of your own."

"Very likely I shall, when the time comes for it. At present I have a great deal too much on my hands to have time to think of anything of the kind."

"In what way?"

"Why! every way of course! There's Daddy, and mother, and Eileen, and the aunties." She paused a moment, but something in his eyes made her run on recklessly. "Oh! and the Sunday School, and the garden, and the hockey club, and the aunties' cats, and Jack—!"

"It's quite a long list," looking amused, "and O'Hara at the far end."

"He's in good form to-night," she said, gazing down at the group in the hall.

Ted followed her eyes.

"He seems to have cheered up since supper."

"He can't bear Lawrence Blake, he never could, and they were sitting rather near together at supper."

"I fancy there's a little rivalry," he suggested.

"Oh, I don't know!" with an attempt at unconcern. "He never did like him at any time."

"Blake is a very clever man," thoughtfully.

"Yes—but he's awfully conceited. I'm always trying to take him down a little."

There was a short silence, then Ted remarked very quietly:

"This time to-morrow I shall be on my way home, and my holiday will be over—the very best holiday I ever had in my life. I suppose I shall not see you again until next summer, when I hope to come back!"

"I guess not."

"I'm sorry Omeath is so far from London—"

Paddy began to fidget, and kept her eyes fixed on the group in the hall.

Ted watched here again with that keen gaze of his; and a great tenderness all unknown to himself spread over his strong face. He seemed to see instinctively, that in some way, a hard time lay ahead for this eager, impulsive girl; and that with all his love and devotion, he would have to stand aside and look on, without being able to help her. If so, he knew that whatever it proved for her, it could not be less hard for him, and his heart sank a little. He wanted very much to tell her about his love before he went home, but her very attitude told him the uselessness of it, and he did not want to vex her their last evening.

So instead, he asked with a smile: "Would it be too sentimental to say 'thank you' for all you've done to make my holiday the best I've ever had?"

"Yes, decidedly. Besides, I haven't done anything at all except torment you occasionally. Let us go down to the hall. I want to know what they're all laughing at," and she got up without another word and led the way downstairs.

Jack glanced toward them as they approached, and Paddy saw vaguely an expression of pain underlying the gaiety of his manner, that hurt her like a blow. She could not bear to be miserable herself, but she could bear it still less if those she loved were miserable. She looked round vaguely for Eileen, feeling an impulse to annihilate Lawrence, and make Eileen see how things stood. But neither were to be seen. Under the large palm by the fountain in the conservatory, Lawrence was again feasting his eyes on his partner's loveliness, and skillfully drawing that changing colour to her cheeks, and those lights and shadows to her beautiful eyes.

Chapter Fourteen.

The Conservatory and the Den.

The fountain had a little tinkling, singing sound, and there was a delicious odour of flowers, which mingled entrancingly with the shaded lights and graceful bending ferns. Eileen felt it rather than saw it, as though all her senses had become one deep appreciation and enjoyment.

Long afterward, when recalling every moment of that quiet half-hour, she was conscious of exactly the light, and the scent, and the sound, and would shrink away from certain hot-house flowers as if they hurt her.

But for the present there was only a deep content in her heart and a vague dream of happiness, shedding a soft light over all her future. In all their intercourse, it seemed to her that Lawrence had never been quite so fascinating before, and though now and then he seemed to draw himself up sharply and suddenly adopt a very matter-of-fact tone, she scarcely heeded it. In truth, though Lawrence meant to enjoy his half-hour to the full, he had no intention of becoming lover-like; and when he found her charm growing too much for him, he did indeed pull himself up with a jerk and try to resist. Yet he could not bring himself to be sufficiently honest to speak of his approaching departure for India. He felt there was time enough, and if he told her now, he might be led into explanations that would be troublesome.

And Lawrence hated anything at all disturbing or troublesome, or in the nature of an explanation.

Eileen was not blind to his failings, and many a time his callousness had hurt her, but, like so many good women, she had a boundless faith in the power of goodness, and believed she could make anything of him once he loved her. In this she was doubtless right, but she was too pure-minded and honest herself to perceive double-dealing in others, and she did not realise that a man like Lawrence might act one thing and feel another.

If he had loved her, she might have made anything of him; yet—but what if he did not? Lawrence admired her beauty and respected her goodness, but he did not love her—he only pretended to himself that he liked her better than any one else when they happened to be together. Possibly, if "love" came at will, he would have chosen then and there to love her with his whole heart and make her his wife. But Love is a fugitive, wild thing—bold as a robin, and timid as a lark—and usually none can fit any "why" or "wherefore" to its erratic wanderings. And hand in hand with Love is usually Pain—pain against which we cry out blindly, and wrestle and struggle to escape—childishly indifferent to the teaching of the Ages—that Pain alone is the soil in which grow Strength, and Courage, and Joy.

In the worst hour of her suffering afterward, Eileen was yet, in a sense, happier and richer than the man who caused the pain.

But now the fountain tinkled and the lights glowed softly, and the scent of hot-house flowers filled the air.

"I thought it would be deadly at Omeath," Lawrence was saying. "If it had not been for the mater, I should not have come, and, instead, it has been very pleasant. How often it happens that we start off on some trip we expect to enjoy thoroughly, and are disappointed all through; whereas we make martyrs of ourselves and undertake something we detest, and it turns out a pleasure from beginning to end."

Eileen looked a little thoughtful. The thought crossed her mind that he had not, then, came back for her.

"Yet you seemed happy enough here before?" she remarked at last.

"So I was," he replied at once; "and I had just the same feeling about coming in the first place. But then I did not know about you, Eileen."

"But you did this time," smiling.

"Three years is so long," he answered unblushingly; "and I imagined, of course, you would have changed, or got married, or something. Most girls change very much in three years."

"Do they?" quietly.

"Yes; but you and Paddy are evidently different. I might have known you would be." He turned the subject deftly to a less dangerous theme, speaking of mutual friends, until a sudden cutting censure brought a remonstrance to her lips.

He looked into her face and changed his tone suddenly.

"All the black sheep are white to you, Eileen. You are too ideal. You look at everything through the spectacles of idealism, and expect too much of life. You would be wiser to try and harden your heart, and care a little less about everything. You seem to regard most of your fellow-creatures as possible angels, and all the time we are most of us rogues and scoundrels."

"I don't believe it," firmly.

"That's because you don't want to. All the same it is true. Half the world knows it, and makes no fuss; and the other half pretends to be blind for their own satisfaction."

"You only talk like this to tease me," she said; "but I like your honesty. A man who pretends to nothing and is something is so much nicer than the man who is nothing and pretends much."

"I am neither," he answered, "for I combine the two. I pretend nothing, and I don't care." She smiled a little in spite of herself. "You do pretend something, for you pretend that you do not care."

He looked into her eyes a moment, with a curious expression in his, and Eileen glanced away with embarrassment. He was thinking for the hundredth time how sweet she was, and how—if only—?

He knew vaguely that the man who won her would win a treasure; but he loved his liberty, and his heart said "not yet," and so he contented himself with a look that might mean volumes, or nothing.

And Eileen was satisfied. He had paid no real attention to anyone but her, merely doing his duty as host to the rest of his guests, and, undoubtedly, that meant a good deal.

As a matter of fact it was so. Lawrence was nearer proposing that evening than he had ever been in his life before, and he could hardly himself have told what deterred him. Perhaps it was a question of the bandsmen finishing their supper five minutes earlier than was expected—upon so slight a thread hang the issues of life. Certainly, leaning forward with his arms resting on his knees, and his whole soul drawn toward the sweet-faced girl beside him, he felt himself on the brink of the plunge that would have changed all her life and his, when, quite unexpectedly, the band struck up in the distance.

At the first note, he sat up suddenly, as if he had been awakened, and instead of the question trembling on his lips he smiled a little, and said: "How cruelly the time has flown! I had no idea we had been here half an hour!" and then they both got up, and he gave her his arm back to the ball-room.

Eileen felt a queer little tremor that was almost fear, but she only answered in her usual quiet tone, and smiled up at the partner who came forward to claim her for the dance.

But the evening was not over yet, and another incident had still to add its mark upon the unfolding of the hours. Lawrence had still to have his dance with Paddy.

It came toward the end, when some of the guests, who had a long drive, had already departed, and the formality of the commencement of the evening had merged into a more free and easy air for all. Paddy had had a set of lancers with Jack, and Doreen and Kathleen and their partners, that had bordered upon a romp, and had made her eyes shine, and her cheeks glow with radiant enjoyment, for she had the happy knack of throwing herself heart and soul into the moment, and in this instance the moment had been full of delight.

Lawrence found her trying to get cool again, while carrying on her usual flow of chatter, to the amusement of the others; and with a smile, he remarked:

"I'm sorry to deprive you all, but this is my dance with Miss Adair."

"Goodness!" exclaimed Paddy in alarm. "Do I dance with you next?"

"According to my programme you do."

"Oh, that's all right," frankly. "I was only thinking my hair was rather untidy, and my face somewhat highly coloured for such an august occasion as a dance with your majesty."

"Your hair never looked better," he replied, "and your colour is most becoming."

"Really!" with a gay laugh. "If you keep this up for five minutes I shan't know myself. You must be careful, for the high honour of dancing with you alone is almost sufficient to unhinge my giddy brain."

"You could hardly dance with me and someone else at the same time," with corresponding lightness; "but I'm glad that you appreciate the honour so thoroughly."

"Appreciate it! Why, my dear man, I've been dying for this dance all the evening."

"May you be forgiven," he retorted as they glided away. Paddy was quite as good a dancer as Eileen when she gave herself up to it, and, with such a perfect waltzer as Lawrence, she could not fail to do so, even if she could not be prevailed upon to enjoy it in silence. So, as they glided round, she plied him with a string of eager questions relating to dancing and gayeties in far-off lands.

"You ought to get your father to take you abroad," he told her presently! "you'd enjoy all the novelty so tremendously."

"Should I meet a lot of nice, superior, cultured young men like you?"

"Well, hardly up to my standard," he laughed.

"Then I don't want to go. When I can talk to you, and dance with you, and gaze upon you here, why cross the sea to other climes?"

"I was thinking more of the countries."

"And have you ever seen anything in all the world so beautiful as the Mourne Mountains and Carlingford Loch?"

"Yes, many things."

"I don't believe it," stoutly.

"Well, come and see some of my photographs in my den."

"What! Enter the throne-room!" in mock amaze.

"Yes; why not?"

"Oh no 'why not' at all. I'm simply dying to go. I have been, ever since I can remember.—I'm wild with curiosity to know what kind of things an animal of your lofty nature collects in its den," and she followed him eagerly down a long passage, and through a little conservatory into the large, airy room known as Lawrence's den.

When he had switched on the electric light, her eyes grew wide with interest and admiration.

"Well! if this isn't just all right," she exclaimed. "How daddy would love it!"

"It's somewhat warlike," glancing at his swords and weapons, "so you ought to feel at home."

"I?—Why?" in surprise.

"Because you are always trying to quarrel with me."

"Nonsense! I only tell you a few home truths for your good."

"I hope you find your pupil progressing favourably."

"Very middling," with a shake of her head. "You know perfectly well you have been bored to death nearly the whole evening, because there were only two or three people you thought worth talking to."

"And if so—it is hardly my fault."

"Why, of course it is! The people were just as nice as you, really—rather nicer in fact—the only difference is a mere question of having studied Browning, and Darwin, and a lot of musty old German and French writers, whom, I'll be bound to say, you don't half understand."

"Possibly not. But they have a way of developing the mind."

"Developing the mind!" scornfully. "What's the matter with my mind?—it develops itself. I don't pore over musty books."

"Perhaps you are naturally more gifted," with light satire.

"Sarcasm is wasted on me," she retorted. "It flows off like water from a duck's back. Why not tell me straight I'm an ignoramus? Just as I tell you straight that all your learning and experience does not give you the right to think yourself so superior to other people, and give yourself such airs."

"You are very outspoken," smiling a little in spite of himself.

"Yes; but I can take plain speaking, too, so if you want to have your revenge, fire away. I know that I've got a snub nose and no complexion, and am always more or less untidy, because I've been told so often, but you can tell me again if you like."

"I'd rather set you an example in good manners."

"That's good," appreciating it at once.

"Besides," he added slyly, "I don't see that it isn't just as bad to be proud of a snub nose and untidiness, as of a beautiful nose or book learning, and from the way you speak you positively revel in them."

"You have me again," she replied frankly. "I guess we'll be friends for ten minutes and you shall show me your views."

They sat down, and he opened an enormous album, but after the first few pages she looked up at him entreatingly, and said with a delightful little air of pathos:

"I'm so sorry, but if you only knew how I hate sitting still. I—I'm just dying to prowl round, and look at all the queer things on the walls."

He closed the book with a laugh, and she sprang up at once, saying:

"I'll look at the views when I'm old and rheumaticky. You must save them for me," and then she went into raptures over a beautiful case of foreign butterflies, afterward fingering with delight his guns and swords.

"You ought to have been a man," he said almost regretfully.

"Why, of course I ought. I've known that ever since they put Jack in trousers, and not me. But I guess I'll have to stay a woman now to the end of the chapter, and make the best of it."

"Then you're sorry?" he asked, with interest.

"Sorry!" she repeated impressively. "Oh, yes, I'm that all right, but I don't believe in crying over spilt milk."

He watched her silently a moment.

"I shouldn't wonder if you haven't got a future, Paddy," he remarked. "There's something about you that has the ring of achievement—only there's not much room here," signifying the surrounding neighbourhood. "Quite room enough," picking up a Mauser pistol and examining it with the eye of a connoisseur. "Can't I ride straight, and shoot straight, and sail anything with a rag and a mast—that's achievement enough for me. What more do you want?"

He drew a bow at a venture, out of idle curiosity. "I wonder where the opposite sex will come in? Don't you want to have adoring males at your feet by and by!—most women do."

She looked frankly into his eyes with a gay laugh. "Not me! I haven't time. I'll leave that for Eileen. Of course, if your lordship—!" with a sudden irresistible twinkle.

He could not help laughing, and watched her with growing interest as she wandered on from one curio to another, until she came to his writing table. Here she came to a sudden standstill, and a little involuntary exclamation escaped her. Lawrence looked past her quickly, to find she was gazing with wide eyes, and a strangely mingled expression, at the beautiful full-length portrait of Gwendoline Carew, noticeably in the position of honour on his table.

Chapter Fifteen.

Dread and Wrath.

"Who is she?" she asked at last, with her customary out-spokenness.

"Do you mean the big portrait?" carelessly.

"Yes."

"Miss Gwendoline Grant-Carew."

Paddy gazed at the portrait silently for another space, and then remarked:

"She is very beautiful."

"Yes, very," dryly.

Again Paddy was silent.

If she had tried she could not have analysed her feelings just then. She was only conscious that in some way the photograph was a shock to her. Though she had scarcely confessed it to herself, she undoubtedly shared the opinion of the neighbourhood, that Lawrence was paying Eileen such marked attention with a view to marriage, and since the incident of the clasped hands she had grown to think of him as a prospective brother-in-law. Unaccountable divination told her the rest.

"Why do you look at her like that?" asked Lawrence at last. "Don't you like her?"

"No," said Paddy slowly, "I hate her."

"But how can you," he laughed, "when you don't even know her? As a matter of fact she is just your sort. Up to any fun, full of life, and not the least bit conceited, though half Calcutta is at her feet."

"Calcutta," echoed Paddy a little sharply.

"Yes, why not?"

Again there was a moment's silence.

"Doreen told me you were going to India," she said at last. "Is it true?"

"Yes."

He picked up a paper knife and toyed with it. Something in Paddy's honest face made him avoid her gaze.

"When are you going?" she asked.

"In about three weeks."

She gulped down an exclamation.

"For long?"

"What a list of questions!" with light sarcasm; "it feels like an examination paper."

But Paddy would not be put off. She fidgeted restlessly with a letter weight, and then asked again:

"Are you going for long?"

"I haven't the least idea."

"And this—er—Miss Gwendoline Grant-Carew," with a slight curl of her lips, "you are engaged to her, or—going to be?"

"Can't a man have a chum's photograph on his table without being engaged to her?"

"I don't know. I am not a man."

There was a long pause, then she added: "I don't know much about men, either, but I believe a good many of them think it very amusing and entertaining to make love to three or four girls at once, and not care a snap of their fingers for any one of them. It may be amusing, but to my thinking, it is the trick of a scoundrel. I'd hate such a man," and she tossed her head and drew up her slight form, with a defiance that was almost a challenge.

Lawrence paled slightly, but he watched her with his keen eyes in a way that bespoke a sudden and unusual interest.

He tried, however, to counteract the sense of strain in the situation, by chaffing her.

"I believe your real name is Patricia," he said, "but this is the first time I have seen you look the part. I shall have to start calling you 'Patricia the Great.'"

She flashed a glance of scorn at him.

"'Patricia,' to me, means loyalty," she said, with significance. "You may call me what you like, but whether it is Paddy or Patricia, 'loyalty' is my watchword."

He felt almost as if she had struck him. As if a glove, flung passionately down, should lie on the floor between them. He got up from his chair, and half turned away, at a momentary loss for words.

"I hear the band," she said, and moved toward the door.

And it was noticeable this time that Lawrence had not heard it, and instead of leading he followed. Moreover, there was something about Paddy's manner that forebade him offering his arm, and at the ball-room door she turned her back on him without a word, and commenced chattering to her next partner.

It would be difficult to describe the feelings of the different occupants of the omnibus which took the party from the Vicarage and the Ghan House home again that night, but undoubtedly the elder folks were now the gayest.

The General was very lively, doubtless because he had got through the evening without the dreaded mishap to his clothes, and was at the same time relieved from the weight of anxiety they occasioned.

Miss Jane had enjoyed herself immensely, and was lively also, and even little Miss Mary was aroused to an unusual gaiety for her. Mrs Adair saw the subdued light of happiness glowing in Eileen's eyes, and anxiety gave place to hopefulness.

But for Paddy and Jack, there was only increased dread, though they both strove bravely to continue to hide it beneath an assumed merriment.

Paddy saw, as her mother, the light in Eileen's eyes, and something seemed to grow cold within her, and she bit her teeth together, murmuring savagely, "I'll kill him, if he's been trifling with her."

Jack saw it, too, and his hopes grew weak, for he believed he was already worsted; and he saw, with an inward yearning, the vision of all the happy, careless, sunny days at Omeath passing slowly and surely away. "What should he do?" he asked, "and where should he go?"

His two devoted aunts noticed there was something wrong later on, before separating for the night, and in Miss Jane's bedroom, they asked each other anxiously.

"What is it?—what is wrong with our boy?"

Miss Mary having the greater intuition, was the first to offer a solution. "Can it be Eileen?" she asked with dread—"Eileen and Lawrence Blake?"

They looked into each other's eyes with a sudden sense of awakening.

"Surely not—" murmured Miss Jane, but her face belied her words.

"Oh, sister," breathed little tender-hearted Miss Mary, "if it is true he will suffer so. I can't bear to think of our boy suffering," and two big tears gathered in her eyes.

"Don't fret, sister," said Miss Jane bravely, blinking back a suspicious moisture in her own eyes, "I don't think it can have gone far enough for that. You see we have lately somehow associated Eileen and Lawrence, and Jack, of course, knew, so he would be guarded against caring too much. Probably it is just the sudden realisation that a change must come over their old happy life, and he will quickly get accustomed to it. There is still Paddy, and I have always hoped so —" she paused, and then concluded with a little smile, "What a dear, wild, irresponsible pair they would make!"

Across at The Ghan House, in a room from which a bright light shone through the trees, in view of Jack's window, the two other sisters were taking off their pretty dresses, and preparing to slip into their two dainty little white beds. Now and then they laughed over something that had happened at the ball, but for the most part Eileen was dreamy and Paddy preoccupied.

"Was Lawrence very nice to-night?" asked the latter at last, longing to know what had transpired.

"Yes," Eileen answered simply. Paddy looked round suddenly and opened her lips to speak, but something in her sister's face held her back.

She was going to ask if he had told her about going to India, but realising how it might hurt Eileen if he had not, she changed her mind.

"I can't—I can't," she said to herself. "She looks so happy. I can't damp it; if he has been playing with her, I will kill him—kill him—kill him," and she clenched her hands together and tumbled into bed, forgetting for the time her own trouble in her wrath against Lawrence.

Chapter Sixteen.

The First Awakening.

It was through her father, a few days later, that Eileen first heard of Lawrence's plans. He came blustering in from his usual daily walk one morning and exclaimed:

"That fellow Lawrence is off again—going back to India to kill a few more tigers—never knew such a chap—can't stay quiet scarcely a month—pity he doesn't look after his estate at home, I think, instead of gadding off over the seas again, and I nearly told him so."

Mrs Adair, at the first words, had looked up in surprise, but Paddy, who was interested in a small sailing boat at the window, turned and covertly watched Eileen. As she half expected, she saw her turn deadly pale, as if the news were a shock, and Paddy knew at once that Lawrence had not told her the evening of the dance, although his plans were already formed, and she hated him yet more vigorously.

Meanwhile, Mrs Adair asked wonderingly:

"Are you sure you are right, dear! Nothing was said about it the evening of the dance."

"I had it from Lawrence himself half an hour ago. I asked him if he would aid me in getting something done to the drainage in Omeath, and he said he would give me a subscription, but he was going away himself for some time. He then told me he was going to India in three weeks."

Eileen looked up. A sudden thought had come to her.

"It must have been decided in a great hurry?" she said a little questioningly, and hung on the General's reply.

"No," came only too promptly. "It was all arranged before he came back to Omeath. I don't know why he did not mention it sooner, but he is never one to talk of his arrangements. If I had only known, I would have hurried on this scheme of sanitation, for I want his personal support as well as his money. It is very tiresome. Bless the man! he's like a wandering organ-grinder."

There was a pause, and presently Eileen rose and left the room. Her mother's eyes followed her with a look of suffering, but Paddy bit her teeth together and said under her breath: "I'll kill him yet."

Half an hour later they all sat down to lunch, and Eileen joined them with just her usual calm manner; only the shadows under her eyes had deepened, and she seemed to avoid every one's glance.

After lunch she and Paddy were alone for a few minutes, and Paddy asked with seeming carelessness:

"Didn't Lawrence tell you he was going to India, shortly?"

"I don't think so," very quietly. "He may have, but if so I didn't catch what he was saying.

"I am not very surprised," she continued with an effort, "as he said something about not staying at home long when they first returned."

Paddy was non-plussed.

She had hardly expected Eileen to take it so calmly, and being at a loss for an answer she wisely dropped the subject.

Presently she went in search of Jack.

"Have you heard that Lawrence is going to India in three weeks?" she asked him.

"The General told me this morning," replied Jack. "I can't say I'm particularly sorry."

He was sitting on a gate that overlooked the bay, and Paddy leaned against the top rail beside him.

"I didn't suppose you would be," she retorted; "but it's not very nice for Eileen."

"Why not?" setting his mouth squarely, with an obstinate expression.

"Well, you know a lot of the people about here think they're engaged."

"And if they do—isn't it a thundering good thing they're wrong?"

"No, it isn't," getting nettled. "If Lawrence has been trifling with Eileen I'll kill him."

"Eileen has too much sense to care for a man who would behave so."

"You don't know anything about it. You're just a great, big, blundering baby," and Paddy looked as if she were on the point of tears.

"Whew!" whistled Jack. "What have I been doing now?"

"Nothing, and that's just it.—If I were a man—if I were Eileen's brother, I'd shoot Lawrence. She hasn't got a brother, but you're the next best thing and you ought to do it."

"I fail to see how I could benefit Eileen by getting myself hanged."

"I don't care," exclaimed Paddy. "I don't care for any of you. I'll have it out with Lawrence some day, and make him pay for this."

"My dear child! you're making no end of a fuss about nothing," sententiously.

"Child!" echoed Paddy derisively. "And I should like to know what you've ever done to prove yourself a man."

Jack was so astonished, for a moment he could hardly speak. In all their lives he had never known Paddy adopt that tone to him, and he regarded her as if she had suddenly developed into a new species of wild animal.

"Oh, you needn't look like that," ran on poor Paddy, getting more and more beside herself with exasperation; "you know perfectly well you are little better than a mere boy. If you had gone out into the world like other men, and made a way for yourself, you might have come back and won Eileen, and saved her from all that's coming. And instead, you have just sat still and stared at her, and let another man come in and spoil everything!—and you call that loving! If you'd any possible chance of providing a home in a year or two, you might be able to do something even now, but there you sit a mere boy at twenty-five years, and nothing achieved except a good aim and a good yachtsman."

Jack was struck dumb.

For a moment they both forgot that Paddy herself had been one of the principal supporters in his idleness—each in his own way saw only his pain.

He got down from the gate slowly.

"Good Lord, Paddy!" he said, "I believe you're right," and without stopping or looking back, he strode off across the garden toward the mountains with his forehead wrinkled into two perpendicular lines.

Paddy watched him a moment, and then rushed away to a lovely little cove by the shore, and throwing herself down on a bank burst into tears.

She did not quite know what she was crying about, but when she finally sat up and dried her eyes she felt better, and was able to review the situation more calmly.

"Perhaps, after all, Lawrence would soon be back," she argued, "and she was making a great fuss needlessly. Or perhaps Eileen did not care so much as she imagined, and things would all come right yet."

At this point she was aroused by voices, and along the little path through the trees, she descried Eileen and Lawrence coming toward her.

"Lawrence was just telling me about his trip," Eileen said pleasantly. "He is going to have a splendid tour. I think he is very wise to go about and see the world while he can, don't you?"

Paddy did not answer, and somehow Lawrence carefully avoided meeting her eyes. Eileen's pluck was making him feel less pleased with himself than anything else could have done. They had met accidentally in the afternoon, and she had immediately, in a charming way, congratulated him upon his good fortune in being able to start off travelling again.

He had been a little surprised and a little chagrined, but he had been nearer loving her then, than ever before.

Paddy's quick eyes saw at once how matters stood, and she followed Eileen's lead.

Thus for the present, Eileen managed to blind the loving, watchful eyes of the home circle.

Only to her beloved mountains, and that distant strip of turquoise, which was the sea, she remained still herself and hid nothing. In her lonely little nook, high up on the mountain side, with the dear wonder of loveliness that she so loved, spread out around her, she passed through the first of those weary Gethsemanes, that sap the joy out of young lives for a season.

At first it was so incredible to her. Had he not looked his love so often!—shown it in so many ways!—done everything, in fact, except confessed it! And if it were all a mistake, if he had meant none of it, how base then he must be.

This hurt her the most. She had never idealised him, she had rigidly made herself see his failings, but because she had believed them only the result of past circumstances and companions, and believed his love would soon lift him above them, she had given him of her best in spite of all.

But now everything was changed. Of a surety he did not love her.

Sometimes, remembering a passage here and a passage there—a look here, a look there—a touch, a tone, a sentence—her whole soul rose up and cried: "It is false, it is a mistake, he does love me, oh! he does—he does—he does—"

There would be a short space of passionate hope, and then calm reason would step in and say with inexorable firmness: "How can that be, since he goes away for no particular reason to the other side of the world, when everything at home needs his presence?"

Then would follow a period of terrible self-depreciation, when poor Eileen's sensitive nature shrank back horrified from the thought of all she had given unasked—and her cheeks burned with a deep sense of shame that she had allowed herself to believe in love where apparently no love was.

Small wonder that her heart grew faint within her. The mountains understood, and the bay, and the lights and shadows, and the strip of turquoise—or it seemed to the sad dreamer that they did —and so upon every possible occasion she stole away to the solitude, to look out upon them all with a world of pain in her beautiful eyes, suffering mutely and alone.

Once or twice her mother had been about to speak, but with quick divination Eileen had seen and stayed her. The wound was too sore yet to bear any probing. She felt, at least, she must suffer alone.

"My child, you are looking ill," her mother said at last, and there was a tremor in her voice that went to Eileen's heart.

"I am quite well, mother dear," she answered in that patient way of hers. "You must not trouble about me; there is no need for it."

For answer Mrs Adair put her hand on the bright head beside her.

"I understand, my girlie," she said in a pain-wrung voice. "I understand so well. God bless and help you and comfort you."

Eileen could not trust herself to speak, but afterward she thanked God that He had given her so dear a mother.

So the three weeks passed, and Lawrence came to say good-by. He would gladly have escaped the ordeal, but that he saw was impossible, so he drove over with his mother the last afternoon, at her suggestion. He need not have minded, for there was no change in anyone. Mrs Adair was far too proud to show by word or sign any symptom of her feelings, and both she and Eileen went through the afternoon with brave, smiling faces and perfectly natural manners.

Only when he was alone with Eileen for a few moments was there any constraint. Then, in spite of herself, she was white to the lips, and her hands played nervously.

Lawrence watched her covertly, and for the first time in his life felt a cur.

"Good-by," she said, to break the almost unbearable silence, looking up with an effort at brightness.

He took her outstretched hand and looked hard into her eyes.

"Good-by, Eileen," he answered, and hesitated a moment as if he would fain say something else. Then he suddenly dropped her hand, and went out to see about the horses.

Paddy was in the stables petting them with sugar and apples, and stroking lovingly their smooth, glossy coats, for she had a passionate love for all animals. When Lawrence came in she glanced over her shoulder, and, seeing who it was, turned her back to him, and continued playing with the horses.

Lawrence watched her a moment, and the thought crossed his mind that in fire and spirit she was a good match for them.

The man went to pull out the phaeton, and Lawrence loosened the headstalls, speaking in a low, winsome voice to his pets. Both horses immediately looked round, and playfully bit at his coat-sleeve. Paddy at the same time drew aside. The voice that enticed them, evidently repulsed her.

Lawrence glanced over one glossy back, with a slightly amused expression, and remarked:

"I am not universally hated; you see. Castor and Pollux put up with me, in spite of my manifest shortcomings."

"You feed them," she retorted. "All animals love the hand that gives them food."

"Ah! I see we are to part enemies!"

"Better an honest enemy than a false friend," icily.

"Yet I'm rather sorry," he went on. "I like you much too well to want to look upon you as my enemy."

"I do not feel as flattered as you may suppose. It seems to me there is little enough to gain in being your friend."

"Very likely," and he shrugged his shoulders with a sudden return of his old cynicism. "This seems likely to prove a striking illustration of my pet theory that it is wisest not to care. I had, forgotten it for the moment."

The horses were harnessed and the man stood at their heads ready to lead them round to the door.

"Go on," said Lawrence, "I will follow."

He turned again to Paddy.

"You have far more occasion to be glad than angry," he said, "but it is hardly likely you will see it yet. By and by—say in five years' time—you will understand. At present you do not know your world."

"Nothing will change my estimate of you," she answered cuttingly. "I wish Miss Gwendoline, what's-her-name—Carew, joy of her bargain."

"Now we are descending to personalities," with a fine sneer, "so perhaps I had better depart."

"A most excellent notion, O Theophilus!" tossing her small head.

A gleam of admiration came unbidden to his eyes.

"You're good stuff, Paddy," he said, almost under his breath. "I like your fieryness uncommon well."

"That is how I like your absence," came quick as lightning.

"Well, good-by," and he held out his hand.

She put hers behind her, with unmistakable meaning.

He shrugged his shoulders expressively, and turned away.

When he had gone a few paces, he looked back. She was still standing where he had left her. A sudden instinct brought him again to her side. "Don't be a little fool, Paddy! Come, be friends. I may never come back."

"It is not of the smallest consequence to me whether you do or not." She still stood with her hands behind her, and her eyes never once wavered before his. He could not choose but admire her dauntless attitude, now she had declared war. He hesitated a moment, unwilling to show himself beaten. Then he gave a little laugh.

"I declare—I believe you've given me an object in life. It will be quite entertaining, some day, to break down your defences." He looked into her face. "Do you hear, Patricia, when I come back, I shall storm the fortress, and make you cry Peace yet. Will you have a bet on it?"

"No," unbendingly, "I do not care to bet with you." She hesitated a second, and then finished with unflinching gaze: "I despise you."

Chapter Seventeen.

Brooding Clouds.

There was a shadow upon the Parsonage. The two little ladies looked at each other with vague dismay, and asked wonderingly, "What is this that has come upon us?"

At meal times Jack was nearly always gloomy and preoccupied, or if he was gay his merriment was evidently forced. Between meals he went for long, lonely tramps, and constantly those two perpendicular lines wrinkled his forehead. Strangest of all, he seemed to avoid The Ghan House, and Paddy was no longer his constant companion.

"Could we ask him, do you think, sister?" little Miss Mary suggested timidly.

But Miss Jane shook her head mournfully. They were feeling rather as the hen who has reared ducklings when they first take to water. This docile, careless-hearted, affectionate boy they had reared, had suddenly become a man, and in one stride passed beyond their tender, watchful care. Illness and weakness alone could ever bring him back as he had been. His troubles, his warfare, his striving, he would henceforth wrestle with alone.

Moreover, there was Eileen's white face and deeply shadowed eyes also. Nothing was said— what was there to say? Only anxious, watchful nights and yearning pain for another mother, whose fledgling was feeling the first cold blast of Life's sorrow.

Mrs Adair's abundant hair, that had been turning grey of late, seemed to go white suddenly in those weeks that followed the dance. She had borne so much; from a very early age Life had held the cup of pain to her lips, and she had tried to drink and ask no questions. But now, it seemed to her that she had met the hardest blow of all. Eileen was all the world to her. Long ago, when life was full of sadness in spite of her good husband and beautiful home—for the sake of the man whose blood had stained the ground on that far-off Afghan frontier, Eileen's baby face had come as her first real comforter, and been life and joy and sweetness to her ever since. Perhaps it was a vague, inward consciousness of this that made the father's heart turn with equal devotion to his high-spirited, boisterous second daughter; while never swerving for a moment from his devotion to her mother.

But now Eileen's cheeks grew white, and her beautiful eyes developed an expression of quiet suffering that went to her mother's heart as little else could have done, and made Paddy rage inwardly.

Until Lawrence had gone away again, and the old routine recommenced, she had not known how much she had thought of him during his three years' absence. All that time she had cared for him secretly, though she had hardly admitted it to herself. Then when he came, and again sought her before all others, and gave her of the best of his charm, it was only as the match needed for the whole to burst into flame.

Vanishing once more, in silence and suddenness, he had left her with all her dreams and hopes and happiness scattered broadcast at her feet.

There were moments when she could not understand, when even her mountains and sky and sea could do nothing to soothe the whirlpool of conflicting emotions in her heart.

"Why?—why?—why?"—she asked, and raised despairing eyes to the heavens that only seemed to smile mockingly down.

She could not vent her feelings in anger like Paddy—least of all anger with Lawrence—so in her misery she became a prey to those questionings and reasonings which torment each soul confronted suddenly by some strange enigma of existence. Questions of faith, questions of doubt, all the boundless "why and wherefore" of daily being thronged round and hammered unceasingly at her brain, stealing the delicate colour from her cheeks, the light from her eyes, and the elasticity from her steps.

In those first troubled days it was curious how Jack and Eileen both turned to the mountains, the one for their companionship, and the other for air. Jack's troubled horizon made him feel as if he could not breathe—it was like something gripping at his throat; so he strode off up the mountain, where he felt there was more air and a wider sense of freedom. It was torture to him to see Eileen's white face and flagging health, and not be able to do anything; and ever since Paddy's outburst he had been ravaged by the thought that had he accepted a man's responsibilities sooner, instead of frittering away his life, he might possibly have been in a position to oust Lawrence before matters had grown serious.

Paddy watched the two of them, and the ache in her heart deepened also; the ache for herself, the ache for Eileen, the ache for him. And with it widened and deepened also her bitterness toward Lawrence.

Suddenly in the midst of their joyous life, it was as though a cloud of darkest menace had descended, and she blamed him entirely. Hopeful by nature, she still cherished the belief that things would come all right by and by, and meanwhile she spent nearly all her time with the General.

In some way he seemed ailing, and one or two spasms, like heart seizures, had given them all a fright. Mrs Adair did not like him to go about too much alone for fear of another attack, so, as she was not strong enough to walk far herself, Paddy quickly fell into the habit of going with him every day. Eileen would gladly have gone, but she could not chatter like Paddy, and she knew, without feeling the smallest pang of jealousy, which of them the father liked best for a companion. It only seemed natural to her that it should be so, for she had such an admiration for Paddy's brightness that she felt everyone must in their hearts prefer her.

So while sorrow drew Eileen and her mother closer together, failing health did the same for Paddy and her father. Day after day, in any weather, the pair might be seen pacing the road either to Carlingford or Newry—the grey-haired, soldierly man, somewhat bent now, leaning on Paddy's arm, and the bright-eyed girl chattering briskly all the time about anything or nothing.

Sometimes the General would tell her about his campaigns, of which she never wearied, or he would go further back still and tell her of the old days at Sandhurst and Aldershot and all the wild things he had done then. Once he brought the quick tears to her eyes by saying:

"Ah, Paddy! they were grand times, and I'd have liked you to go through them; yet where would I have been for a walking stick now? I expect the Almighty knew best. I married too late in life to be trusted with a son. Boys want a father who can be a boy with them, and not a crotchety old man who needs caring for like a child. It's hard, enough on the girls—eh, Paddy!—a father who's too old and decrepit to take them anywhere or be anything but a burden!"

Paddy stood still suddenly. There were tears in her eyes, but she frowned like some ferocious Medusa.

"How dare you!" she said sternly. "How dare you speak to me like that! If you ever say anything of the kind again, you bad, wicked daddy, I shall just march you back home and not speak to you for a week."

The General smiled tenderly.

"Do you now, Paddy," he said a little wistfully, "before you came, I used sometimes to think I'd done the wrong thing in persuading your mother to many me. You see, I loved her so; I was certain I could soon make her forget and love again. But women's hearts are wonderful things. I'm thinking God didn't make anything else quite as wonderful, and it wasn't her fault that she couldn't forget. But she was always just goodness itself to me, and there was no sacrifice she would not have made willingly to please me; but after a time I found it wasn't any good, for I still felt she was mourning secretly. I couldn't bear her to be unhappy, you see, and feel I couldn't help it. At first I thought if she would only come to me, and let me have the right to take care of her always, that in itself would be a world of happiness. Afterward I found it wasn't enough. I wanted more of her love. When Eileen was born she was brighter and happier altogether, and at first I was content. Then I began to feel a little jealous of the newcomer who had succeeded where I had failed, and to feel a new sense of loneliness."

"Poor daddy," Paddy said lovingly. "I expect God said to Himself, 'I must send him something now that won't leave him time to think—the very naughtiest, unmanageable child that can possibly live; and I'll make it a girl instead of a boy, so that she'll be a good walking stick later on.' And behold! there was Paddy."

"Yes, yes, that's just it," he exclaimed delightedly, "the naughtiest, unmanageable child imaginable—that's just what you were—and Lord! how I revelled in it! The first time I saw your bright, blinking brown eyes, and your ugly little face—for you were a very ugly baby, Paddy— my heart just went straight out to you, for I felt you at least were absolutely my own. Eileen was afraid of me; she wouldn't leave her mother if she could help it, but you seemed to like the old man the best from the start. You would lie in my arms and stare up at me with the sauciest expression, as much as to say, 'Just wait till I'm a bit bigger, I'll lead you a dance.' Then you would grab at my moustache and hang on like grim death; or you would start kicking out of pure mischief, and land out right and left like a little demon, till I was afraid I'd drop you. When you could toddle I was little better than a nursemaid, for there wasn't a dangerous spot you wouldn't immediately make for. The moment anyone's back was turned you were missing, and it was a dead certainty you had found your way on to the quay, or taken a stroll along the railway, or tumbled into the cucumber frame. I couldn't bear to go far for fear you would get into danger, and there'd be no one at hand to save you, so I just hung round the grounds all the time; and ever since then, Paddy, I've been as happy as a man need be, for somehow things drew your mother and me closer together."

"Then we've all been happy, daddy, and that's good, isn't it? The aunties, and Jack, and you and mother, and Eileen and me, just the jolliest family party in the world."

The General was silent a few moments, then he said, with a little tremor in his voice, "I'm thinking it can't go on, Paddy."

"Can't go on!" with a sharp spasm of unknown dread. "Why not?—O why not?"

The old man did not answer. Instead, after another pause, he continued:

"When anything happens to me, Paddy, you'll try and look after your mother just as if you were a son, won't you? It will be hard on you, but you're so plucky. I know you'll do your best. You'll always remember your old daddy worshipped her, and nothing'll be too hard then for a brave girl like you."

"Daddy, you are not to talk like this," laughing that she might not cry. "We'll be all together years and years yet."

"I hope so, Paddy—I hope so, but I'm an old man and there's no making the old young again in this world. You'll remember about being a good son, eh!"

"Of course I will, daddy. I'll just work like a slave to give her everything she wants, but we won't talk about it now," and she cleverly changed the subject.

That evening a third seizure took the General, and Jack was called in hurriedly to help to get him upstairs to his bed.

Chapter Eighteen.

The Angel of Death.

Through four long, weary days, and four long, weary nights, the brave old soldier fought his last and hardest fight; and all the time Paddy never left him.

When the others broke down under the strain, she was strong still; strong and calm, as she felt he would have been had he been in her place. She knew it was the last thing she could do for him to prove her devotion, and the thought nerved her for a strain that might well have vanquished older and stronger hearts. Never once did the dying man open his eyes and look yearningly round without seeing the young, strong, pitying face of his heart's darling.

But when it was all over—and with a long-drawn sigh as of great content the brave old General had passed away—she stood up and looked vaguely round with a dazed air. Her eyes met Jack's, and with a sudden low cry she held out her arms to him. Then, as he hastened to her, she broke down in a paroxysm of weeping, all the more terrible from the long restraint.

With great tears in his own eyes he carried her to her own room, and laid her down on her own little bed, while he tried to soothe her in broken sentences; until little Miss Mary sent him away, saying softly it was better she should cry unrestrainedly.

Four days later, in the presence of several hundred people, General Adair was laid to rest in the little churchyard of Omeath. Every effort had been made to keep the funeral quiet and simple, but so familiar and beloved had he been, that from far and near young and old came to pay their last tribute of love and respect. There was no uncalled-for weeping and lamenting; a spirit of solemn farewell seemed to spread over all, encouraged by the brave, white faces of the widow and her two fatherless girls. The widow leaned on the arm of their only relative, a brother of the General's, Dr Adair, from London, and Eileen and Paddy followed together. Jack and the two aunts came next, and that was all the funeral procession.

It was one of those soft, sunny days that come sometimes in late November, as if they had been left over from summer, and must be fitted in somewhere; and early in the evening a young moon looked tenderly down through the trees upon the bereaved home and the new-made grave with the white wreaths spread all around.

The little waves of the Loch murmured tremulously against the beach, as if they would fain be silent, but, since that was not possible, they would make their rippling upon the shingle as gentle and soothing as they could. The tall trees stood like sentinels; now and then a little breathing whisper passed through their scanty leaves, but there was no unseemly tossing or creaking to mar the solemn silence. In the distance, all around, the Mourne Mountains reared their heads to the starlit heavens in a sublimity of majestic steadfastness. It was, indeed, an eve of surpassing loveliness that commenced the watch of that first night around the flower-strewn grave, lulling with ineffable sweetness the last, long sleep of the fine old warrior.

It crept with a tender soothing into Paddy's aching heart also as she silently threaded her way through the shrubs and gravestones to the spot where the flowers lay. The peacefulness of it all, the sense of a work well done and all Nature offering tribute—her sure and certain hope that it was indeed well with her father—kept her eyes serene and her face calm, although there was a drawn look about her mouth that went to the aunties' hearts.

When she reached the grave, she stopped and tenderly re-arranged the flowers, freeing some that had become twisted or crushed, and giving others more room to breathe.

"Daddy would not like any of you to get hurt through him," she whispered, "and you must just try and keep fresh as long as possible."

When she had finished she stood up, and a sudden terrible sense of loss enfolded her.

"Oh, daddy, perhaps you'll be lonely in Heaven," she whispered brokenly. "It doesn't seem possible you can be happy without mother and Eileen and me. We're so terribly lonely without you here. I'm so afraid God won't be able to comfort you without us up there. Only, perhaps, in some way, you are with us still. I expect you will be our guardian angel now, and you'll understand all the things that are so strange and mysterious to us; and you'll know about the glad meeting coming, and how beautiful it will all be some day. I know you won't forget or change, daddy, and I'm glad we should have the pain instead of you; yet, how I'd love you just to come and tell me that it's all beautiful, and you're not lost and lonely among so many strange angels.

"I know it's all right, daddy, I mustn't talk like this, and you're not really far away at all. I can feel you quite close, only I can't see you. Daddy! daddy! how shall I bear to live for years and years without seeing your dear face," and she broke down into low, pitiful weeping.

In the moonlight another form could be seen approaching, but Paddy was not aware of it until an arm was slipped through hers, and a big, sunburnt hand closed over her small one. She knew at once that it was Jack, but for some moments neither of them spoke. At last he cleared his throat and said huskily:

"Your uncle has been asking for you, Paddy. I came to look for you."

"What does he want?" she asked wonderingly. Jack hesitated a little. At last he said: "I think it is something you have to be told. I'm a little afraid it's bad news."

She started and turned a shade paler. Then she glanced down at the flowers.

"It seems as this were surely enough," she breathed half to herself.

"I wish I could help you, Paddy," he burst out. "I wish I could help you all. If you only knew how I hate and loathe myself for having wasted all these years."

"Poor Jack!" she said gently, and stroked the big brown hand.

"You must go now," he said. "Your uncle is waiting in the library. Will you come out again afterward?"

"Yes. Wait for me by the boat-house," and she turned away and crossed the churchyard.

In the library her uncle, a kindly, strong-faced man, was anxiously looking for her, and when she entered he glanced keenly into her face. He had been hearing a good deal about her from one and another during the last two or three days, and it was because of a plan he had in his mind that his glance held such searching interest.

"Did you want me, uncle?"

"Yes, dear."

He hesitated, then went on: "You slipped away this afternoon the moment I had finished reading your father's will, didn't you?"

"Yes, uncle. Ought I have stayed?"

"It did not make any difference, my child, except that I must explain now what has passed since. You heard, I suppose, that your father lived almost entirely on his pension, and that the greater part of that ceased at his death?"

"Yes," wonderingly.

"In fact, he seems to have had nothing left of his private property except this house and grounds, and even upon this there is a mortgage. At some period, though not within recent years, I think, with his usual kind-heartedness, he has put his name to bills for one or two brother officers, and they have not been met, and your father has had to pay. In short, my dear, your father was a noble-hearted man, but he had no business capacities, and what with one thing and another, you and your mother and sister are left very badly off."

A sudden fear seemed to seize Paddy, and with dread in her eyes, she half whispered:

"Yes, uncle. Go on."

The doctor cleared his throat and played nervously with his watch-chain.

"There does not seem to be anything except your mother's pension now, and that is barely enough to support three."

"And The Ghan House—!"

What was it in Paddy's voice that made him turn away a moment and apply his handkerchief vigorously to his nose? What was it in the aching pause that opened those eyes, wont to brim over with fun and laughter, wider and wider with dread? But nothing was to be gained by delay, and at last the doctor said slowly:

"You will have to leave The Ghan House."

Paddy sat as if she had been suddenly turned to stone. On the top of all the rest, this last blow fell like a death-stroke. Her uncle gave her a little time to recover, and then he sat down and, resting his arms upon the table, leaned toward her.

"Paddy, my child, it's terribly hard for you all," he said in a gentle voice, "but I'm so hoping you will help me to do the best for your mother and sister."

He had touched the right chord; no other method could have gone so straight to Paddy's heart. She gulped down the hard, dry sobs that threatened to choke her, and looking up with an effort said:

"I promised daddy I would be a good son."

"And I'm sure you will!" her uncle exclaimed. "You will prove yourself a true Adair—your father's own flesh and blood. You see," he continued more seriously, "what I am most troubled about is your future and Eileen's. While your mother lives there is the pension, such as it is, but when she dies, you two little girls will have practically nothing—except an old uncle who will always do what he can."

Paddy looked up gratefully, but he gave her no opportunity to speak, continuing immediately:

"If I were a rich man, you should none of you want *for* anything, but I am far from it. We Adairs have a fatal gift of getting through money—a truly Irish trait—and a great part of my private means have gone in medical research, and my practice is in a poor parish, where I have to get what fees I can and leave the rest. As you know, your aunt has a little money, but she has insisted upon giving Basil a most expensive education, and now he is only half through his exams. He may not pass his final for two or three years, and meanwhile he is a great expense."

He paused and there was a long silence, then Paddy looked up, and, steadying her voice with an effort, said:

"I must earn money, uncle. I must do something at once."

The doctor knit his forehead together. He knew only too well how, in spite of the widening opportunities for women of earning a livelihood, it is desperately hard for a young girl, fresh from the country, who has done nothing but play most of her life, to gain any kind of a footing in the ranks of women workers.

"It is difficult to begin," he said, "and you have had no training."

Paddy was silent.

"I think it will be better to go away from this neighbourhood first," he began, as if feeling his way a little.

"Oh, must we?" she cried. "I think I could teach or something. It would break our hearts to go away from the mountains."

The doctor shook his head.

"I have a plan," he said, "and you must talk it over together and let me know your answer in a week or two. Comparatively recently, it has become usual for doctors to employ women, instead of men, as dispensers. There is a certain amount of studying necessary and an examination to be passed, but this once over, they are able to demand very good salaries. You are a smart little woman, Paddy, and I have been thinking it would be an excellent arrangement for you all to come to London, and for you to fit yourself to be my dispenser. I would pay you a hundred a year, and that would not only be a help to your mother, but it would mean that you had something substantial to fall back upon when she is gone."

"A hundred a year!" Paddy half gasped. "Isn't that a great deal?"

"Oh, no!" carelessly. "It is what most dispensers get." He knew that it was considerably above the salary of the average lady-dispenser, but he did not want Paddy or her mother to know, and in any case he believed she would be well worth it to him.

"You must just think it over well," he said, "and let me know later what you decide. If your mother does not approve, I will try to think of something else, but if she does, there is no time to be lost. You must begin to study in January, with a view to getting through in July, and I will pay all the fees for you. I was obliged to speak to you to-night, my dear, because I must return to London to-morrow, and I may not have another opportunity. You are a brave girl. God will help you to do the right," and with a suspicious moisture in his eyes he stooped and kissed her forehead, and went out leaving her alone.

Then it was that the flood-gates were opened, and throwing herself down in the chair where her father had been wont to sit so often, she gave way to hopeless, heart-broken weeping. She had said little enough to her uncle, but in reality the news had been a terrible shock to her; it had never entered her head for a moment that they must leave the old home. Even now it seemed utterly impossible—as if it were better that they should all three lie quietly in the churchyard beside their beloved dead, than go away from the loch and the mountains and leave him there in the churchyard alone!

When he weeping had spent itself, she remembered Jack and how he was waiting for her at the boat-house, but just for the moment she felt too exhausted to rise. Presently, however, she dragged herself up, and with a long, sobbing breath, turned to the door and crept noiselessly through the hall to the garden, and made her way down across the railway track to the spot where she and Jack had met so often to go upon one of their many madcap escapades. He was leaning against a post, lost in thought, and he started a little when her light footstep sounded on the shingle.

"Is that you Paddy!" he asked.

"Yes, Jack!" came the answer, and he felt vaguely that there were tears in her voice.

He went forward with outstretched hands, and took her unresisting ones, trying to see into her face.

"I thought you were never coming," he said.

She gulped down a sob, and big tears splashed upon his hand.

"What is it!" he asked, feeling cold suddenly.

The little wavelets hushed their singing, a twittering bird stopped to listen; over the majestic sleeping mountains, the shining stars, the steadfast heavens, the sentinel trees, the shimmering, wistful loch, there seemed to spread the hush of a spirit of pain, as he heard her say in a trembling voice:

"We have to leave The Ghan House, and the mountains, and the loch, and go and begin over again somewhere else."

He said nothing—what was there to say! To both of them the words were like a sentence of doom.

Chapter Nineteen.

In Which the Worst Came.

The shadow upon the Parsonage had become actual distress—deep, poignant, all-absorbing distress. The two little ladies still looked mutely at each other, while this thing that had come upon them began to take actual shape. First there had been the vague anxiety for Eileen and Jack —then the loss of their old friend the General—then the bitter news that The Ghan House must be given up; and it seemed for the time that their cup of trouble was full. And yet the worst was still to come.

But it is necessary first to go back and review the events of the weary week that has dragged past since the flowers were laid upon the new-made grave in the little churchyard.

There had been many consultations, and many tears, and much pain, ere it was finally decided the good doctor's offer must indeed be accepted, and early in the new year the mother and her daughters must start for London in order that Paddy might begin her studies at once.

Meanwhile, Jack had been absent a great deal in Newry, and had returned always with a deeply thoughtful expression, and moved about in the preoccupied manner of one having some project weighing heavily upon his mind.

One evening he had come in quickly and gone straight to his room without saying a word to anyone, and he had not come down again, though Miss Jane had gone upstairs and begged him to come and have some supper, or let her carry it to his room for him.

"I couldn't eat anything to-night, auntie," he had answered, "but I am quite well. Please don't worry about me," and poor Miss Jane had gone back to the dining-room with tears in her eyes, wondering what had happened to make their boy shut himself away even from them.

"Perhaps he has seen Eileen," little Miss Mary suggested. "I know he went across to The Ghan House, and as Mrs Adair is laid up, and Paddy had to go to Newry, there would be only Eileen about."

And little Mary was right.

Jack had seen Eileen. He had had his first uninterrupted talk with her since her father died. He had found her sitting alone over the library fire, leaning back with a tired, wasted look on her face, and a closed book on her knee.

"May I stay!" he asked her, and she had mutely acquiesced, and he had closed the door, with a strange throbbing in his heart.

"Won't you sit down!" she said, and he had shaken his head without speaking, and remained standing with his back to the fire, leaning against the mantelpiece, where he could watch her face the better. He could see that she was looking ill, and the sight smote him. He realised that, perhaps, she was suffering even more than the others. Indeed, it was so, if possible, for in her longing for her father, her heart would turn and turn piteously to Lawrence, and only feel the greater desolation. Yet no word or sign escaped her. Only that frail, wasted expression grew on her face, and the unchanging sadness deepened in her eyes.

"It seems impossible that only a few weeks ago we were all so happy," he said at last. "It's very hard when Life lets you go on being careless and light-hearted for years and years; and then, without any warning, suddenly grips you by the throat and makes you feel half strangled by the weight of it all."

She did not speak, and looking straight before him he ran on:

"It seems as if the death of the dear old General would have been enough in itself, but on the top of that comes this awful separation. Do you know, Eileen, sometimes I think it can't be true— that it is too awful to be true—that The Ghan House should stand here and none of you in it, and that the sounds craning over to the Parsonage should be from other voices than yours. Sometimes I feel I can't bear it; and yet I know it will have to be borne."

Still she did not speak. She was so tired—so tired—and what was there to say?

"And that isn't all, Eileen," in a voice that would tremble in spite of himself. "It seems somehow as if it were my fault that you have to go to London, and Paddy must work."

"Your fault!" she asked wonderingly.

"Yes, Eileen, in a way. You see if I had taken the opportunities that I might have had for the asking when I was eighteen, I should probably have been doing very well indeed now, and been in a position to do something for you all."

"You are very good, Jack, but it isn't likely that we should have let you, though we should have loved you for thinking of it."

"I don't know," he said. "Everything might have been different." He paused, then added: "You know. I think I have always loved you, Eileen, ever since you were a solemn-faced little girl; though it is only lately I have realised just all it meant. I know I have generally ran about with Paddy, and been far more with her, but she was like a boy friend, while you were always my ideal of all that is best and sweetest in a woman. It is only lately I have actually understood that all my life I should love you better than the whole world."

"Oh, Jack!" she breathed, in a distressed voice, "please don't go on."

He smiled down at her, and there was something strangely beautiful in his smile.

"Yes, let me go on," he said. "It does me good to speak of it. I am not one of those men who feel bitter about loving when it is not returned, and too vain to acknowledge that it is so. To me it is such a simple, natural thing to love you; and such an unlikely possibility that you should return my love. Perhaps, if I had been more of a man the last nine years, and had started to make my way in the world, and then come to you with something to offer, it might have been different; but now! ah! that is just the hard part of it all."

"No, no, you mustn't feel like that," she cried. "What should we have done without you?—what would the aunties have done?—and I don't think it would have made any difference, Jack."

He looked at her searchingly.

"If there is someone else, Eileen, perhaps not, and yet—and yet—how often have you lectured me about being idle and good-for-nothing! Would to Heaven I had awakened, and listened to you sooner."

She buried her face in her hands.

"I suppose I ought not to ask if there is someone else," he said, watching her. "It would sound like an impertinence, wouldn't it?"

"Oh, Jack, don't talk like this," she begged. "Please, please forget about me. It hurts me so much to feel that I am hurting you."

"No, I can't forget," he answered very firmly. "I don't want to; but I have no right to bother you with my love, when I have nothing in the world to offer. But I am going away, Eileen. I am going right away out of the country altogether, and some day, if I have succeeded, I shall come back; and if you are free I shall tell you again what I have told you to-day."

"You are going away!" she repeated incredulously, sitting up and gazing at him with questioning eyes. "Going away!—out of the country!"

"Yes. I ought to have gone before."

"But the aunties, Jack!—whatever will the aunties do?"

"I am afraid they will feel it very much, but I know they will understand, and I must go."

"But where to? Have you actually arranged it?"

"Yes. There is a man is Newry named Wilkinson—I don't know if you know him. He is home from the Argentine for a few months' holiday. He has a large cattle ranch out there, and he wants me to go back with him. I have decided to go."

"Oh, Jack!" was all she could say. "Need it have been so far?"

"Beggars can't be choosers," with a wintry smile. "I believe it is a good thing. Wilkinson is a nice fellow, and he has done very well in the ten years he has been out there. We were chums at school, you know, and he offers me a better job than anyone else would."

"Poor aunties! It will half kill them."

There was a long silence, then Jack spoke again:

"I hoped—perhaps—that is," he began hesitatingly—"Eileen, couldn't you give me one word of hope to live on all the years I must be away?" He drew nearer and sat on the arm of her chair, as he had so often done through the time they had grown up together. "You'll miss me a little, perhaps, and wish I could come back sooner—tell me, Eileen, that you'll miss me."

"We shall miss you terribly, Jack," she answered, struggling to keep back the tears. "England will not be the same without you. Mother and Paddy and I will miss you terribly."

"Is that all?"

He leant forward and clasped one hand over both hers, looking hard into her face.

"Is that all, Eileen!" and his voice was a prayer.

"I'm afraid so, Jack. Oh! I wouldn't have hurt you like this for the world. I never dreamt! I never thought! Are you sure you mean it, Jack?—Isn't it just a dream or something?"

"No, it is not a dream—I mean every word of it—but there is nothing for you to blame yourself about, and you must never do so. I think, perhaps, there is someone else—I was half afraid—only I wanted so to think it was a mistake."

There was another long pause, and tears rolled slowly down Eileen's white cheeks.

"I wish I could think that you were happy," he said painfully. "It makes things worse going away and feeling that you are breaking your heart. It isn't as if he were worth it. I don't even think he could make you happy if he tried; he's too set in his own ways and opinions."

"Don't, Jack, please," she said. "It is better not to bring any other name into our talk."

"I am sorry. Forgive me. Only it's so much more terrible than you can know. It's like a raging fire in one's heart to feel as I do about it all. Only it does not make any difference to my feelings for you, and I do not think it ever will, even if you marry him. In any case I want you to feel that I am your slave wherever I am, and that nothing would be too much to ask me to do for you. I shall hear of all that happens from the aunties, and, perhaps, Paddy will write if she has time, and after a few years I shall come back to see you all."

He stood up, and there was a new look of determination in his handsome, boyish face.

"I mean to try and make up for all the time I have wasted," he said, "and prove that there is some good stuff in me yet."

"Oh, Jack! you know we all think the world of you," she urged.

"I know you have all combined to spoil me ever since I was a little chap," with a wistful smile, "and I guess it was about time Mother Fate took me by the shoulders, so to speak, and pushed me out into the cold.

"She seems to have started off with the hardest blows first though," he added. "It just feels like a clean sweep of everything I cared for most. To-morrow I must tell the aunts. I keep putting it off, because I can't bear to begin, but it won't make it any easier in the end. I think I'll go for a tramp now. Trudging over the mountains helps a little and I feel—oh! I feel as if nothing in heaven or earth mattered much because of you, Eileen," and he ground his teeth together to keep his self-command. A second later, feeling himself giving way, he strode across the room, and, passing out, closed the door quietly behind him.

Eileen rested her arms on the table, and leaning her tired head down upon them, sobbed her heart out in the old library.

That was the night Jack went up to his room and shut himself in without appearing at the supper-table, and the two little ladies clasped each other's hands in mutely questioning distress, vaguely conscious that some new blow was about to fall. The next evening he told them.

They were sitting as usual, one on either side of the big, old-fashioned fireplace, and Miss Jane's cap had got tilted a little to one side when she went to the door to speak to Eliza Spencer, whose baby had the whooping-cough. Miss Mary's looked to be preparing itself to follow suit. They both wore little white shawls folded crosswise on their breasts and pinned with large Cairngorm brooches, which looked as if they might have come out of the Ark; and black silk mittens over their pretty little hands. In the morning the shawls were grey or black, and the mittens of fine wool, but in the evening, all through the winter, they sat on each side of the fireplace, dressed precisely the same, with the same species of knitting in their fingers, reminding one of two china ornaments. Almost ever since Jack could remember it had been the same, and he took in each little detail now with a new tenderness, from the quaint little elastic-side boots just showing on each footstool, to the softly waving white hair growing perceptibly thinner each year and the dainty caps that had such a habit of getting awry. Until that evening he felt he had never quite known how dear his two second mothers had become to him.

He sat now over by the table with his arms on a newspaper he was supposed to be reading. He felt as if he could control his voice better if he did not come too near.

For a little while they talked in their kind, sympathetic way of Eliza Spencer and her sick child, and then there was a breathing silence. All felt that something unusual was in the air. At last Miss Jane looked up from her knitting, and saw that Jack was not reading at all, but sitting with his eyes upon their faces, and a deeply troubled expression on his own.

"Is there anything wrong, dear?" she asked.

He cleared his throat, but the rising lump would not go, and he waited several moments before he answered. A pained look came into each little, wrinkled face. They knew then that something fresh was to come upon them.

"I'm afraid you'll both be very upset," he said at last, and again he had to pause.

"Go on, dear," said Aunt Jane encouragingly, seeing what ah effort it was to him.

"I am going away," he blurted out, almost like a schoolboy. "I am going to South America to earn my own living," and then he buried his face on his arms, for he could not bear to see the distress come into their eyes.

"Going away!" He heard Miss Jane repeat it as if she could not believe her own ears; and then: "South America—going away—to South America—"

Each piece of knitting went down into each lap, and two wrinkled faces looked at each other as if they could not understand, and then turned slowly to the man's bowed head—the fair head that it seemed only yesterday had nestled to their hearts in babyhood.

"He can't mean it," breathed little Miss Mary. "Indeed, sister, he can't mean it—" There was a long silence, and then with tears coursing silently down her cheeks Miss Jane said very quietly:

"Yes, he means it, sister. The time has come for our bird to leave the nest and fly away."

Chapter Twenty.

Explanations.

"It's just this way, aunties," he explained. "Somehow, while you and father made me feel you only wanted me to stay at home with you, I was too easy-going and happy to care about the future at all."

He had come over to the fire place now and pulled a chair between them, so that he was quite close to each. The ice being once broken, it was easier, and Miss Jane was helping him by her brave self-control.

"Then, a little while ago something happened which made me suddenly think of what I meant to be or do in the future, and I realised how I was wasting the years. Since the dear old General died, and we heard that Paddy and Eileen and their mother were poor, I have felt awful about it, as if, had I only been making the most of these years, I might have been able to help them now."

"Poor Jack," murmured Miss Jane gently, and little Miss Mary laid her small withered hand upon one of his big ones. "I am afraid it is chiefly our fault, sister," she said sadly. "In our love we have been selfish."

Miss Jane pressed her lips together tightly. She was thinking the same thing, but it was hard to say it.

"You will have all that we have some day, Jack," she said presently. "You will not be poor."

"I know you will do all you can for me, aunties," he answered, "but I hope it will be a long, long time before anything that is your becomes mine."

Then he told them all about his plans and about his friend, and they tried to listen as if they were glad for his sake, and finally arranged that Mr Wilkinson should be brought over to the Parsonage the following day, so that they might get to know him and hear all about the country he had come from. It was quite late when they finally went upstairs to bed, and no one spoke as they kissed their usual good-night in the sisters' room, for their hearts were too full. Five minutes later, however, there was a gentle tap upon Jack's door, and in answer to his voice little Miss Mary slipped into the room and softly pushed the door to behind her.

Jack was sitting on his bed, feeling utterly wretched, and he had remained so since he came upstairs. Miss Mary sat down beside him and slipped one arm through his.

"Jack dear," she said, "you know that sister and I don't really care for anything in the world except you and your happiness, and that if we thought you were unhappy it would be impossible for us to be otherwise?"

"Yes, auntie, I know," he answered, with a catch in his voice. "You are just too good to me, that's all."

"No, dear, because no words could ever tell all you have done for us. If you had not come into our lives to keep us young and hopeful, a sorrow that nearly broke my heart, and Jane's for my sake, would probably have ended in making us sour, embittered old maids."

Jack shook his head; he knew how impossible that would have been.

"But it might, Jack," the little lady urged; "and so we must always feel we cannot ever do enough for you."

That Jack had had no choice in the matter of coming into their lives did not appear to strike her; but what of that?—she could not love him less or more either way.

"What I want to say, Jack dear," she continued, "is that sister and I have often thought how foolish it was that you should have to wait until we are dead to have our money when we would much rather you had it now. As you know, we have three hundred pounds a year each, and however much we try we cannot spend more than fifty pounds each, living in this quiet country parsonage. So we think if you would take the remaining five hundred pounds a year you might be able to win something of all you want, and we should never miss it at all."

"How good you are—how good you both are," was all he could say.

"And you will take it?" with unconcealed eagerness.

"No, no," hastily. "It is impossible—quite, quite impossible. Oh, auntie! how could I—a great strong fellow such as I—with my health and strength, take away the income of two frail women?"

"Jack dear," she urged tearfully, "don't look at it in that way. It is only that we long to repay you for all the happiness you have brought into our lives."

"It is impossible, auntie," he said, and his eyes glistened.

"Jack,"—there was a new note of tenderness in Miss Mary's voice—"is there anything between you and Eileen?"

For answer he dropped his face in his hands with a low groan. For some moments Miss Mary was silent. She could not trust herself to speak.

"Don't think your old auntie over-curious, Jack," she said at last. "I love you so. It is just as if the pain was mine again, as it was long ago. It is because I suffered so once, and understand it all, I came to you to-night. Perhaps if you could tell me about it—"

"You are an angel, auntie," he murmured, and gripped the little hand in his until he hurt it.

Miss Mary waited.

"She doesn't care, auntie," he said at last, as if the words were wrung from him. "It just seems as if nothing in heaven or earth matters since Eileen does not care."

"Poor boy; poor laddie," and a hot tear fell on his hand.

"And I don't know why she should care," he ran on, finding relief in speaking. "What have I ever done or been that she should care for me? I must always have seemed just a great, lazy schoolboy, and not a man at all. And yet I have loved her since she was a little serious-faced thing in pinafores. I can't think why I did not realise it sooner, and try to do something that might teach her to care. Instead, I have just waited until the wolf came and stole her heart away, and found out how terribly I cared when the mischief was all done."

"Poor laddie, poor laddie," the little lady said again, letting her tears flow freely. "I don't think it was so much your fault as sister's and mine. We ought to have let you go out into the world sooner. It would probably have made all the difference. Are you quite sure there is no hope?"

"There is none now, but if he does not come back I shall still hope in the future. She will not care for anyone else, I think, and by and by, perhaps, she will forget. I shall go on hoping that if such a time comes she will turn to me."

"I believe it will come, Jack," Miss Mary said hopefully, "and that in the end she will indeed turn to you."

"But I must do something to feel more worthy of her auntie, and when I come back I must come with something to offer. I feel as if I had yet to prove to her that I am a man," and he half smiled with a very wistful expression. "She has lectured me so often on being idle and wasting my life; and I always meant to begin at something but somehow it got put off. Perhaps it was just staying in Omeath spoilt everything. I feel as if I should be different altogether when I get away from the fishing, and shooting, and boating, among hardworking chaps." He paused, then added: "You must tell me everything about her that you possibly can, and perhaps—perhaps when I come back she will be waiting for me."

"I believe she will, Jack, I do, indeed," and then the little lady kissed him lovingly and went back to tell her sister.

But it was a long, weary night for all of them. Jack's hopefulness was only intermittent and vanished again almost as soon as it came, leaving him a prey to vain, pitiless regret and longing.

As for the two little ladies, it was many years since they had spent sadder hours. Far into the night they wept silently, quite unable to comfort each other. That he must go away was so terrible to them; that he must go away in trouble was only worse. In a few weeks The Ghan House would be empty and their birdling flown, and the desolation in Omeath would be terrible beyond words. Once before life had dealt them a bitter blow, and for years joy had been crushed beneath it. Then Jack had come, and their old friend the General with his young wife, and life had smiled on them again, and it had seemed that they had found a "desired haven" for the remainder of their years. And now, suddenly, the cup was dashed from their lips again, and the old, old bitterness offered, instead, and for that one night poor human nature rebelled.

Only the next morning it was as if the words, "Peace be still," had been spoken through the silence of the starlit heavens, and two sweet, calm faces greeted Jack at the breakfast-table. For sorrow does not come *so* hard upon the old as upon the young, since when half the journey is over and can be looked back upon, for those who have eyes to see there is ever the God-light visible shining through the darkest hours.

That day Jack told Paddy, and the news began to spread swiftly, until it was known in all the neighbourhood that not only was The Ghan House to be let to strangers, but Jack O'Hara, everybody's favourite, was going away across the sea to seek his fortune in foreign lands. And in every direction there was manifold sorrow and regret. People did not like to intrude upon Mrs Adair yet, but every day someone drove or bicycled to the Parsonage to know if it was indeed true, and tried the two little ladies sorely with their exclamations and questionings.

Moreover they were extremely busy. Going away to a foreign land—for all they knew, of heathens and cannibals—where there was never a woman to sew on a button nor darn a sock, it was, of course, necessary for Jack to have a regular trousseau. Everything had to be new, everything of the best, and every button and every tape sewed and sewed until it would really have puzzled Jack to get them off if he had wanted to.

In vain he expostulated and pleaded as the heap of clothes grew bigger and bigger. They would not listen to him, and were deaf to his plea that it would necessitate chartering a private ship if he were really to take ill the things they were preparing for him. When there was the slightest indecision about anything, it was always, "What do you think, sister?—will he want this?" or "Will he want a dozen suits of pyjamas" or "Three dozen pairs of socks?" or "Do you think he would be likely to require silk handkerchiefs?" And always, whichever sister asked the question, the other answered gravely, "He *might*," and that was considered final.

The Parsonage rapidly assumed the appearance of a clothing warehouse or permanent jumble sale, and Paddy's first real laugh broke out one afternoon when she came over to help sew on name-tapes. The order for the socks had accidentally been repeated four times, with the result that they were so literally swamped in socks that it seemed quite impossible to get away from them go where you would. All over the drawing-room socks lay everywhere. They hid in corners of the dining-room, disported themselves in the kitchen, smiled at you from the stairs, where they had been dropped in driblets when Miss Mary carried one armful to the first story, to spread themselves over the bedroom. In many places they were hopelessly mixed up with woollen underclothes, which also lay broadcast around, waiting for name-tapes; while flannel shirts and sleeping-suits of every hue and description draped themselves, gracefully and otherwise, over chairs and on the dining-room sideboard. The half-dozen cholera belts, that he *might* want, managed even to get into the rector's study, though how or when no one knew, and it was only after a frantic search they were discovered. His suits of clothes he had always left lying about since he left off petticoats, also his boots; and now, as if unwilling to see old friends outdone, these were tossed pell-mell among the rest, and walk where one would you were pretty certain to stumble over boots or get entangled in trouser legs.

When Paddy first saw it all there was a sort of aching pause, and then she laughed till the tears ran down her cheeks. Indeed, being somewhat out of practice, she laughed so much that she could not stop, and finally Jack attempted to stuff socks, and cholera belts, and woollen garments down her throat, to help her, while, governed by instinct, the two little ladies once more flew round collecting the breakables.

"I'm—I'm—so afraid you won't have enough things to keep you warm," gasped Paddy between her struggles. "It's only about ninety degrees in the shade, you know, in South America; you really ought to have two or three fur coats and caps and a dozen nice warm blankets."

Two minutes later nothing was to be seen of her except a pair of feet, emerging from a promiscuous heap of coats, waistcoats, socks, woollens, shirts, handkerchiefs, and an odd boot here and there.

Chapter Twenty One.

Two Love Stories.

Christmas Day broke clear and frosty—the last Christmas Day of the old order. Everyone woke up with an oppressed feeling and a vague wish that for just this once the season of merry-making and gladness might have been omitted. For The Ghan House and the Parsonage it had always been such a particularly joyous time, the aunties always spoiling the young folks in every possible way, and Mrs Adair had been wont to say laughingly when they were children, that she had to develop into a sort of griffin armed with salts and soothing draughts, and follow them all around. And there had always been such presents too—ever since Jack, as a four-year-old youngster, managed to slip out of the Parsonage in his night-clothes and no shoes, on a cold Christmas morning, to get over to The Ghan House to show Paddy and Eileen his wooden horse. The gardener found him trying to drag the animal over the breach in the wall, his poor little feet blue with cold, but his eagerness was so great that he could think of nothing but getting to The Ghan House with that precious horse before any of the Parsonage folk caught him. So the gardener picked him up, horse and all, and carried him into The Ghan House kitchen to be warmed, and then went back to tell the aunties and fetch his clothes. Meanwhile Eileen had heard him in the kitchen, and managed to drag herself, burdened with an enormous doll, to the head of the stairs, where she was only just rescued in the nick of time from going down head first, doll and all.

But at breakfast-time things had looked a little more cheerful, for a delightful surprise awaited everyone. The two families had arranged to spend the whole day together, and The Ghan House had been selected, so that quite a large party sat down to the table. Two minutes later the postman arrived and Jack and Paddy once more raced and fell over each other to the door. They came back with their arms loaded. It just seemed as if everyone who knew them had seized the opportunity of expressing their sympathy by means of a little present.

There were books, and handkerchiefs, and pictures, and purses—never had there been such a Christmas before as far as presents were concerned, and even Mrs Adair smiled to think her girls were so genuinely beloved. The greatest surprise of all came last, in the form of an envelope on each of the three young folk's plates. With eager fingers Paddy got hers open first, and then uttered a little cry of amazement, and in two seconds was hugging both aunties at the same time with a vigour that added consternation to their discomfort.

Each of the three envelopes contained a cheque for twenty pounds, and the three recipients could find no words to express their thanks.

Later they all went to church, the Adairs sitting as usual in the top pew on one side of the little aisle, and the Parsonage folks in the top pew on the other side; just as they had sat ever since Jack and Paddy as children had had to be closely watched, because they would peep at each other and make signs behind their elders' backs. Vivid recollections thronged the aunties' minds that last Christmas before the boy left them. They remembered how he and Paddy would try to see who could sing the loudest, all out of tune of course, and had considerably disturbed the music of the whole congregation; how Jack, as a little chap, loved to slip out of the pew when his father was reading the Lessons, and stand beside him—and how once, when Paddy had happened to be sitting on the outside of the Adair's pew as a reward for being a good girl, the temptation had been too much for her and she had slipped after Jack; of the Sunday Jack had put a little frog in her pocket, and she had found it and screamed out in church; and of another time when Paddy, exasperated because he would not look at her, had deliberately, in a fit of naughtiness, thrown a hymn book across the aisle at his head.

For one and all there were recollections that saddened and gladdened at once, but perhaps for Eileen were the saddest of all, because the most hopeless.

Close behind, on one side, where his thin profile had been distinctly visible, was the spot where Lawrence had often sat on a Sunday evening after coming to church, as she could not but know, especially to see her. The Blakes' parish church was at Newry, but Lawrence was never seen there; if he went to church at all he walked over to Omeath, and went in to The Ghan House to supper afterward.

It was in vain Eileen told herself he was unworthy, fickle; struggle as she would she could not tear him out of her heart, nor forget for a moment all he had been to her. The effort to do so, combined with her mourning for her father, and the dreariness of the future, had seriously affected her health the last few weeks, and just as they were finishing the first prayers, everyone was startled by the sound of a fall, and discovered Eileen in a dead faint. A second later, with a set, compressed expression, Jack had picked her up as when she was a child, and carried her out, across the churchyard and into the Parsonage. When he laid her down on the sofa, his own face was scarcely less white than the face on the cushions, and he smothered a sound that was almost a sob, as he turned away to make room for Mrs Adair and Aunt Jane.

So the day ended in sadness after all, for though Eileen came round quickly, she was almost too weak to stand, and in the evening Jack helped her across to The Ghan House, and then went to fetch the doctor. It had been arranged for her and Paddy and their mother to start for London the first week in January, where Dr Adair had already taken a house for them, and they were to stay with him while the furniture followed, but in Eileen's state of health this seemed very unwise, and it was finally decided Jack and Paddy should start off together, and Mrs Adair and Eileen should move over to the Parsonage, and remain there for a week or two following to London when their own home was ready.

Mrs Adair and Aunt Jane and Paddy and Jack planned it all in a consultation that Christmas evening, while little Miss Mary sat upstairs with Eileen. It was an opportunity she had wished for some time, for her understanding heart saw that Eileen would be better if she could be induced to speak of her pain, and she believed that she held a key that would unlock her confidence. She carefully closed the door and made up the fire, before she drew an arm-chair beside the bed, and sat down, saying:

"I think we shall have a quiet hour now, dearie, for the others are talking business, and that will be so nice, won't it?"

Eileen smiled her consent, and Miss Mary went on talking softly, in a soothing way that was natural to her. Presently she laid a little wasted hand on the invalid's and said simply:

"Eileen, my dear, you have always been especially precious to me. It goes to my heart to feel that you are unhappy and none of us can do anything."

The quick tears sprang to Eileen's eyes, but she made no reply.

"I have been thinking, perhaps, if you could trust me—" Miss Mary continued a little hesitatingly. "I know how difficult it is to speak of anything like this—I know how terrible it is to bear. I once suffered in just the same way myself, dearie, only perhaps for me it was a little harder, for we were actually engaged."

Eileen was crying quietly now, wholly undone by Miss Mary's tenderness, and made no attempt to speak.

"I always meant to tell you about it some day, if you cared to hear," Miss Mary went on, softly stroking the girl's hand, "and I have been thinking I would like to tell you now, or shall I weary you?"

"No, please tell me," murmured Eileen, and her fingers closed lovingly over her companion's.

"My dear, as you know, many people about here wonder why sister and I have never married, but I doubt if anyone knows the real reason except just she and I." She paused a moment, and then continued simply: "You have heard of old General Quinn, who used to live at Omeath Park? He was a hard-drinking, hard-living old man, and he had three sons, two of whom took after him in everything. The third son was quieter, but he was terribly weak, though none of us quite knew it at the time. He took after his mother, who was a beautiful Irish girl from the South, but she died young, and none of the boys had anyone much to look after them as they grew up. There was no real harm in any of them, but the two elder were terribly wild, and the younger was very handsome and very fond of popularity, though he followed none of the excesses of his brothers.

"They all three went into the army and were away some time, and then Patrick, the eldest, and Allan, the youngest, came home on furlough. My sister and I were twenty and twenty-one then, and I believe we were considered very pretty, but we had never been away from the Parsonage much, and we knew nothing of the world beyond the mountains.

"Patrick fell in love with Jane, and Allan with me, and you can understand, I think, how easily and naturally we were conquered, though sister never actually got so far as Allan and I, who were secretly engaged after a few weeks. We were afraid to tell my father, because he was angry with the old General about something, and we knew well it was wiser to wait until his anger had blown over, as it always did pretty quickly. The only person who knew was my godmother, and she happened to come and stay with us just then. Fortunately for me she liked Allan, though indeed she was certain to, for he was just as handsome and popular as Jack, only without Jack's backbone. She promised to help us if she could, and advised us not to say anything to father just yet. Of Patrick and Jane she thought less, perhaps because they quarrelled so often, and it seemed so very doubtful if they would ever be actually engaged; though, when they were good friends, no one need wish to meet with a happier pair. Looking back since, I have not been able to help feeling deeply sorry for Patrick. Though he was wild he was not bad, and Jane could have done as she liked with him. I know now that he was far the best of the three brothers, and it seems strange that he should have been the one who had to suffer for the other's sins.

"Things were going on in this way when the Egyptian War broke out, and Allan's regiment was ordered on active service. It was a terrible time, my dear. Getting Jack's things ready now brings to my mind so clearly that last week with Allan, and the misery of the parting when at last he sailed away.

"Had I known what was to follow I could not have borne it all. My only fear, night and day, was that he would be killed in battle, and yet before so very long my cry was changed to—'Oh, God I would that he had been killed fighting for his country!'

"We did not hear from him for some time, and then his name appeared among the wounded, and I was nearly distraught. My godmother was staying with us again, and through her influence we managed to get many details we could not otherwise have done, and we heard he had been rather seriously hurt, and as it might prove a long case he was going to be taken to the hospital at Cairo. I was not very strong at that time, dear, and what with worry and dread, the winter tried me exceedingly, and godmother grew anxious. Then she hit upon a plan. I must tell you she was rich and she had no children of her own, which doubtless made her care so deeply for me. When she saw how I was suffering about Allan, she made up her mind to take me to him—and when she made up her mind about anything she always carried it through. It took her some time to talk my father round, but in the end he agreed to let Jane and myself go away with her for three months, and a few days later we started for Cairo."

She stopped, and remained thoughtful for a few minutes, as if recalling all the facts more vividly to her mind. Eileen did not speak, and presently she added:

"It was nine months after Allan first sailed that we reached Cairo. It is no use to weary you with the details of the trip, or of what happened when we arrived. All that matters is, that in three days we discovered he was married."

"Married!" gasped Eileen incredulously.

"Yes, dear, he was married to a great friend of the hospital nurse who had nursed him—a rich heiress."

"Oh! auntie, what did you do? How terrible for you, how terrible!"

"I was very ill for some time, there at the hotel in Cairo, and my godmother and Jane nursed me night and day. Afterward, as soon as I could be moved, they got me away to Switzerland, and there I gradually grew well again. I thought it was hard at the time, Eileen, for I wanted so to die, but I have lived to understand how poor and weak that was." She stroked the girl's hand tenderly.

"It is cowardly to want to turn and run away directly the path gets hard and stony. I was a coward. I see it clearly now, and I have lived to feel ashamed. I am thankful that God did not hear my passionate pleas, for it has comforted me often to feel I am trying to make up for the weakness of that terrible year. But it was so hard at the time; oh! my dear, I know so well, when the future looks all black and hopeless. But it is never really so. What God takes away from us with one hand, He repays with the other. I was quite certain no joy was left in all the world for me—nothing but a long, lonely single life. And instead, it has all been so blessed and so sweet. What I have lost in husband and child, I seem to have found again a thousand times in you and Paddy and Jack, and all the young folks and children around that I love so well. It has been the same with Jane, I think. For twenty-five years—that is since Jack was born—we have been intensely happy in this dear, quiet spot. It is hard to lose him now, and you and Paddy also, and most of our happiness will go with you, but we shall still have each other, and it is not right to repine when one is drawing near old age and the portals of the great New Day. I only pray I may live to see you all happy, for yours is not the only aching heart, Eileen—My poor boy!" she added softly.

"I wonder you don't feel angry with me," Eileen whispered.

"My dear, how should I?—though it hurts us to know that Jack is unhappy, we have lived long enough to see that sorrow is a great teacher and a great helper, and we believe that by and by he will be glad again, and bless the Hand that let the sorrow come."

"How good you are!" Eileen breathed. "It helps me only to hear you talk."

"I want very much to help you," the little lady said sadly. "You are going away to a hard change, my child, and carrying more than one heavy cross with you. I wish I could bear something for you. But you must try not to brood, lest it injure your health and add to your mother's sorrow; and you must try to be bright to help poor Paddy. London will be terrible to her, poor child I fancy I see her now straining her eyes to the horizon, dreaming of her dear mountains and loch."

There was a short silence, and she said in a changed voice:

"But I have not finished my story yet. I have not told you what happened to Jane and Patrick. It was not until we came back to England, a year later, that I knew, and then it was a shock to me. I am afraid I was very selfish all through that year, or I should have drawn it from Jane sooner. It seems that Allan's conduct made her very angry with the whole family, and while in Cairo nursing me she learnt a great deal about the world generally that she had never known before. Among other things she heard how wild Patrick and his brother had been, and she made up her mind she would have no more to do with anyone of the name of Quinn, for my sake. By a strange chance, Patrick's regiment came to Cairo, and he sought her out at once and asked her to marry him. A very stormy scene followed, in which Jane vented her wrath against Allan upon poor Patrick and denounced the whole family. Then she accused him of drinking and betting, told him she believed no one of his name could keep faith, and sent him away.

"Poor Patrick; poor Jane—looking back now, I believe theirs was, after all, the saddest case. You see she loved him all the time, though she did not know how much until she had sent him away. And he loved her, too. For her sake he would have changed, and there was much good in him; only when she sent him away like that he just gave in and sank deeper, and not very long afterward he died of sunstroke in India. For a long time Jane never breathed a word concerning him, and then one day I found her accidentally with her head down on his photograph, and I made her tell me all.

"It was a strange mystery how one man's perfidy should be permitted to spoil three lives, but it is good to think that what looks so mysterious to our dim eyes is perfectly clear to Him, and in the end we shall understand and be satisfied.

"That is all, dear! Now you know why sister and I have never married, yet are rich because we have known the deep wonder of Love. It is worth some sorrow to have that knowledge, and there is no life so barren, whatever else it holds, as the life that has not known a deep and true Love."

She got up, and in the firelight it seemed to Eileen that some inner radiance lit up her sweet, lined face, reflecting a faint aureole round her silver hair.

"I hear them coming upstairs. God bless you, dear," and she stooped to kiss Eileen's forehead before the others stepped softly into the room.

Chapter Twenty Two.

Good-Bye.

It was the early January twilight the day before they left that Jack and Paddy went round to take their last farewells. They slipped out quietly and went alone on purpose, as neither felt particularly sure of themselves, and they were determined not to upset the others. This very fact made Paddy remark resolutely, as they walked down to the quay:

"Now, we're not going to be sentimental, Jack, and we're not going to act as if saying good-by was awful. We've just got to pretend we like it, do you see!"

"I'm with you," he answered at once, "only you'll have to show me the way."

"Let's take hands and pretend we're children again to begin with," was the prompt reply, and then, hand in hand, they stood and looked across the water to Warrenpoint.

"We've had some fun there, haven't we!" said Paddy. "Do you remember the first time we crossed alone, when you were about ten and I was six, and what a row we got into afterward!— and three weeks later we decided it was worth it and went again? Jack! what a scoundrel you were!" and she laughed up into his face.

"I, a scoundrel indeed! I like that! Why, you put me up to nearly everything, and called me a coward if I held back."

"Did I?" innocently. "How wrong of me! Good-by, my dear loch, we're only going away for a little while, and well soon be back. Mind you don't forget." And she turned briskly away, pulling Jack after her.

All through the grounds of The Ghan House and the Parsonage, path by path, they trampled, laughing at a recollection here, an escapade there, each pretending not to notice how near to tears they both felt. Last of all they came to the churchyard, and the hand in Jack's tightened involuntarily.

"It will be the making of us, you know, Jack," she said, throwing back her head with an odd little jerk, and speaking at random. "I can see it well enough now. If you had not been suddenly awakened to the true state of things, you'd just have hung on here, and never been anything at all but two dear little old maids' spoiled darling. By and by you would have taken to sipping tea, and knitting, and having your slippers warmed, and a hot-water bottle at nights, and grown very stout, and quite forgotten you were ever meant to be a man. You'd have been for all the world like one of Lady Dudley's precious kittens, that are not allowed out in the rain for fear of getting their feet wet. You wouldn't have been able to help yourself—just everything would have tended to it.

"Oh! of course it's a splendid thing for both of us," running on. "I'd have developed into an oddity of some sort, you may be sure, and been a kind of show person of the neighbourhood. Or perhaps I'd never have grown up at all. I'd just have remained a rowdy kid—and fancy a rowdy kid of thirty-five! wouldn't it be awful! Now I'm going to be a good son—it sounds lovely, doesn't it? I'm so glad daddy put it that way. Being a good daughter sounds namby-pamby and Sunday-schoolish, but being a good son, when you happen to be a girl, sounds just fine. And then it's splendid not having to teach, isn't it? Not that I could, for I don't know anything; but I might have had to be a nursery governess and worry about after tiresome children. Mixing medicines sounds much more exciting, though, I think, if I might have had my choice of anything, I'd have been one of the keepers at the Zoo. It would be just lovely to be with the animals all day long, and find out all their funny little ways, and make friends of them. But best of all would have been to come to the Argentine with you," hurrying on without giving him time to speak. "You'll ride bare-headed over endless grass plains, and have great times with the cattle, and shoot and fish, and have wide-spreading skies all around you still, while I'll be suffocated among the smuts and chimney-pots. Oh, Jack, Jack!" clinging to him with sudden weakness, "God might have made me a man, mightn't He? Then I could have come and been a cowboy with you, instead of mixing silly medicines among the smuts and chimney-pots."

Jack put his arm round her, but for a few moments he could not trust himself to speak.

"It'll be all right by and by, Paddy," he said at last. "You'll get married, you know, to some awfully nice chap, who'll take you back to the country again and just spoil you all day long."

She shrank away from him suddenly, almost with an angry gesture.

"No, I won't get married," she said. "I tell you I won't—I won't—I won't!"

Jack looked taken aback.

"Why ever not!" he asked.

"Because I won't, that's why. You're no better than the other men, Jack—and you're all a lot of blind owls. You think a girl can't do without getting married—that just that, and nothing else, is her idea of happiness! Such rubbish—you ought to have more sense."

Jack was quite at a loss to understand in what way he had so unexpectedly offended, and for the matter of that Paddy was not much wiser but under her show of determination and spirit her heart was just breaking, and she felt she must go to one extreme or another to keep up at all. And then that he could talk so calmly of her getting married and belonging to someone else? Was it possible he would not care the least little bit if his old playfellow could be the same to him no longer? Did his love for Eileen make her no more of any account at all? Of course it was so— she could see it plainly now; he did not really mind leaving anything or anybody except Eileen; the rest of them were all in a bunch—just people he had been fond of once. Her goaded heart ran on, exaggerating every little detail in its misery, and adding tenfold to its own loneliness; while in every thought she wronged Jack.

Before all things he was intensely affectionate and true; and so deep was his distress at leaving his aunts and the old home and each inmate of The Ghan House, that he had given less thought to Eileen than usual, as the day of departure approached.

"What have I done, Paddy?" he said, seeing the wild, strained look in her eyes.

"Go away," she said. "Go away to Eileen, and leave me with daddy."

The tears rained down her cheeks, as she turned from him to her father's grave, and leaning against a tombstone behind it buried her face in her hands, murmuring passionately:

"Why did you go away, daddy, when I wanted you so? Didn't you know I hadn't anyone else?—that I'd be just all alone? Mother loves Eileen best, and Jack and the aunties love her best, but you and I belonged to each other, and we didn't mind. It wasn't kind to go away and leave me. It wasn't good of God—it was cruel. I'll be a good son, because I promised, but I'd much rather come to you, and no one would mind. Daddy, daddy, can't you hear me? Ah! I know you can't or you'd come to me. You couldn't stay in Heaven or anywhere else if you knew your Paddy had this awful—awful lonely feeling—you'd just make God let you come back to me. Only you can't hear, you can't hear, and I'm all alone—alone. What shall I do through all the long years to come?"

She was now in a paroxysm of weeping, all the more intense that she had kept up so long, and Jack was frightened. His impulse was to run and fetch one of the aunts, but something held him back. Instinct told him that there was in Paddy a kindred soul, which would shrink from letting anyone see her in tears if she could possibly help it. So he stood and waited beside her silently, as he would have wished her to do had he been in her place. And when Paddy grew quieter, this action in itself appealed to her more than anything else could have done, and all her anger against him died away.

"I'm awfully silly, Jack. I don't know what you'll think of me," she said, trying to stay the tears.

"I think you're rather unkind," he answered.

She seemed surprised and asked "Why?"

"You know I think the world of you," he blurted out, feeling very near tears himself. "You know you're just the best pal a chap ever had."

Paddy gave a little crooked smile.

"Then you ought not to want me to get married," she said.

"You know I only want you to have a good time, and that I'd rather a thousand time you were a man and could come with me to the Argentine."

Paddy slipped her arm through his and rubbed her face against his coat-sleeve caressingly. "I know you would, Jack. I'm just horrid, but you must forget and make allowances. I feel—oh, I don't know what I feel—it's so positively awful."

"I know," he said feelingly. "That's just it, positively awful. But it's not any good minding, so we'd better go on trying to pretend we don't. I'll be glad when we're started now. I dread to-morrow so."

The next evening they stood together leaning on the ship rail, and straining their eyes up the loch while they steamed away from Greenore. The terrible day was over at last, and both felt quite exhausted. "How had they ever kept up at all?" they wondered, through those three meals of forced conversations, forced smiles, and poor attempts at merriment. How had the aunties ever kept up? Of a certainty they were sobbing their hearts out now in the empty, empty Parsonage.

There had been no tears until the final good-by and then the strain had become too much for them. But Jack had still held on manfully.

"Don't you fret, aunties," he said, with an odd little crack in his voice. "I'll be back almost before you've had time to tidy up after me, with pockets full of gold; and Paddy and I will be flying over the furniture again, and you'll both be collecting the ornaments, and you'll just forget we've ever been away at all."

"That's if I don't poison somebody and get hanged meanwhile," said Paddy in a cheerful way that made them all laugh in spite of themselves. "I'm sure I'll never know one medicine from another."

And now the ship is steaming away, and the two travellers strain their eyes to the familiar mountains, outlined distinctly against the star-spangled sky in the bright moonlight.

"I'm glad we can see the old giant on Carlingford Mountain," Paddy said. "I've always had a kind of fondness for him. He lies there so calmly through all weathers, and when it's bright and sunny and not too hot I can always imagine him heaving a sigh of content that it's not raining, or snowing, or anything unpleasant. Good-by, old man," waving her hand to him. "I'll be back again soon, and mind you don't change in any way. I want you to look exactly the same when I come again.

"There are the lights at Warrenpoint," she ran on. "Isn't it odd to think that the people there are going about just as usual; and next summer the Pierrots will come again, and we shall all be so far away? The mountains look specially beautiful to-night, don't they? My dear Mourne Mountains, it's just as if they put on their very best dresses, to look their nicest for our sake. I'm quite sure they're sorry, Jack. They're just awfully sorry, but they can't say it. You see they've watched us grow up, and we must have amused them a good deal at times. They know all about that first rabbit we shot, when we stole daddy's gun. How proud we were, weren't we? And they were so angry at home, instead of delighted as we thought they ought to be, when we carried in the trophies of our big game expedition. You were Selous, you know, and I was Captain Bailey. We had been reading about them just before. I expect they know about every time we have got capsized in the loch, and each time we were lost and nearly got in bogs, and just all about everything. Good-by again!" and she waved her handkerchief slowly. A bitter sea wind struck them.

"You'll catch cold," said Jack. "Come in."

"All right," and she turned away. At the entrance to the salon she looked back once more. "Good-by," she said softly to the night. "Good-by, daddy's grave—try and keep nice. Daddy himself will be in London with me."

Chapter Twenty Three.

Gwendoline Carew.

Lawrence Blake found Calcutta even more to his liking than he expected. When he left England what conscience he possessed pricked him rather severely, but when he reached India he was able to plunge into a round of gaieties that left him little enough time to think. Still, whenever he remembered Eileen he felt the same twinge. He recognised that she was not quite like other girls. She had not in any way laid herself open to the blow he had dealt her, and she had certainly not led him on. All through she had been just her own natural self, and he could not but know this only placed his conduct in a still less pleasant light. It would have been nothing to be proud of with any girl, but it does sometimes happen that a man is not wholly to blame when he has gone further than he meant.

At the same time Lawrence was a little surprised. He had several times paid quite as much and even more attention to members of the fair sex without meaning it, and gone quietly away, but he never before remembered experiencing the unpleasant sensation that he had acted like a cad. Did he then care more than he supposed? he asked once or twice. No, this was not the solution, for if anything, he felt relief as the distance between them lengthened. It was then, perhaps, the fearless measure of scorn that Paddy had dealt out to him, forcing him to see himself as he looked in the eyes of anyone who loved truth and sincerity. This, and the growing consciousness of how infinitely above him in all that matters most, was the girl whose heart he had carelessly trifled with.

The passengers on that particular P. and O. steamboat bound for India found Lawrence taciturn and morose to a degree, and in the end left him severely alone. When he arrived in Calcutta he revived, for there was so much to distract his attention. Gwendoline was charming. Earl Selloyd's attentions were more pronounced than ever, and playing at rivals amused him. And there was no risk of any serious harm this time either, for Gwen was a wholly different type of girl from Eileen, and perfectly well able to take care of herself. She liked queening it over him, and he was useful to her, and for the rest she was more likely to trifle with him, than give him a chance to trifle with her.

They saw a great deal of each other because Lawrence was a great friend of both her father's and mother's, and their doors were always open to him. So, while living at his club in Calcutta, he spent a part of each day with the Carews, either lounging in the morning-room in the morning, or dining with them in the evening, or accompanying them to some of the endless social festivities they attended.

People soon began to talk, and generally designated him the Earl's chief rival, but neither Gwendoline nor Lawrence paid any attention, only amusing themselves with the Earl's discomfiture. Mrs Carew was rather set upon the coronet, however, and endeavoured to enlist Lawrence upon her side. The topic was brought up in the drawing-room one afternoon about a month after he arrived, and just in the middle of it Gwen herself burst into the room.

"He is an extremely nice man, and it is such an excellent position," her mother was saying, and then, she stopped short to find her daughter standing before her with laughter in her splendid dark eyes.

"So mamma is making a countess of me off-hand, is she?" she asked, turning to Lawrence, who was looking on with an amused smile from the depths of a big easy-chair.

"We were just considering how a coronet would become you," he replied.

"Oh! the coronet's all right," shrugging her shoulders, "but the man! Heaven preserve me from marrying a woolly lamb with a spring inside, that says 'Baa-a-a' when you squeeze it."

"I didn't think you had got so far as that," said Lawrence wickedly.

"Don't try to be funny," retorted Gwen; "it doesn't suit your peculiar style of cleverness. Look here, mother," turning to Mrs Carew again with the air of a young queen, "don't you go setting your heart on Selloyd for a son-in-law, because I won't have him. I won't have anybody yet. I'm having a glorious time, and I mean to keep on. It's all rot wanting to tie a girl up her first season. I mean to have three seasons, and then, if no one else will have me, I'll take Lawrence," and she flashed a bewitching glance at him.

"Lawrence won't want a wife who's been in the lists three seasons," said her mother.

"Lawrence will do as he's told," promptly. "It will be a new experience, and very good for him."

"And afterward I suppose you'll allow me the same beneficial course with you," he remarked.

"Oh, no," laughing. "Women who are reigning types of English beauty never have to do as they are told. They simply reign."

"All the same I'm afraid Lawrence would know you far too well to put his head in such a noose," said Mrs Carew. "If any man would let you do as you liked, Selloyd would, and they say he is fabulously rich."

"I don't care. He can keep his old riches and his old title: I tell you I'm having a good time, and I don't mean to change it. With half Calcutta at your feet abroad, and Lawrence at your feet at home, what could I possibly want more?"

"You will wake up one day and find Lawrence gone, and the others rapidly getting tired of stooping."

"I don't care—and Lawrence would have to come back."

"That wouldn't be much good if he were married."

"Married!—Lawrence married!" and a ringing laugh sounded through the room. "Why, he'd never have the energy to propose, much less be bothered to get fixed up. He'll just lounge about in easy-chairs all his life, smiling his cynical old smile, and rousing himself occasionally to make cutting speeches. The only way to marry Lawrence would be to propose yourself, and arrange everything, because he'd give in rather than have the bother of refusing. That's how it will probably end, and I shall take pity on him and be the victim. I shall say, 'Wake up, Lawrie, you've got to marry me,' and I shall have the licence all ready and drag him off then and there."

"Who did you say would be the victim!" he asked.

The butler entered with a letter, and, after hastily reading it, Mrs Carew explained that she must send an answer that evening, and excusing herself to Lawrence went out, leaving the young folks alone. Gwendoline seated herself on the arm of a chair near him and commenced a running conversation.

"How did you like that photograph I sent you?" she asked presently. "I don't believe you ever had the manners to write and thank me."

"If I didn't it was because I knew I should be seeing you so soon."

"Well, how did you like it? You don't seem inclined to go into raptures over it, as you ought."

"All the same, I thought it excellent."

"What did you do with yourself in that deadly little Irish hamlet? Wasn't it perfectly awful? Why didn't you come away sooner?"

"I rather enjoyed it than otherwise."

"Oh! you rather enjoyed it, did you?" pricking up her ears. "I thought you never could be bothered to enjoy anything."

"I can't say I put myself out much over this."

"Are there any nice girls there?"

"Yes."

"Many?"

"Two."

"So ho!" impressively. "Yet I didn't think country bumpkins were much in your line."

"One of them is as good-looking as you."

"Is she dark?" with a little pout.

"No, fair."

"Umph—Insipid?"

"No, good."

"Good!" she echoed in a tone of laughing derision. "How amusing! Have you really been able to find entertainment in a goody-goody girl?"

"I didn't say 'goody-goody.'"

"Well, you implied it, and that's the same thing."

"Not in this case."

"And I say it is. We'll change the subject. Goody-goody girls don't interest me in the least. What's the other like?"

"Like you."

"Like me!"—in surprise. "Then she's pretty, too?"

"No. On the whole she is plain."

"You wretch! I protest she is not in the least like me!"

"And I tell you she is."

"But how?"

"In manner and ways."

"My dear Lawrence, you are talking nonsense. Do you mean to tell me that after my Parisian education, and presentation in London, and year of travel, and the gayeties of India, I resemble a little, countrified Irish girl?"

"I said that she resembled you, which is quite a different thing."

"Well, go on."

"She is quite your equal at repartee. She has quite your number of admirers, though they may not be of the same social position, and she treats them with precisely the same disdain."

"I hate her," said Gwendoline pettishly.

"That is exactly what she said about you."

Gwen sprang up. "Oh, she did, did she!" she exclaimed, "and pray why!"

"I don't know."

"Yes you do. Don't try and back out of it now, after telling me that much. What have you been saying to her about me!"

"I haven't been saying anything."

Gwen clenched her hand and bit her teeth together.

"In two minutes I shall shake you. There is nothing either funny or clever in being exasperating."

"I am sorry," he replied, with imperturbable humour. "If you will tell me what you want to know, I will try to enlighten you."

"Then 'why' and 'when' did this country bumpkin say she hated me!"

"The incident took place in a sanctum at Mourne Lodge, known as my den, upon the evening when Kathleen and Doreen 'came out.'"

"And what was she doing in your den, pray, in the middle of a dance!"

Gwen spoke peremptorily. She had somehow, unconsciously, grown to consider Lawrence her property, although there had never been anything but good-fellowship between them. Ever since she was ten and he was twenty she had ordered him about, and Lawrence, while teasing her, had usually acquiesced because she amused him.

"To the best of my recollection she was playing with my foreign swords."

"And how could that have anything to do with me?"

"She chanced to weary of the swords, and on a voyage of further discovery came across your photograph, in the place of honour, on my desk."

A pleased gleam passed through her eyes.

"Ah!" she said, "and she was angry because she is in love with you."

"On the contrary, she hates me even more than you."

Owen frowned and looked incredulous.

"Now you are talking riddles again—how silly you are! If she hates you, why did she go into your den, and why was she angry with me? I believe you are making the whole thing up."

"I am not. I do not think she spoke half a dozen civil words to me after the dance, and when I came away she would not shake hands. She told me she much preferred my room to my company."

"Really?" with dawning interest.

"Really," emphatically.

"Well, she's rather interesting after all," said Gwen, "for no doubt you are the eligible man of the neighbourhood."

"She wouldn't care a snap of the fingers for that."

"Not any more than I do for the woolly lamb's coronet?"

"Exactly. Now you are getting at the resemblance."

"But you haven't yet told me why she hates you and me."

He shrugged his shoulders. "I'm not very clear," he answered, "and anyhow it would be too tedious to try and explain. It's a trifle enough anyway. Hullo!" breaking off, "isn't that your baa-lamb I hear?"

Gwen listened with her head on one side.

"Yes, that's his bleat," she said. "Mamma will lead him in by a blue ribbon, so to speak, in a minute, and I shall want desperately to recite:

"'Mummie had a woolly lamb,
Its fleece was white as snow,
But 'twas everywhere that Gwennie went
That lamb would always go.'"

She jumped up and commenced patting her hair into place and straightening the lace of her dress, remarking that, after all said and done, there was no harm in captivating. A moment later her mother came in looking worried.

"My dear," she said, "Earl Selloyd wishes to speak to you alone. He is in the library."

"Good Heaven!" exclaimed Gwen. "Has it come to this!"

"It's very wrong to speak of it in that way," said her mother reprovingly. "I'm sure I don't know where the girls of the present day get their queer manners from. Do try and realise that Earl Selloyd has come here this afternoon to pay you the greatest honour it is in the power of any man to pay to any woman."

"Baa—a—a—a," mimicked Gwen wickedly, and Lawrence bit his lip.

"At least then, remember that you are a gentlewoman," continued Mrs Carew severely, "or that Providence intended you for one."

"Now you're getting sarcastic, mummie." Gwen went up and put her arm round her mother's neck. "Don't you get sarcastic with Gwennie, mummie, because she's just all right underneath. It's only on the top die's queer. Because you thought you were going to rear a stately swan, and found you had only a wicked duckling, you needn't frown and pucker up in that fashion. Stately swans are very tedious, and wicked ducklings do at least keep you going; so you ought really to go down on your knees and thank the good Providence that spared you the monotony of perpetually sailing about with your neck at an uncomfortable angle. Don't you think so, Lawrie? Now, I'll go and see his Earlship and be good. To him I shall put the case differently, and explain how infinitely preferable the calm of the stately swan is, beside the tiresome duckling,"—and she crossed the large drawing-room to the door. Here, however, she turned again.

"Lawrie."

"Yes."

"Do you know, I've an odd notion that if you haven't already fallen in love with that Irish, country-bumpkin girl, you very shortly will!" and without giving him time to reply she vanished.

Chapter Twenty Four.

Lawrence Hears Some News.

"Now, you know this is very foolish," said Gwen.

When she entered the library Earl Selloyd had hastened to meet her with exaggerated courtesy, and dragged forward a big arm-chair, begging her to be seated. Gwen poised herself on the arm of it, and swung one foot.

"Very foolish, indeed!" she repeated, eyeing gravely the thin, nervous, foolish-looking young man, who, nevertheless, represented one of the oldest and most illustrious families of England.

"I hope you don't mean that," he said. "Indeed, Miss Carew, it is only your happiness I have at heart."

"And a little your own, I hope," with a faint smile. Then she went on before he could interrupt: "You know I have the name for being very original, Lord Selloyd, and I'm going to be original now. You've evidently come here this evening to propose to me, and I'm not going to let you propose. I'm not the sort of girl who likes to count up her conquests and tell all the other girls. All I ask of things generally just now is, let me have a good time, and I don't care whether I get any proposal or not. Of course I think it is awfully good of you to want to give me your name and title and all that, but since I can't accept them, we won't say any more about it."

"But my dear Miss Carew," he implored, "your mother led me to suppose that she—"

"That doesn't count," interrupted Gwen. "To be very candid, you know as well as I do that no mother can help fancying a coronet for her daughter, and it's just the same the world over. Now, although I'm supposed to be very up to date, I'm really positively antique about some things, and one of them is the question of matrimony. I'm so old-fashioned that I mean to marry for love, even if I marry a plain Mr Nobody. There! now you must see that it is a mistake to continue this interview."

His lordship fidgeted nervously. "But couldn't you?" he began—"couldn't you—don't you think —?"

"I'm afraid not," Gwen said kindly, helping him out. "Isn't there anything I could do?" pleadingly. "Perhaps if you would tell me what you want in a man—?"

Gwen felt inclined to say it was a *man*, just that, pure and simple: that she wanted, but she was naturally a kind hearted girl and had no desire to hurt his feelings.

"It's no use," she said frankly. "Let's part friends, and you'll soon find someone you can care for heaps more than me, who won't worry the life out of you a bit like I should have done."

His lordship shook his head sorrowfully, and looked very woebegone.

"No," he said, "I shall never love another, and I shall never be happy again. I might as well go and shoot myself at once."

Gwen felt desperately inclined to laugh, but managed to keep her face sufficiently to say:

"Oh no, I wouldn't do that. When you've got a fine estate, and a title, and all that sort of thing, it's a pity to clear out and let someone else snatch it up."

His lordship seemed rather struck with the idea, for he said no more about shooting as he dragged himself to the door. He did, however, contrive to look the picture of wretchedness, though somehow not in a manner that appealed to Gwen's heart, and when the door finally closed behind him she hid her face in her hands a moment as if she would hide her smile even from herself. She had to pause to straighten her face again before she reappeared in the drawing-room, though Lawrence read everything directly in her eyes.

"Well," said her mother, "have you sent him away?"

"I didn't send him, mummie—he went," she answered coaxingly.

"He wouldn't have gone if you had answered him sensibly."

"Answered him about what?"

"Why, his proposal, of course."

"But he didn't propose."

"Didn't propose!" dropping her work on her knee, and lifting her eyes in astonishment.

"No, mummie. I advised him not to."

Lawrence's rare smile spread over his face.

"My dear, what do you mean?" said Mrs Carew with a helpless look.

"Well, mother, what was the good of Lord Selloyd making a fool of himself any more than he could help by asking me to marry him, when I was certain to decline with thanks? I didn't put it to him quite like that, but it came to the same thing in the end, and he had the sense to see it and go away."

"You are hopeless, quite hopeless; and I believe you make her worse, Lawrence."

"No, indeed," answered Lawrence from the depths of his easy-chair. "I have been at great pains to point out to her the ineffable benefits of a coronet, to say nothing of a husband who is—well —like cotton-wool in the hands of a strong-minded woman."

"You are both leagued against me," continued the mother, shaking her head. "If the same thing happens again, Lawrence, I shall just expect you to marry her yourself, and what will happen to your quiet Irish home then I'm afraid to think." She spread out her hands with a gesture of hopelessness, but there was a twinkle in her eyes that made the mother and daughter for a moment wonderfully alike. "Gwen buried in the Mourne Mountains would result in a social tornado, and a year of libel actions. She'd just scandalise the whole countryside and set every one quarrelling to break the monotony, and though you think you are very strong-minded, Lawrence, you'd find your match in Gwen; and I ought to know, being her mother."

Owen laughed gayly, without the smallest shadow of self-consciousness, for marriage between herself and Lawrence had been so long talked of with jesting freedom that it embarrassed neither of them in the smallest degree, although there were many who firmly believed it would eventually ensue.

"We'd get mummie to come and smooth things over, wouldn't we?" she laughed, and sauntered to the piano, afterward singing several songs in a rich and beautiful contralto. When she was tired of singing she came back to the fireplace and, seating herself upon a low footstool, remarked to her mother with a side-glance at Lawrence: "Has Lawrie told you about his Irish friend yet, mummie?"

"No," looking up questioningly. "Hasn't he?" in feigned surprise. "I am astounded. He's just full of her."

"Her?" repeated Mrs Carew, raising her eyebrows significantly.

"Yes, *her*—and she *hates* me, mummie. What do you think of that?"

"But surely she doesn't know you?"

"That's of no account at all. She's rather given to hating, for she hates Lawrie too—at least she says she does."

"I hardly see how she can be his friend then."

"Oh, yes! it's simple enough. If I say I hate a man, I find it's generally a sure sign I rather like him. Only I'm surprised she's found the trick out, buried among those old mountains."

"All the mountain ranges in the world piled up round a woman wouldn't make her other than contrary," remarked Lawrence. "I can imagine her wrestling and struggling to get away, and then a deliverer of the male sex comes along and proceeds to help her, says something she doesn't like, or doesn't say something she does like, and she would promptly sit down and say she adored mountain ranges and wouldn't be in any other spot for the world."

"Of course," exclaimed Gwen, "you wouldn't have us grow as milk and watery and monotonous as the male sex, would you? That's just what makes us so interesting."

"Irritating would be nearer the mark."

"Well, both if you like. One is just as good for you as the other. But touching this Irish girl, what's her name, Lawrie?"

"There were two I told you of. Which do you mean?"

"Why, the one who hates, of course. The other doesn't count, especially if she's goody-goody."

"The hater is Paddy Adair."

"Paddy!" cried Gwen in amusement. "What a name, but I rather like it! I'm beginning to feel quite interested in this Paddy. At first I was furious with her for daring to hate me, but now I rather like her for it. Tell me something about her."

"There isn't anything to tell."

"Of course there is. What does she do all day long, living in that deadly place!"

"Fishes, and shoots, and sails."

"Oh, does she shoot!" with eagerness.

"She's the finest shot of her sex that I've ever come across, and she can sail a boat as well as any man. She gets capsized into the loch periodically, but thinks nothing of it. Her father is a soldier, and the wilder the things she does, the better he likes it, because then he is half able to persuade himself that she is a boy. I believe the dream of his life was to have a son, but as it is he considers Paddy the next best thing and dotes on her."

"She must be very jolly," said Gwen. "What a pity she isn't pretty too."

"I never knew anyone who cared less. She won't even take the trouble to make the most of her hair, and yet, with a little pains, it is so beautiful that she could easily pass for a good-looking girl."

"I'd like to know her," said Gwen.

"I daresay you will when you find there's nothing for it but to take me and reign at Mourne Lodge instead of Selloyd Castle," with a twinkle.

"I wonder if she'd still hate me," thoughtfully.

Lawrence said nothing, but he was of the opinion that Paddy would hate more than ever.

Owen's father came in then from an official interview with Lord Kitchener, during which grave matters concerning the welfare of India had been discussed. The Hon. Jack Carew, as he still continued to be called, in spite of his forty-three years, held a Government post in India, and was one of the popular rising men of his day, great things being predicted for him in the future. Like all the rest, he idolised Gwen, and when told of the Earl's visit and its result he took her side entirely, secretly only too glad to feel the question of a wedding once more thrust in the background. The subject was quickly dismissed, and affairs of state, as far as was permissible, discussed with great interest between the father and daughter and Lawrence, until the latter departed for his club.

Here he was surprised to find a letter with a thin black edge awaiting him, in his mother's handwriting, and, once more sinking into the depths of a big easy-chair, he proceeded to read it. As he did so his brow contracted somewhat, and once or twice he glanced over the top of the paper with a half-anxious, worried expression. Then he folded it up slowly, and sat for a long time lost in thought.

So the General was dead—the kind old soldier he could remember almost as soon as he could remember anything—and, beyond doubt, Omeath and its neighbourhood was greatly the poorer. And The Ghan House was to be let, was probably already let, and Mrs Adair and her daughters were going to London. This was the news that set him thinking the most deeply—at first it seemed so utterly incredible. Omeath without the Adairs was like a problem he could not solve. Omeath without Jack O'Hara—without the Adairs or Jack—was only more extraordinary still.

And then to go to London! Eileen and Paddy cooped up in a little stuffy London house, after their lovely home among the mountains on the loch-side. It was not possible—surely it was not possible that this had to be.

He read the letter again, lingering over the part that explained how all the General's private means had gone and there was nothing left but the widow's pension, and how the post of dispenser had been offered to Paddy, and rather than be separated they were all going to London together.

So Paddy was to be dispenser? What in the name of fortune could have put such an idea into their heads? Paddy dispensing was so ludicrous to him that he could scarcely forbear to smile. But he soon grew serious again. The Adairs' misfortunes touched him more nearly than he would have thought. His mind ran on. If he went back and persuaded Eileen to marry him, he wondered if there would be any difficulty about his renting The Ghan House, and installing Mrs Adair and Paddy there for good. He believed not. If it were arranged that the gift came from Eileen, they could hardly object, and, for the matter of that, why should they?

Far into the night Lawrence sat in his big easy-chair, oblivious to all that was going on around him, thinking out his new idea.

Chapter Twenty Five.

A Curious Engagement.

For several days Lawrence had only a flying interview with Gwen, so occupied was she with balls and receptions and gayeties of all kinds, and meanwhile he still pondered the question of the Adairs. At last Gwen noticed he was unusually quiet, and taxed him in her customary outspoken fashion.

"There's something the matter with you, Lawrie," she said. "You've been looking as solemn as a boiled owl for days. Is it an attack of liver, or the hundred-and-ninety-ninth love episode? Come, out with it, and let me give you the benefit of my sage advice."

They were standing on the large staircase at the Viceroy's, having met at a reception there, and she had detained him in passing.

"Why not choose a more public spot?" Lawrence asked. "Only half Calcutta would hear us here, and they might as well all know."

"You goose," she laughed. "I suppose you want a *tête-à-tête*. Oh, dear!" with a sigh; "and I've got such a lot of special friends here to-night. Never mind, I'll manage it. I'll go with you to have refreshments at eleven o'clock, and then we'll—well, we'll go and look at the idols and mummies and things," and she passed gayly on.

Later they found their way into a quiet alcove that overlooked the big reception rooms, and Gwen at once plunged into the subject.

"Is it anything to do with the little Irish girl?" she asked.

"Partly."

"Well, what's happened."

"Her father is dead."

"Dead!" echoed Gwen, in a shocked voice.

"Yes. He died after a few days' illness, about six weeks ago, of some heart attack."

"Goodness! How sudden it seems. When did you hear?"

"The night I told you about them."

"Fancy! And I've never given you a chance to speak of it."

Lawrence was silent.

"I can see that's not all," she said.

"No. The money all seems to have gone, and they have to leave their home and go and live in London, and Paddy's going to be a dispenser."

"What in the name of wonder is a dispenser?"

"A person who makes up prescriptions."

"In a chemist's shop!" opening her eyes wide.

"Sometimes; but in this case it would be in a private doctor's surgery."

"What an extraordinary occupation! What on earth put it into their heads! If I had to earn money I'd go into a big establishment where you did nothing all day long except try on lovely dresses and pat yourself on the back because you knew you looked infinitely better in them than the annoying people who had the money to buy them."

"That wouldn't suit Paddy. She'd probably end by throwing the dresses at the people's heads. It's quite likely that's what she'll eventually do with the bottles of medicine."

"Poor Paddy," said Gwen softly. "Do you know, I don't hate her a bit now! I'm just awfully sorry."

Lawrence was silent a moment.

"It will be terrible for those girls to have to live in London," he said at last.

"What—are they sisters?" she cried. "Do you mean Paddy and the goody-goody girl?"

"Yes."

"But you didn't say they were sisters before."

"Didn't I?" carelessly. "Well, probably I didn't think about it."

Gwen watched him thoughtfully.

"Do you know," she said at last, "I think you'll just have to go home and marry Paddy, and make the mother and the other one a present of their old home."

"Paddy would almost as soon marry the Sultan of Turkey."

Gwen looked at him with a sudden light of understanding.

"Lawrie," she exclaimed, "you don't mean to tell me that you've been foolish enough to make love to the goody-goody one!"

"I told you she was not goody-goody," shortly.

"Well, what is she, then!"

There was a pause.

"She's like my mother," he said slowly; "only mother was never as good-looking."

"Yes, that's all very well," quoth Gwen; "but men never want to marry their mothers, even when they worship them. I can just see the whole thing now, and you've behaved like an idiot, for all your brains and cleverness. If I had been there to look after you it wouldn't have happened. A man of your type does not *love* a girl of her type; he only admires and respects from a distance. If you had married her you wouldn't have made her happy, so it's a very good thing for her you've come away. Why! your morose, taciturn moods would have broken her heart, and your temper would have been like an icy blast to a delicate hot-house flower. She would never have understood you at all; and being sweet-tempered and unselfish herself would only have left her more hopelessly in the dark, and in the end have irritated you awfully. Oh! I am very wise, Lawrie, about some things. I don't know how I got it, but it's there, and possibly father spared me a biggish slice of his brains. Now the other girl, Paddy, would suit you well, but it's a pity she's plain. If you were moody and sullen with her I expect she'd throw something at your head, and that's just about what you need."

"You are very kind."

"Glad you think so," with a little laugh; "but meanwhile, what's to be done with your friends!"

Lawrence was annoyed with her plain speaking, probably because she was so distinctly in the right.

"I think," he said coolly, "that I shall return to England and marry Paddy's sister."

Gwen looked into his face, and saw with her usual intuition exactly how matters stood.

"Very well," she said airily, getting up. "Go and make the funeral pile of your own happiness and hers as well. I'm sure I don't care, and I've got quite as much on my hands out here just now as I can well attend to, so I'll be quite relieved to leave you to look after your own affairs entirely. But when you've managed to fit a square block into a round hole by becoming a pattern, stay-at-home country squire, just let me know, as by that time I shall be wanting to see something unique. Good-by! I have an important engagement," and without giving him time to offer his escort she was off.

Lawrence remained where he was, and thought of Eileen, drawing back into deep shadow, and staring moodily down at the gay throng below him. After a long time, getting no nearer to a decision, he went below again and joined a small coterie of men about the Hon. Jack Carew, discussing the probability of disturbances on the Afghan frontier in the spring.

A few days later, while still in a state of indecision, he made the discovery that Gwen was in a fix. He came upon her unexpectedly in the morning-room, and caught her with tears in her eyes before she had time to brush them away. She did so angrily enough directly he entered, but by that time he had seen them. Lawrence looked at her a moment, and then crossed and carefully closed the door and came back again.

"What's the matter?" he asked, as if he meant to be told.

"Nothing," she answered shortly.

"When I came in your were crying."

"No, I wasn't!" and she tossed her head.

"Fibber," from Lawrence.

"Well, I suppose I can please myself."

"Not much good though, when I know the truth."

"I tell you I wasn't crying," stamping her foot.

"Very well, then, we'll begin again. How did you manage to get such a cold, Gwen?"

"I haven't a cold."

"Indeed! I thought your eyes were running."

She made no reply. Lawrence drew near and leaned on the table beside her.

"What's the matter, chum?" he said coaxingly.

"Oh! just everything," she broke out. "I can't think why Heaven made men such fools."

"Admirers getting entangled?" he asked.

"Yes," pettishly. "I believe Captain O'Connor is going to make Lord Selloyd fight."

"You needn't worry. Woolly lambs don't fight—they run away."

"Oh, but can't you see how silly it is!" she cried in exasperation. "It is bound to get round to the clubs, and then to the women, and mother will be furious. I must make them come to their senses somehow."

"What's it all about?"

"Oh, I don't know," expressively. "A storm in a tea-cup, of course, but you Irishmen are so ridiculously hot-headed. Take a hot-headed Irishman and an Englishman who is a fool, and they're sure to do something silly.

"I don't mind about them," running on, "but I do want to keep it from mother and father. You see, they give me a lot of liberty, and they'll think I've been abusing it, and it really wasn't my fault this time," and the tears sprang to her eyes again.

"What happened?"

"Well, it was at the Inglis' dance. Lord Selloyd would follow me about, and Captain O'Connor got angry. I think they had both had too much champagne for supper, and in the end they had a row."

"Probably it has all blown over by now."

"No, it hasn't. They will both be at the Markhams' to-night, and it will be very unpleasant."

"I shall be there," said Lawrence. "Can't I see you through!"

Gwen was thoughtful a few moments, and suddenly she looked up with an idea.

"Look here, Lawrence," she said, "if I could once for all convince both of them it wasn't the least use thinking any more about me, I believe they'd just leave Calcutta, and no one would ever know there had been this bother."

"And can't you?"

"I can't by merely talking. I must try and prove it—and I have an idea, Lawrence."

"Say on."

"If I could tell them I was engaged it would just simplify everything." Lawrence nodded, to show he was following, and waited. "I can only do that with someone to corroborate it, and I've been thinking, Lawrence, if you wouldn't mind helping me, you're just the man."

"I am ready for anything. What do you want?"

"I want you to be secretly engaged to me for this evening."

Lawrence looked up, and there was amusement in his eyes.

"It's a splendid idea," she exclaimed, warming to her subject. "I shall tell Captain O'Connor and make him understand it can't be announced for some particular reason, and he'll be flattered at being told, and just keep it to himself and say no more. You must, of course, be there yourself to sanction it or he might not believe it."

Gwen talked on, and Lawrence listened, falling in with her plans easily enough because he saw no harm in the trick and it was the least trouble. When Mrs Carew joined them later, Gwen was radiant again and rather looking forward to her evening. Afterward she was still more radiant, for everything had gone well. Captain O'Connor, a fiery young officer, spending a month's leave in Calcutta before starting to England, was quickly brought to reason by Gwen's charming way of confiding in him, and, while announcing his intention of running himself through, in the same moment grasped Lawrence's hand, and told him he was the luckiest chap on earth.

The next morning he did actually start for England, a week sooner than he intended, leaving Lord Selloyd to congratulate himself upon having got out of the quarrel so simply.

The incident dispersed Gwen's passing displeasure with Lawrence also, and she condescended once more to mention the subject of the Adairs, asking him if he had decided what to do. He was standing with his hands in his pockets looking out of the window, and for a moment he did not reply. Gwen came and leaned against the window-frame beside him.

"If you go, Lawrie, are you quite certain it would have to be the pretty one?" she asked.

"Yes—quite," he answered.

"Then stay here. I'm awfully sorry for them—at least I'm sorry for Paddy," she continued, as he did not speak, "but I'm absolutely certain it would be a mistake for you to marry the other one. Deep down in your heart you think so yourself, don't you?"

"I have long been under the impression that I had no heart."

"Rubbish! Why, that's what people say about me, and do you think I don't know better! When 'John Right' comes along you'll all see I've got just as much heart as any one else, but until he does—a short life and a merry one, say I! That's how it will be with you, Lawrie. When Mary Jane Right turns up you'll tear your hair—what there is of it—and stamp, and rave, and storm, just like any other love-sick male. Till then, if it pleases you to be cynical and *blasé*, and all that nonsense, why, be cynical and *blasé*; it doesn't hurt any one else—in fact, it's rather amusing," and she rested her hand on his arm and looked into his face with roguish, laughing eyes. "I'd have just loved to have a brother," she said, "but, like that nice old General Adair who wanted a son, I guess I've got the next best thing."

So, in the end, Lawrence did not return to England, and nothing happened to avert the hard change for Paddy and Eileen and their mother.

Chapter Twenty Six.

Paddy Makes Her Cousin's Acquaintance.

One of the first things Paddy did when she got to London was to quarrel with her cousin, Basil Adair. Basil was a medical student, a young man who had somehow got a notion that the world would be in no end of a queer fix without him; but that, as long as he remained in it, he had no occasion to work or strive after anything except having a good time, spending a great deal of money and talking big. He was rather curious about this new cousin who was coming to stay a few weeks with them, and inclined to be pleased at the idea of some one quite fresh to impress daily with his new clothes, immaculate boots, glossy head-gear, and generally magnificent appearance. When he saw a black-robed, sallow-faced girl, with serious eyes and badly dressed hair, he was inclined to be satirical. Paddy's mourning, hastily procured in Newry, did not meet with his approval at all, as indeed it was hardly likely to do, and black was the most unbecoming colour she could possibly wear. Still, he had a great idea of always doing the correct thing, so he came home to dinner the flint evening, and addressed various polite remarks to her, in a grandiloquent, not to say condescending, tone.

Paddy looked at him as if he were a clothes-horse, and Basil was not pleased. Half divining the same, Paddy looked again. After dinner, when she had the opportunity of a nearer inspection, she looked with interest at the immaculate patent-leather boots, and took a calm survey of the whole effect. Basil felt he was making an impression, and though he thought she was very plain and dowdy, he was a young man who could not have resisted trying to make an impression on a crossing sweeper. He took up his stand on the hearthrug, with his legs astride and his hands behind him, and looked down at her over his two-and-a-half-inch collar, prepared to continue his magnanimity.

"Er—you don't know London, I believe—er—Miss Adair?" he began.

"I have been here before," Paddy answered. "I was at school here for about four months."

"It is unfortunate," he continued, "that father's practice happens to be—er—in Shepherd's Bush, and that, therefore, you should have to become acquainted with London from such a—er—plebeian locality."

"I don't see that it matters where you are, if you've got to be in London," said Paddy more bluntly than grammatically.

"But London is a glorious place," he cried. "To be in London is life, to be out of it is death. London is—er—the centre of the world. The centre of learning, and commerce, and—er—art, and—er—progress."

"Don't they say the same about Paris, and Berlin, and New York, and lots of other places?" she asked calmly.

"If they do, it is a lie. London stands at the top of the pyramid built by the cities of the world."

"Well, anyhow, I'd sooner have Omeath," said Paddy.

"It is heresy," he cried, "rank heresy—and you an Englishwoman."

"Irish," corrected Paddy, very decidedly.

"Ah, yes, to be sure! And I suppose you're—er—very proud of it. Funny thing how the Irish fancy their nationality."

"Not half so funny as some of the things you fancy yourselves for over in England," she retorted, getting a little exasperated.

Basil glanced down over his collar rather as if he were taking stock of a curious kind of animal, and Paddy began to fidget. She was becoming more and more conscious of a desperate impulse to ruffle his hair, and tumble his collar, and disarrange generally this painfully well-dressed young man, with his air of extreme condescension.

"Ah!" he said satirically, "you cultivate the art of repartee in Ireland—as well as potatoes."

"We cultivate men, too," with scorn. "You ought to go over there and finish your education."

This rather took his breath away for a minute, and while he was recovering Paddy's mood changed.

"That was rude," she said. "I'm sorry."

This surprised him still more, and he mentally designated her the oddest fish he had come across.

"Oh, don't mention it," he replied with a paternal air. "I like people who say what they think." There was a pause, then he asked: "I suppose you are fond of theatres?"

"I have never been to one."

"Never been to a theatre!" he gasped. "Impossible! Why you haven't done anything!"

Paddy leaned forward suddenly. "Have you ever shot a snipe?" she said.

"No," wonderingly.

"Well, I have," and she closed her lips with an expressive snap, and there was a slight pause.

"You're a—er—sportswoman then?" at last.

"I don't shoot my bird sitting, if that's what you mean."

Basil had no mind to reveal his ignorance upon sport generally, so he tried another tack, asking: "I suppose you have read all the new novels."

"I have ready scarcely anything, except 'The Jungle Tales,' 'A Voyage in the Cachalot,' and the Bible. I never had time to read."

"Never had time!" he echoed. "I thought people who lived in the country had no other way to kill time."

Paddy did not reply, so he asked, "What did you do beside shoot, then!"

"Oh, I could sail a bit, and fish a bit, and climb a bit. Then there was the hockey club, and tennis club, and golf club. The days weren't as a rule half long enough."

Basil looked down with some show of interest.

"You'll rather miss all that in London," he suggested.

"I guess so," was Paddy's short, laconic response, and she fixed her eyes on the fire.

"Still, there'll be lots of other things," he went on. "Dances, and theatres, and—er—shops. The guv'nor's awfully easy-going, you know—you won't have to do much work."

"Do you mean Uncle Frank?" raising her eyebrows a little.

"Yes, of course. Why?"

Paddy did not answer, and just then her aunt come back.

"Basil, my dear," said his mother anxiously, "I don't like to think you are working so hard. I'm sure you're not strong enough. Last night it was quite one o'clock when I heard you moving about overhead."

"Oh, that won't hurt me," carelessly, "and it's so much easier to read at night."

Paddy looked at him keenly.

"But, my dear boy, you must remember your health," continued his mother fondly. "You must not let your zeal make you rash."

Paddy grew meditative. She had distinct recollections of her uncle saying Basil could not get through his exams, and implying that he did not work. Her aunt turned to her.

"You know the medical profession is such a hard one to get on in, my dear," she said, "and Basil has to be nearly always working. I assure you it is a most unusual thing for him to spend an evening in the drawing-room like this. He nearly always goes to the hospital, or works at a friend's rooms. It is entirely for your sake, my dear, and I was very glad when I heard him say he could manage it."

Paddy murmured something about being honoured, and a little later asked if she might be excused and go to bed, as she was very tired.

Basil had something of a shock. It was incredible for any girl to want to go to bed at nine o'clock when he was there. When Paddy actually stood up and prepared to go, he concluded she had a headache and could not bear the light. As a matter of fact poor Paddy was momentarily getting nearer breaking down altogether, and the instant her aunt closed the door and left her alone, she went down on her knees by the bedside and burst into tears.

It had been such a terrible day—she thought she would never forget it as long as she lived.

She and Jack had breakfasted together at Holyhead, where they remained until morning, and then he had seen her safely into the train to London. There had been tears in his sunny eyes, and Paddy had felt awful, but it had to be borne, and now he was on the sea sailing away—away from England and all of them. It did, indeed, seem as if all the hard things possible had come upon them at once, and when she at last slipped into bed, she cried herself to sleep.

The next day she went with her uncle to see about her dispensing and was fortunately able to start working at once, which left her less time to think.

Nevertheless, often across her studies would steal the memory of the mountains and loch. In fancy she would smell the heather or the peat, hear the curlews calling or the cry of the plover, the lapping of the little waves against the keel of the boat, or their light murmuring on the shingle; she would wonder what the aunties were doing, and how the hockey club was getting on with its new captain, and whether they all thought of her sometimes and missed her! One big tear would gather and then another, and she would dash them angrily away, fighting day by day with steady persistence the passionate longing, the sometimes passionate determination, to throw everything to the winds and go back and live on crusts, if need be, beside her beloved lake. Sometimes these fits left her very sore and irritable, and it was in such a mood she had her first real quarrel with Basil, about three weeks after her arrival. She hardly knew what it was all about, neither did he, but he started holding forth in his usual high fashion upon London and Londoners being the salt of the earth, with certain vague innuendoes about well-cut, tailor-made dresses and a smart style, until Paddy grew exasperated beyond endurance, and informed him, none too politely, that he was only fitted to stand in tailor's window, as a model of an empty-headed, well-dressed, curled and pampered modern young man, with about as much real manhood in him as a wax doll.

Having delivered herself of this somewhat pointed speech, in a highly impressive fashion, she flung out of the room and slammed the door behind her in a way that shook the jerry-built Shepherd's Bush villa to its very foundation. It shook his lordship, Basil Adair, gasping into a large arm-chair with open mouth and eyes, for the onslaught had very literally taken his breath away.

"By Jove," he breathed, "I hope the roof's securely fastened on. What in the name of fortune did the guv'nor bring this whirlwind—this tornado—this positive monsoon—into a suburban villa for?"

Chapter Twenty Seven.

Paddy has a Visitor.

When Paddy was alone in her room her anger quickly evaporated, and was as quickly replaced by an overpowering sense of loneliness. Why, oh why, had they let her come to London alone? Why had Fate dealt her this double blow! "Daddy, daddy," she breathed piteously, and buried her face in her hands. For a moment she longed to be away there in the quiet churchyard beside him. It seemed to her quite impossible that life would ever be glad again, since he was gone, and Jack was gone, and strangers were probably already moving into The Ghan House.

But presently the mood passed and she was calmer, remembering all the responsibility on her shoulders.

"Don't forget you're an Irish Fusilier's daughter, Paddy," she admonished herself severely, "and you promised to be a good son. Irish Fusiliers' daughters don't cry like babies, just because everything seems to have gone wrong; and a good son is more sorry for his mother than himself."

A few minutes later there was a knock at her door, and the maid told her a gentleman had called to see her.

"A gentleman?" asked Paddy in surprise. "What is his name?"

"I'm afraid I didn't catch it," the maid answered. "It was a long name."

"Are you sure he asked for me?"

"Yes."

"Where is he?"

"In the drawing-room. Mr Basil has gone out, and Mrs Adair is in the master's surgery."

Paddy smoothed her hair and bathed her eyes, feeling very curious, but when she walked into the drawing-room her visitor saw at a glance that she had been crying.

"Mr Masterman!" she exclaimed in glad surprise, and Ted came forward eagerly enough. After the first greetings, however, there was a slightly awkward pause.

"I only heard about everything last week," said Ted at last. "My aunt is a very bad correspondent. I need hardly say how her letter shocked me."

Paddy had motioned to him to take a chair, and sat down on the sofa; but Ted, being no less masterful than of old, and quite as certain as to his mind, sat down on the sofa beside her instead.

"I can't tell you just all I feel," he said, in that quiet, convincing way of his. "I wish I could, but I think you must know it has all been like a personal sorrow."

"You are very good," Paddy murmured gratefully. She was so glad to see him—he was like the first link from the old home since she parted from Jack at Holyhead.

"How did you know I was here!"

"I wired to my aunt for your address directly I received the letter. I wanted to call sooner, but was prevented by business. We have been kept late at the works every night for a week. I'm afraid this London arrangement will be very hard on you," he said, so kindly that Paddy felt the tears coming back.

"A little," she answered, trying to pull herself together, "but it won't be so bad when I'm used to it."

She tried to meet his eyes, but could not, and instead looked away, blinking hard.

"Poor little girl," said Ted in a very low voice, half to himself, and covered his eyes with his hand a moment, as if there was something in them he felt he must hide from her. She little knew how that pair of strong arms beside her ached to fold her tight, and take her away then and there from this London she so hated.

"I wish I could do something," he said at last. "It's hard to have to sit still, and feel as I feel, and see no way to help."

"You mustn't take it like that," trying to speak brightly. "Mother and Eileen will be here soon, and then it will be much better for me."

"What has become of O'Hara?" he asked. "Will you tell me all about everything?"

Paddy was only too glad to have someone who knew all about Omeath and The Ghan House, and she readily described all that had happened since he left. Ted listened quietly, leaning back a little, as once before, that he might the better watch her, with his own strong face in the shadow.

"It will be the making of him," was his comment when she came to Jack's plans, and Paddy agreed with alacrity.

When she had finished he looked at her, with a slightly wistful look in his grey eyes, and said:

"Now may I tell you about my affairs?"

"Yes, do."

"I'm following O'Hara's lead and leaving England," and he looked hard into her face.

"Leaving England!" she repeated, with frank dismay—indeed, far too frank for Ted, who was sufficiently wise in these matters to know that such a complete absence of self-consciousness left but little room for him to hope in.

"Yes," dropping his eyes gloomily to the carpet. "At once."

"I *am* sorry," she said expressively. "Why do you go? What is happening to England that you and Jack and Lawrence Blake and everyone must all go abroad?"

"Lawrence Blake?" he asked, in some surprise.

Paddy coloured painfully.

"Yes, didn't you know? He went to India a month after the dance."

Ted watched her inquiringly, uncertain whether or not to ask a particular question.

Paddy settled the matter for him.

"It was rather a good thing," she said, trying to speak naturally. "He and Eileen were hovering on the brink of an engagement, and it would not have been a suitable match. He would never have made a girl like Eileen happy."

Ted drew his own conclusions, but all he said, was:

"O'Hara will get his chance now—lucky beggar," and then suddenly relapsed into thought, as it dawned upon him it might in the end mean his own chance, too.

"You have not told me why you are going abroad?" she said, after a pause.

"I am going to South Africa for the firm I am with."

"For good?"

"For several years, I expect."

"Why do you go?"

"Well, you see," he began slowly, "it's a very good opening for a man who wants to get on, and I want that even more now than I ever wanted it before." She waited, and he continued: "Engineering is rather overdone in England, and it's very hard work to get any kind of a real footing at all. The firm is opening a big, new branch in Africa, and they have offered me the managership. It is a very good thing, and I have accepted it."

"But still," reasoned Paddy, "you were all right as you were before."

He smiled a little.

"No, that's just it. I wasn't all right. You see, Miss Adair, there comes a time in a man's life when he suddenly wakes up to the fact that he'd desperately like a home of his own, and that makes him think more seriously of the pounds, shillings, and pence. I want my home to be right in the country, too," he added whimsically, half to himself, "if possible, where there are mountains and a loch and plenty of fishing and shooting."

Paddy said nothing, but she felt a queer little thrill all down her back. She turned her head away and stared hard into the glowing coals. She knew his eyes were fixed searchingly on her face, but she would not look round, nor give him the chance to see the consciousness in her own. He leaned back presently with a little sigh.

"I'd rather have thought of you running wild at Omeath still," he said, "but it can't be helped, and I shall have to make the best of it. Perhaps, sometimes you'll be glad to feel there's some one thinking of you, some one awfully sorry for you, across the sea. At least, I hope you won't forget altogether?"

Still Paddy kept her face averted.

"I shall not forget," was all she would say.

"I wonder if it would be too much to ask for an occasional letter," he went on. "Perhaps, if you remembered what a boon it would be to the exile—?"

"Oh, yes, I'll write to you sometimes," with frankness. "I dare say I shall be glad to air my opinions upon London and things generally, now and again."

"Not so glad as I shall be to get them. How I wish I could have been here and, perhaps, helped you all a little, and still had the good position. I could at least have taken you to theatres, and down the river."

"It would have been nice," she assented.

"I may get back in four years," he continued, "but hardly before."

"When do you sail?"

"Next week."

"Next week!" in astonishment. "How near it seems."

"Yes." He hesitated. "May I come and see you again!"

"Of course you must come and say good-by."

"Very well then. Next Friday evening!"

It was agreed so, and just then Mrs Adair and the doctor came in, and after a little Ted rose to go.

The following Friday, as luck would have it, Basil took it into his head to remain at home, and ensconced himself in the drawing-room as if he meant to stay. When Ted arrived he was still there, and Paddy felt vexed. Her feelings, however, were nothing to Ted's. He would gladly have picked the young man up by his collar and dropped him out of the window into the street below. After half-an-hour of vain efforts to keep the conversation going naturally, the kindly doctor himself came to the rescue.

"I'm sure these young people would like to talk over old times together without us," he said, "as they're not to meet again for so long. Come along, my dear, we'll go to my room as usual, and Basil can come too."

Basil looked annoyed, but could hardly do other than follow the others from the room, though he loftily declined the invitation to the surgery.

"Is that young man your cousin!" asked Ted when they were alone.

"Yes, but I'm not proud of the relationship," said outspoken Paddy.

Ted only smiled. He could afford to be more magnanimous now he had gone. He got up and strolled round the room, not because he was tired of sitting at all, but because he was thus enabled to make an entirely free choice of where he would sit down again. Paddy was on the sofa, so as it is much easier to talk to anyone from the same sofa, instead of shouting from another chair, he chose the vacant space beside her. Paddy fidgeted with her hands, and again took to studying the glowing coals as if she had never seen a fire before.

"Do you know I have taken a great liberty?" he said presently.

"Yes!" looking up.

"I've—well, I've taken upon myself to bring you a small talisman. You won't be angry with me?"

"I think it is very nice of you."

"And you'll accept it?" eagerly.

"What is it?" turning to the coals again.

Ted took a little parcel from his pocket, and unfolded a very valuable old gold coin with a hole in it.

"It's a lucky coin," he said. "I noticed you had a chain bracelet and I thought, perhaps, you wouldn't mind letting me fix it on for you. It's rather a rare one. My father was a great collector, and it used to belong to him."

"Oh! but you mustn't give it to me then," she cried.

"Yes, I want to," firmly, "and I am going to fix it on myself."

She gave him her bracelet, impelled by some unseen force, and watched him silently while he carefully fixed the coin to one of the links. A little while afterward he wrung her hand, looked a whole world of love into her eyes, and hurried away.

When Paddy was alone, she became unusually thoughtful, and fingered the coin gently. Then for the first time she discovered something had been engraved on it, and held it curiously to the light. In small writing, across the centre, were the two words, "Dinna forget," and underneath the date of the morrow when his ship would sail.

"Poor Ted," murmured Paddy softly, and a little flush crept into her white cheeks.

Chapter Twenty Eight.

The New Home.

It was not until March, when Paddy had been in London over two months, that her mother and Eileen joined her. By that time she and the doctor had the furniture all in place and everything ready. A letter Paddy received the last day rather surprised her.

"Do not meet us," Eileen wrote, "nor wait at uncle's for us. We particularly want to receive you in our own little home, and shall be eagerly watching for you about six o'clock."

Paddy thought it rather queer, but fell in with their wishes, and went off as usual to her classes. When she reached home in the evening Eileen was watching at the little front bow-window and flew to the door, her mother following closely, and none of the three knew quite whether to laugh or cry, they were all so glad and so sad together.

"It's just good to have a home again," said Paddy, and bustled into the little sitting-room while her mother and Eileen exchanged glances. No sooner had she entered than she gave a cry of delight, for there, on each side of the fireplace, in their usual manner, sat the two aunties. The next moment they were both pleading for mercy in stifled tones beneath her vigorous hugs.

"You dear, *dear*, dear aunties!" she cried; "to come all this long way at such a cold time of year. How I just love you both! I shall have to go on hugging you all the evening. However did you make up your minds to come?"

"Well, you see, dear," said Aunt Jane, "we could never have rested content without being quite sure you were all as comfortable as circumstances would permit, and so we felt the only thing to do was to come and see for ourselves."

"Yes," nodded little Miss Mary, "we have come to see for ourselves."

The tea-table caught Paddy's eye then, and she had to go into raptures over again.

"Omeath eggs!" she cried. "Omeath ham!—cream! honey!—marmalade!—parsonage tea cakes! —parsonage scones—parsonage apple pie! Oh, goodness! how ill I shall be to-morrow! Was ever such a delicious-looking meal! I shall be practising dispensing upon the whole household, I expect, in a few hours." And then, just to relieve her feelings, she started hugging everybody over again, until the two poor little ladies' caps were at such an impossible angle they were obliged to retire to put them straight.

"If only Jack were here," Paddy said longingly, as they sat down, "what a lovely occasion for a scramble it would be!"

"We have had a letter from him," said Miss Jane, in a glad voice. "You shall see it afterward. He has reached Buenos Aires safely and had a good voyage, and he gives a wonderful description of the flowers and loveliness of Montevideo. It is nice to think that the boy is seeing something of the world at last. We ought to have sent him abroad before. I am afraid we were very selfish." And little Miss Mary chimed in with mournful agreement.

"Oh, no, you weren't," asserted Paddy; "nothing of the kind. Jack was lazy, and I encouraged him, and it just serves us both right to have to work hard now."

They asked her how she was getting on with her studying, and she looked gravely mischievous and said, "Pretty middling."

"You see," she continued, "medicines are very confusing. They're nearly all water, with a little colouring, but the various colourings have long Latin names to give them an air of importance, and it's very hard to remember which high-sounding name belongs to which colouring. I have to study a very learned book called the 'Materia Medica,' but I haven't yet succeeded in making any sense of a single page and I have my doubts whether there is really any sense in the whole book. But I like going to the hospital," she ran on. "The matron is nice and the nurses are jolly. The dispenser and I generally contrive to get tea in the dispensary in the afternoon, and whichever of them can manage it slips down and has a cup with us. Both the tea and bread and butter usually get flavoured with the nastiest drug lying about, but that is a mere detail."

"What is Aunt Edith like, and how do you get on with Basil?" they asked.

"Aunt Edith is like Mrs Masterman, and looks as if she was left over from a hundred years ago. She always speaks of Basil as '*dear* Basil' or '*poor dear* Basil,' according as he has been over-working or over-spending, and she spends a great deal of time in church, and talks about the 'poor dear clergyman' and the 'poor dear choir boys,' and discusses a different guild every evening in the week. She has only two real ideas in the world—one is the church and the other is

Basil; and they agree in one thing—they never stop asking her for money. Uncle is a sort of fixture, like the blinds or the kitchen range, but he doesn't seem to mind so long as he can follow his profession in peace, and he is just the dearest and kindest man in the world."

"And how do you get on with Basil?" they asked again.

"Well, I don't get on at all," and Paddy looked amused. "I don't think we're on speaking terms just now—we are not as a rule. Before I had been there a month I told him he was not fitted for anything but a dressed-up mummy in a tailor's window, and a few other similar things, and for a time our relations were very strained. We indulge in home truths concerning each other so often that I find it difficult to remember when we are on speaking terms and when not. He is rather fond of making sarcastic reflections upon Irish dressmakers and countrified style, and of course I have to hit back from the shoulder for the sake of the old country."

They could not help laughing, but her mother quickly grew grave and looked a little anxious.

"I hope you don't carry it too far, my dear," she said. "I would not like to hurt your uncle's and aunt's feelings after all their kindness."

"Don't you be afraid, mother," cheerfully. "Uncle enjoys it, and aunt doesn't understand half we say. She generally misses the point, you see, and thinks I am paying Basil compliments. Uncle, on the other hand, sees that it is only his welfare I have at heart."

She then went on to tell them about Ted Masterman—all except the incident of the coin—and the doctor at the classes, and her friends the 'bus drivers, chattering away like her old self again for very happiness at having them all round her. They sat in a semicircle over the fire until late into the night, and finally went to bed too tired after their long day, and too pleased at being together again, to have time to be miserable.

Only when they were alone Paddy asked Eileen if she had heard from Lawrence, and with a faint blush Eileen acknowledged that she had. After a moment's hesitation she produced the letter and gave it to Paddy to read.

"It is a nice one," was all Paddy said, as she folded it up afterward. "He could always be nice if it happened to please him."

Eileen made no reply. It was not a subject she could discuss, and she knew, moreover, that it was one upon which she and Paddy could never agree. For she had not forgotten Lawrence at all, and still, deep down in her heart, lived a hope that she could not extinguish. When we desire a thing with a great and terrible longing, it is very hard to honestly and squarely face the fact that it can never be ours. If there is any possible chance of fitting in a "perhaps," that "perhaps" is pretty sure to be there. Eileen had managed to find more than one chance, and the really nice letter that Lawrence had written her directly he heard of the General's death, and while the news still had a softening effect upon him, had only more firmly entrenched them.

It was unfortunate, but it was the way of the world. The fine-strung nervous system that holds the deepest capacity for suffering is oftenest jarred upon and hurt by rough, careless hands and cold, selfish hearts. And always, too, are these the sufferers who hope and remember the longest in spite of all.

Paddy felt vaguely that Eileen still loved and still hoped and her loyal heart was furious with Lawrence. But she was obliged to content herself with scathingly picking his letter to pieces in her own mind, for she recognised that no good could some of saying these kind of things to Eileen, and she would just have to stand aside and let matters take their own course.

"I suppose he might come back," she reasoned, with a worried feeling; "but it is not very likely, and a very questionable benefit if he did."

Yet, when, as the days went by, she saw the quiet sadness still paramount in Eileen's eyes, and knew that all her happiness was forced, she felt a great longing to have it settled one way or another for all their sakes. The shadow hung heavily upon the mother also, and Paddy easily saw that it was not London and her loss only that kept her so worn and ill-looking.

It was just when things were in this state, by a most strange coincidence, that Paddy heard news of Lawrence partly through her cousin Basil. Now that they did not five under the same roof, they managed to keep better friends, though Paddy never missed the smallest opportunity of a taunt at Basil's effeminacy, and Basil still persisted in veiled hints at her general lack of elegance. However, as both were already profiting by the other's plain speaking, it was very harmless. Paddy, on her part, had become very friendly with another girl student, who, in the matter of appearance, was the exact opposite of herself, and she was beginning to benefit by the friendship. Ethel Matheson was a true Londoner of the modern type, which represents a girl quite as fond of outdoor games as a country girl, but at the same time having the unmistakable cut of London about her clothes. Well-cut tailor-mades, simple, smart hats, hair well dressed, gloves and boots always neat, made Ethel a pleasing picture in any weather and at any time, and before long Paddy began to envy her. After a time she got so far as to mention it, and from that day the change commenced. Ethel took her in hand altogether, and guaranteed that in a few months, if Paddy would give her mind to it seriously, she would turn her out as neat and smart as herself, and only spend a fraction more money. Consequently, when the spring was well advanced, Paddy invested in her first smart "tailor-made," a very pretty hat, and began to take pains with her hair. The very first time she was out in them, feeling not a little conscious, but on the whole well pleased with herself, she ran into Basil going home on the top of a 'bus.

"By Jove!" said Basil. "If it isn't Paddy!—all in new clothes!"

"Well, there's no occasion to be rude," retorted Paddy. "Any one would think you were not accustomed to new clothes instead of dreaming and thinking of little else."

Two men, who, unknown to her, were accompanying Basil, began to laugh, and Paddy blushed a fiery red when her cousin, with considerable enjoyment, proceeded to introduce them to her.

Chapter Twenty Nine.

A Strange Coincidence.

"Let me introduce my friends to you," he said. "This is Pat O'Connor, of your own proud nationality, known as the lady-killer of Middlesex Hospital, and this is his brother, Captain O'Connor, of Dargai renown, now home on leave from India. Gentlemen," he added wickedly, "allow me to introduce you to Miss Paddy Adair, the snipe-shooter."

Paddy blushed again, which was most becoming to her, and Basil could not help looking candidly surprised, though he forbore from any more personalities at present. The individual introduced as Captain O'Connor was sitting next to Paddy, and she was rather glad, as "lady-killers" were not in her line, and she liked the look of this sunburnt soldier. She commenced chatting to him at once in her pleasant, friendly way, and Captain O'Connor was more than pleased. With the delightful humility of his nation, his first thought was—"Any one would have known she's Irish, she's so nice."

Presently the topic of India was introduced, that of their respective Irish counties and the general perfection of the Emerald Isle becoming a little exhausted, and the Captain told her about the gayeties of the hill stations, and of Calcutta during the season.

"I stayed two or three weeks in Calcutta," he told her, "on my way home, as I knew I should have quite as good a time there as in England." He suddenly became thoughtful, as if struck by some memory, and with equal suddenness turned upon her with the startling remark:

"By the way, Lawrence Blake comes from near Omeath. Do you know him?"

Paddy was so taken aback, she caught her breath with a little gasp before she answered.

"Yes, very well indeed."

"How odd," said the Captain and paused.

"Why?" eyeing him keenly.

He coloured under his sunburn.

"Oh, nothing," and then after a moment—as if changing his mind—"He's engaged to a great friend of mine."

"Engaged!" exclaimed Paddy, too taken aback to hide her astonishment.

"Yes; why!" and this time it was Captain O'Connor's turn to look with keen eyes.

"Oh, nothing!" she answered, "only I'm rather surprised I hadn't heard of it. Whom is he engaged to?"

"The Hon. Grant-Carew's daughter. She's well known over there."

"Do you know her?" unable to hide her curiosity.

"Yes, very well."

"What is she like?"

He paused a moment.

"She's the most beautiful girl I've ever seen," he said at last, with conviction.

For some minutes Paddy was silent.

"Are you quite sure they're engaged?" she asked presently.

"Quite. I had it from her own lips, and congratulated the two of them the same evening. It hadn't been publicly announced yet, but she had her own reasons for telling me then. He's rich, isn't he? I hope so, because she's the sort of girl who ought to have just everything she wants. He's a thundering lucky chap," and poor Guy looked sufficiently miserable to make his own part in the story very plain.

"Yes, he's rich," Paddy answered, "and he has a lovely place near Omeath. I wonder when they will be married? I don't like the idea of somebody fresh coming there at all. I'm sure I shan't like her."

"I think you will. She's very popular in India. Everybody likes her."

"I'm rather difficult to please," asserted Miss Paddy with her nose in the air and Guy O'Connor wondered why she seemed so unnecessarily down upon both Gwendoline and Lawrence.

At Lancaster Gate the two brothers got off, and Paddy and Basil proceeded alone. Paddy was very thoughtful, and Basil wanted to talk, which made her somewhat cross.

"I don't know what's happened to you," he said. "You're looking real stunning! I could scarcely believe my eyes when I first saw you."

"Don't talk nonsense," snapped Paddy. "I've only got a new dress on, and there's nothing so very extraordinary in that."

"But there is," he insisted, "it's all very extraordinary. The last time I saw you, you were just dressed anyhow, and suggested milking-stools and hayfields; now you're—well, you're a Londoner."

"I'm *not*," emphatically. "I wouldn't be a Londoner for all the world—grasping, conceited, money-grubbing lot."

"Whew!" whistled Basil softly. "What's Captain O'Connor been saying to get her little temper up?"

"Nothing, only you're so silly, and I haven't the patience to talk to boys."

Basil proceeded to do a little sum on his fingers, looking abnormally grave.

"Umph! thirty-five I should think," he said musingly, "though you hardly look it. No chicken that! eh—what?"

Paddy was obliged to burst out laughing.

"Do you know I think you're improving rather," she told him. "You aren't half such a namby-pamby coxcomb as you were when I first came to London at Christmas."

"Not easy when you're about," he commented, adding, "I think we might be said to have formed a mutual improvement society. If you only knew what you looked like that first night! A sort of antediluvian Joan of Arc! I thought you were the oddest fish I had ever come across."

"Why Joan of Arc?"

"Because you had war in your eyes from the first moment we met. I didn't recognise it so quickly then as I should now, but I couldn't help seeing you didn't mean to waste much cousinly affection on me."

"I thought you were an awful idiot," she remarked, with smiling candour.

"And you tried to show it with more force than politeness; which was cheek when you weren't anything much to boast of yourself."

They had reached the terminus and now climbed down, walking off homeward together at a brisk pace.

"By the way, how's that long-legged, broad-shouldered British bull-dog specimen who came to say good-by before going to South Africa?" he asked.

"Umph! sour grapes!" with a little snort.

Basil was pleased. He felt as if he were getting a little of his own back again.

"Feeling a bit love-sick, eh?" he asked.

"If I were, I should think I had caught it from you," scathingly.

"Oh, I've given all that sort of thing up now; but I'm naturally interested in your affairs, being a cousin. When did he say he should be back?"

"I didn't ask him."

"Ah! I expect he had already told you."

"He had not."

"What! not when he asked you if you'd have diamonds or emeralds?"

"He wouldn't be likely to be so silly, and if you can't talk sense, Basil Adair, for heaven's sake don't talk at all."

Basil laughed outright then with great enjoyment.

"It's such fun to tease you, Paddy," he said. "You do get so deliriously wild about nothing. Good-night," as they reached her door. "Don't fling the plates about when you get in, it's such an expensive amusement," and he went off down the road.

All evening Paddy remained moody and preoccupied, revolving in her mind how to tell Eileen about Lawrence. In the end she waited until bed-time, and they were alone. She then began a long rigmarole about the extraordinariness of coincidence, which made Eileen look at her with wonderment, and question in her own mind if she had a bad headache or anything. Paddy noticed it, but held on until she was hopelessly and inextricably mixed up, and then, after all her fine preparation, she suddenly blurted out:

"Lawrence Blake is engaged. I heard it from a friend of his this afternoon."

Eileen turned deathly white and gripped a table near her. She looked as if she were going to faint.

"Oh, Eily! don't look like that!" cried poor Paddy. "What a blundering idiot I am. Oh! don't take it to heart dreadfully—he isn't worth it—really, really, he isn't."

It was too late for Eileen to prevaricate, so she just sat down and leaned her face in her hands and said, "Tell me about it."

Paddy told her all she knew, and how she had heard of Gwendoline Carew before and seen her photograph, but how, when she taxed Lawrence, he had denied there was anything between them.

"I suppose he was just hesitating," she finished, "and as soon as he got back to her he made up his mind."

Eileen said nothing. It was a bitter blow to her, but no words could ease it now. Paddy, however, slipped down on her knees and threw her arms round her.

"Eily, Eily!" she cried. "I'll kill him, I will indeed, if you take it to heart so. I don't know how he dare hurt you, but you are well rid of him; he is just a scoundrel and no gentleman at all, and he would never have made you happy. I am quite sure he never would. You didn't know him so well as I did. I used to hear from Kathleen how queer he was at home. Sometimes he would scarcely speak for days, and he just damped everything for them all; but he was so selfish he did not care. And I hate to tell tales, but I am not sure that he doesn't drink, Eileen. He used to at one time. I feel awful to think you are unhappy through him, but I'd feel more awful still, I think, if you were going to marry him."

Eileen kissed her, but still remained silent. What was there to say? She had loved this man, she had given him of her best, encouraged and attracted by his attentions, and now at last she knew indeed that what he had won he did not want, and all he had said meant nothing. She remembered the incident in the boat—she remembered the half-hour in the conservatory at the dance—ah! she would not easily forget that; but how it hurt her, oh! how it *hurt* that this man she loved had proved himself fickle and false. She hid her face in her hands—her eyeballs burnt and scorched, her head throbbed wildly, but she could not cry. She felt as if all her tears were dried up for good.

"Don't say anything to mother, Paddy," she managed to plead at last. "Keep it just between you and me. By and by I shall feel better about it, and then I will tell her myself."

Paddy was crying quietly now; she was devoted to her only sister and cared as much as if the pain had been hers. For the time all thought of her own feelings went out of her mind, and with true unselfishness she pleaded for Jack. But Eileen only shook her head.

"I couldn't love Jack in that way," she said with quiet resolve. In her heart she felt she could never love any one in that way again, but she did not say so to Paddy. She waited until her sister's regular breathing told her she was asleep, and then had it out by herself in the kindly darkness of the night.

And Paddy went to sleep vowing vengeance black and overwhelming upon the cause of her sister's misery.

"He shall suffer for it yet," she told herself. "I, for one, will never forgive him; and if I can make him pay, I will."

Chapter Thirty.

An Encounter.

In July Paddy had to go up for her examination, and for days she was in a fever of nervous anxiety about it.

"What's it matter!" Basil said. "Examinations never worry me."

"They wouldn't me if I didn't care whether I passed or not."

"Well, why do you? It's silly, I think."

"Umph!" expressively. "If I were a man I'd sooner sweep a crossing than live on my mother."

Basil flushed and bit his lip. Things had been going so easily and pleasantly with him for years, that it was extremely trying to have these pointed remarks hurled at his head.

"The mater likes it," he grunted.

"Well, you see, she has your delicate health so much at heart," sarcastically. "I wonder she let you come out without an overcoat this morning. I do hope you won't take cold."

"Chuck it!" and he frowned gloomily. Presently he glanced up.

"Look here, Paddy!" he said. "If you get through your exam, I'm hanged if I don't buck up, and get through mine, too."

"You'd better begin working to-night," she answered, "for I mean to pass," and she shut her lips with a determination that spoke volumes.

And she did pass too—one of the three girls out of the whole number who had only worked for six months, and there was great rejoicing in the little jerry-built villa. Eileen went with her to the hall where the examination was held, and waited all the time she was there. Before Paddy appeared Basil joined her.

"It matters a good deal to me," he told Eileen, "because if she passes I've got to start working to pass too."

When Paddy came her eyes shone so, there was no occasion to ask her anything.

"Oh, Eileen," she said, "do you think I might dance a jig right here! Faith! and indaid!—I'm that plaized—!"

Basil was pleased too, though he would have thought it bad form to show it too much.

"Let's go and have a beano," he said. "We'll dine at the Trocadero and then go to Daly's."

"Oh, but I must rush home and tell mother."

"We can wire," and he succeeded in persuading them to go with him to the nearest telegraph office and dispatch telegrams to Mrs Adair and the aunties; and then they trooped away delightedly to the Trocadero. Paddy dearly loved dining out in this way, and all those sitting near them could not refrain from glancing again and again at the table from which such a genuinely happy laugh rang out. Even Eileen was gay that evening, and Basil surpassed himself with tales of the medical students and the comic side of hospital life.

When they at last got home they found Mrs Adair waiting with tears of gladness, for she knew how bitterly Paddy would have felt it had she failed. The following week they all went off to Seaforth for a month, neither Mrs Adair nor Eileen being well, and consequently the long journey to Omeath was pronounced too trying, and the nearer English seaside place decided upon.

When they came back Paddy was duly installed as dispenser in her uncle's surgery; and her hours being nine to eleven and half-past five to eight, she was kept fairly busy. This was fortunate, as it left her little time to mope, as she would otherwise have done. For as the weeks sped by Paddy could not in any degree grow reconciled to London, and when they first returned from Seaforth it seemed more hideous to her than ever. She hated Shepherd's Bush with all her strength, and secretly much missed the daily journey to Chancery Lane, which had at least been interesting. To this free-born mountain-child the cramped streets, the dingy rows of ugly little houses, the whole atmosphere of this London suburb, were positively repulsive; and she felt as if she were in a cage, against which she was ever beating and bruising her wings in a vain longing to escape. It was much the same to Eileen and her mother, only they were made in a less vigorous mould, and it was not so hard for them to bear up, helped as they were by a religion which was very real and very true. Paddy's religion, it must be confessed, was chiefly her father. She stuck to her dispensing manfully because she had promised to be a good son, but deep in her heart she nursed a silent soreness against God that He had let things come to this pass. It was, perhaps, wrong of her, but no doubt that brave loyalty to her promise, covered much weakness in the eyes of Him who understandeth the secrets of every heart, their soreness as well as their patience. Also, when Eileen's defences did break down, she suffered even more for the time being. Paddy could fling about and hurl out vigorous sarcasms, in which poor Shepherd's Bush got even more than its due of opprobrium, but which relieved her feelings a good deal, while Eileen could only fight it out silently alone. And whereas the mountains and loch represented so much fun and adventure to Paddy, they had been actual friends and companions to Eileen, and no one knew how terribly she missed them, nor what an utter loneliness there was in her heart. At these times she could not but turn gladly to Jack's occasional letters. They were not brilliant specimens of either penmanship or composition, but there was the true ring of the man himself about them, with his breeziness and humour and unmistakable sincerity. He made no direct allusion to anything that had passed between them before he left, filling them chiefly with descriptions of the free, wild life on an Argentine cattle ranch, but there was something in the way he put things, and in the fact of each letter being addressed to her, that whispered a secret message to Eileen's heart. She was not ready for the message yet, but when she was very lonely it was a soothing thought and she let it linger in her mind gladly. Paddy, meanwhile, with true pertinacity, remained staunch to her old chum. What Jack had been to her he still remained, and seemed likely to do at present, to the detriment of any other would-be suitor. Paddy felt she liked them all, but not any one more than another, except Jack O'Hara. Poor Ted Masterman only came in for an equal share with the rest, though she still continued to wear his coin, and he never ceased to think of her, night and day, in his far-off African home. Then there were the two O'Connors, to say nothing of Cousin Basil. At first it had been the gallant Captain, who soon found himself in a ripe condition to be consoled for the loss of Owen Carew; but he had made no headway whatever, not even as much as with the gay society belle, and finally had to return to India needing consolation all over again. Then his brother Pat, the Middlesex lady-killer, took a turn, but with still less success, for Paddy would not even bother to amuse him, and pitilessly summed him up in the same breath with the meek young curate, who had meanwhile become hopelessly enamoured of Eileen's lovely face.

Basil, on the whole, she began to rather like, though she still taunted and teased him mercilessly; but if he got at all sentimental, as he very much wanted to do, he was shut up in such a very summary fashion that it was quite an exercise in courage ever to approach the dangerous ground at all.

With the doctor's patients she was a great favourite. Being a poor practice, those who could usually fetched their medicines themselves, and others sent children; and for one and all Paddy had a cheery greeting, or a merry jest, from behind her rows of neatly-wrapped bottles. To a police sergeant, who started airing all his grievances at things in general at great length, she once said: "What's the good of grumbling; it doesn't really help matters a bit. Do you know, if I stopped to think now, and then tried to express my feelings, I should just hurl all these bottles at your head, and anyone else's head who happened to come to the surgery."

The sergeant of police was so impressed that he went away quite thoughtfully, and the next time he fetched medicine he brought her half a score of new-laid eggs from his own fowl run.

"I was thinkin' about you findin' it dull work corkin' up them bottles," he said a little shamefacedly, "and them'll be as good as you got in the country, which you can't say of many eggs in London."

But it was one day the following spring, fifteen months after she had first come to London, that a chance meeting in Regent street brought about the beginning of a great change in Paddy's life. It was amazing how trim, and neat, and smart she had become now; London must certainly have been said to suit her, for she had rounded and filled out into a charming figure; and, while taking pains with her dress and appearance, she still walked with the old light, free step of her country days, her head thrown well back and her eyes clear and frank as of old. Without the least effort or wish on her part, wherever she went she was almost sure to be noticed, even when with Eileen, who, however, must always absorb the lion's share of passing homage. Mrs Adair was, indeed, justly proud of her two girls' increasing charms; while far away, under the sunny South American sky, across endless reaches of rolling grass, raced Jack—the other part of the Irish trio —likewise developing into a fine, strong, deep-hearted specimen of his sex, immeasurably the better for his hard work and various hard experiences in the matter of roughing it generally.

On that particular spring afternoon, however, it is with a thin-faced, clean-shaven man, and a very striking, dark-eyed girl, who passed up Regent Street and went into Fuller's to tea, that we have now to do. The man was mostly silent, as was his wont; but the girl was chattering gayly, now and then drawing a smile to his lips; and from the amount of nods she dispensed in different directions it was very evident she knew and was known very well. After they had commenced their tea, the girl bethought her of some special kind of cream bun she particularly wanted, and her companion must needs go and hunt for it. While he was gone she looked round casually, and was presently enjoying in no small degree a lively altercation between two girls seated near as to which should pay for their tea. There was not much question from the beginning as to which would win, for the girl who first caught and held the watcher's fancy was unmistakably a young person who usually got her own way by hook or crook, and in this case she informed her companion of her intention in quite as original and outspoken a way as she did most things. Finally, they departed, and the dark-eyed stranger was quite sorry to see them go.

When her attendant knight returned with the cream buns in question, his usually impassive face wore the faintest suspicion of surprise, but he only placed her delicacies before her and said: "There! now you can make yourself ill to your heart's content."

"You ought to have been here a minute ago," she said. "There was such an amusing discussion between two girls about which should pay. I was immensely taken with one of them—she wasn't exactly pretty, but she looked so jolly, and she just carried everything before her in a most entertaining fashion. She's just the sort of girl I'd fall in love with if I were a man. Did you notice her? She was paying at the desk while you hunted up these cakes."

"I did. It was Paddy Adair."

"Paddy Adair!" in tones of amazement. "Was that really Paddy Adair, Lawrence?"

"It was."

"Goodness!" and Gwen grew quite contemptuous. "Why you said she was plain and dowdy!"

Lawrence calmly continued his tea.

"So she was the last time I saw her."

"Well, she isn't now, anyway. I call her quite striking, and she was distinctly well dressed." There was a pause, then she added: "Perhaps she's married, and got a man to choose her things for her. That's one thing husbands are sometimes good for; and some of them know a fair amount about hair-dressing too."

"No, she's not married," said Lawrence. "Doreen was talking about them only the other day. They're living in Shepherd's Bush."

"Shepherd's Bush!" echoed Gwendoline. "How awful, after their country home. But how London has smartened her up, hasn't it?"

"Astonishingly."

"I wish you had come back in time to speak to her," continued Gwen. "I'd like to be introduced."

Meanwhile, Paddy walked down to Piccadilly Circus with Ethel Matheson, and then hurried back to get her 'bus in Oxford Street. On the way she dashed into a shop and bought some tomatoes, a favourite dish of her mother's—true to her nationality, acting on the spur of the moment, blissfully regardless of the fact that she could have got the same article for half the money at the other end of her 'bus ride. As she hurried past Fuller's Lawrence and Gwendoline came out, the latter catching sight of her instantly.

"There's Paddy Adair!" she exclaimed. "Do stop her."

Lawrence hesitated and in that second Paddy brushed too near a boy with a basket, the basket caught against her bag of tomatoes—carried no doubt in somewhat careless fashion—the paper split, and out sprawled the tomatoes all across the pavement in the midst of the rank and fashion of Regent Street.

"Christopher Columbus!" exclaimed Paddy under her breath and blushing crimson, but quite unable to help laughing, as she commenced diving for her belongings among the feet of the passers-by. A dark-eyed girl, enjoying the scrimmage immensely, rescued one from the gutter, while the man with her succeeded in getting three from various directions, and when Paddy at last turned to thank them, a lovely colour in her cheeks and a bewitching roguishness in her eyes, she found herself face to face with Lawrence Blake and his companion, each offering her a tomato.

Chapter Thirty One.

Paddy Makes a New Friend.

For one moment Paddy was utterly at a loss, and bit her lips in evident vexation, while the colour deepened still further in her face.

"How do you do, Paddy?" said Lawrence. "You seem to be in difficulties as usual. May I introduce you to your other timely helper, Miss Grant-Carew?"

Paddy bowed very stiffly, but as Gwen promptly held out her hand, she was obliged to take it. She managed, however, to avoid doing likewise with Lawrence. Gwen pretended not to notice her coldness, and remarked laughingly:

"I'm so glad I didn't miss that. You can't think how funny it looked—in Regent Street of all places, too?"

Paddy was constrained to laugh again at the recollection, but she busied herself trying to rearrange the tomatoes in a secure fashion, and absolutely refused to look at Lawrence.

"I think they will be all right now," she said. "Thank you so much for helping me to pick them up. I'm in rather a hurry, as I have to be at the surgery by half-past five—if you will excuse my running off. Good-by!" and in two seconds she was vanishing in the crowd.

Gwen looked at Lawrence drolly.

"She's a good hater," she remarked. "Gwen isn't used to being put off in that summary fashion. She doesn't like it, Lawrie."

"It's your own fault. You practically pushed me into the introduction."

"Because I wanted to know her. It isn't often people don't want to know Gwennie. I don't understand!—me *ne comprenez pas*, Lawrie. This is going to be interesting," she ran on. "I shall insist upon Doreen inviting me to meet her in Cadogan Place."

Paddy meanwhile scrambled on to her 'bus, tomatoes held safely this time, and started homeward feeling furious.

"How dare he introduce me!" she mused angrily. "He knows I hate her. How dare he stop me at all in that cool fashion!" calmly ignoring the fact that the tomatoes and her own carelessness, not Lawrence, had done the stopping. "How pretty she is!" she went on in the same angry way. "She's as pretty as Eileen. I wouldn't have cared so much if she had been plain, I think, but she's just lovely. Oh, I hate her, I hate her—I just hate them both!"

The bottles got rather banged about that evening, and the good doctor looked up once or twice from his writing, in his little inner sanctuary, and gently marvelled. Basil happened to be at home, and strolled into his father's den, though only with the idea of strolling out again through the surgery door upon suitable pretext. While hovering round there was a sudden crash, which made the doctor start somewhat violently. Basil looked amused.

"Rather stormy this evening, eh?" he suggested. "Perhaps I'd better go and help to pick up the pieces," and he strolled out at the other door.

"Is it blowing great guns and glass bottles, to-night?" he asked of Paddy, showing himself somewhat gingerly.

Paddy vouchsafed no reply.

"I understand it rained tomatoes in Regent Street this afternoon," he went on, nothing daunted.

She could not forbear to smile.

"Who told you so?"

"Pat nearly lost his life trying to scramble off the top of a 'bus in time to pick them up for you. As far as I can make out, when he arrived on the scene a gay Lothario and a wonderful Diana were in possession of the field, and he thought well to decamp, and nearly broke his neck over again boarding another 'bus, with his eyes occupied in the wrong direction."

"Tell Mr O'Connor he shouldn't tell tales out of school."

"Is it the tomato incident that is making you cross?"

"I'm not cross."

"Well, of course I can't contradict you, but, like the parrot, I can still think a lot."

"I shouldn't if I were you. The unusual strain may hurt your brain."

"Whew—as bad as all that, is it? No letter from Africa this mail, I suppose?"

Paddy preserved a contemptuous silence.

"Too bad," said Basil.

"What's too bad?" said Paddy. "Your last attempt at a joke?"

"The pater's getting anxious." he went on without heading her. "He's sitting in there," nodding toward the surgery, "strung up to an awful pitch of nervousness lest you should be blind with—er—well, we'll call it annoyance, and poison someone by accident."

"Go away," said Paddy.

"I've nowhere to go."

"Go and look for a picture book to keep you quiet."

"Don't be a silly kid, Paddy," persuasively. "What's the matter? I've a strong right arm you can command as you wish. Do you want someone hit?"

"No."

"Well, let, me help anyway. I'll wrap up the bottles for you."

She demurred, but he finally ensconced himself on a high stool beside her and presently talked her into a better humour, afterward going home with her, which was really rather kind of him after the manner of his reception.

Three days later, Paddy received a most affectionate letter from Doreen Blake, begging her to come to tea, as she was quite alone.

"Mother and Kathleen are slaying in Eastbourne," she wrote, "as Kathleen has been ill, and I had to remain in London because I had accepted so many invitations. Miss Wells is here to look after the house, but you and I can have a long, cosy chat all to ourselves. If you don't come I shall be dreadfully disappointed and hurt. I want to hear all about the dispensing and everything."

As Doreen had always been Paddy's special chum, there was nothing unusual in Eileen being left out of the invitation, but Paddy tried to make it an excuse not to go. Her mother would not hear of it, however.

"I want you to go, dear," she said, "because I like Mrs Blake and Doreen and Kathleen very much, and if they are going to remain in town for the season it will be nice for you to go and see them sometimes while Eileen and I are away."

It had been arranged that they two should go to Omeath and stay at the Parsonage for three months, leaving Paddy at the doctor's, and later on Paddy was to join them for her summer holiday, and Mrs Adair and Eileen to come back. This arrangement had been made owing to Eileen's ill-health and the doctor's advice that they should not remain in London all the summer, and as there was barely room for three visitors together at the Parsonage, they decided to go in detachments.

In the end Paddy gave in and accepted the invitation, and at half-past three on the appointed day presented herself at the Blakes' house in Cadogan Place. A butler ushered her in, in a lordly fashion, which Paddy afterward mimicked much to Eileen's and her mother's amusement, and she presently found herself alone in an enormous drawing-room, which seemed to her just a conglomeration of fantastic chairs and looking-glasses. A few seconds later there was a swish-swish outside and Doreen appeared. For one second the girls looked at each other with the unspoken question, "Are you changed?" and then with little exclamations of delight they literally flew at each other.

"Paddy, this is just lovely!" exclaimed Doreen when they had finished embracing. "I've been longing to see you for months."

"Silk linings!" said Paddy, walking round Doreen quizzically. "We are grand nowadays! If there's one thing I want more than another, it's to go swish-swish as I walk."

"Nonsense!" said Doreen. "I know better. You don't care a fig about it, and neither do I for the matter of that. It's as much Lawrence's fad as anyone's. When Kathleen and I go out with him he likes us to be lined with silk," and she laughed merrily, adding, "But what a swell you are, Paddy, and how pretty you have grown!"

"It's only my hair," answered Paddy. "I spend ten minutes on it now instead of two. It's awfully jolly to find you just the same, Doreen. What a heap we've got to tell each other. Are we going to say in this 'throne-room' or what?"

"Don't you like it? We can sit on the rug by the fire, and no one will come. I told James to say 'not at home.'"

"Is James the overpowering individual who condescended to show me upstairs? I nearly said 'Thank you, sir!' by mistake."

Doreen pulled up two big cosy chairs, and they were soon talking nineteen to the dozen, or rather Paddy twenty to Doreen's ten, with such vigour, that neither of than heard the door open and a light footstep enter. At the sound of a bracelet jingling, however, they looked round in surprise, to find Gwendoline, resplendent in a lovely new spring costume, standing watching them with laughter in her glorious eyes.

"I knew you would be 'not at home,' Doreen," she said, "so I just made Lawrence lend me his latchkey. Don't be vexed. I'm sick of private views, and spring shows and things, and I just wanted awfully to come and see you and Miss Adair."

Doreen sprang up and made room for her eagerly, not noticing Paddy's sudden stiffness.

"Come along," she exclaimed, "I'm delighted to see you. I know you and Paddy will get on first-rate."

Gwen held out her hand to Paddy and looked frankly into her face, as much as to say, "I know you hate me, but I mean to change all that," and Paddy, slightly disarmed, shook hands and said, "How do you do," with a little less starchiness.

For ten minutes, results hung in the balance. Gwen was at her best; she was indeed most charming; but Paddy was obstinate, not to say somewhat pig-headed, and when she was in that mood, to quote Basil, you might almost as well try to persuade a lamp-post to walk across the road.

But Basil was not Gwen, and if he had tried for a life-time, he could not have cultivated such powers of persuasion as hers and in this she meant to win. Paddy would have needed to be made of adamant to withstand her. In the end, of course, she gave in, and by the time the stately butler condescended to serve them with tea, a merrier trio it would have been difficult to find.

Lawrence heard their gay laughter down in the hall, as he hung up his hat, and smiled a little grimly.

"Gwen's won," he said to himself. "I wonder what sort of a reception I shall get?"

He walked slowly upstairs, and as slowly entered the drawing-room. Paddy was entertaining the other two with some of her dispensing adventures and for a moment he remained unnoticed. Paddy saw him first.

"I was reaching to a high shelf—" she was saying, and then she stopped short suddenly, with her eyes on the door.

The other two looked round quickly, as Lawrence advanced, saying, "Yes, you were reaching to a high shelf, and—"

"Nothing," said Paddy, "or at least nothing that would interest you."

"Try me."

"Come along, Lawrie," cried Gwen. "We're having a regular, jolly old school-girl afternoon. You'll find it an education gratis, and you can eat as much cake as you like. We are all eating as if we had never ate before, to make up for the times we went hungry at school."

Lawrence sat down by Doreen, opposite to Paddy.

"Delighted," he murmured. "Always thought the *rôle* of school-girl would suit me down to the ground. Touching this high shelf—don't let me interrupt you, Paddy."

Paddy looked furious and got scarlet in the face. She was determined she *would not* be friendly with Lawrence, and yet here she was, almost on intimate terms with his *fiancée*, and fairly caught as regards himself.

Gwen dropped her long lashes to hide a decided gleam of amusement, while Doreen, pouring out tea and noticing nothing, said, "Go on, Paddy, you needn't mind Lawrence."

"Of course not," he said, keeping his eyes fixed on her. "Why should she?"

Still Paddy bit her lip and hesitated. "It's time I was going," she said at last, very lamely, looking around for her gloves.

Gwen's mouth twitched desperately at the corners and Doreen looked up in surprise. Doreen's expression made Paddy pull herself together.

"It wasn't really anything worth telling," she said, "only that, instead of standing on something to make myself taller as I ought to have done, I tried to tilt the jar over into my hand, and while doing so the stopper flew out. The jar was full of black powder, and before I could help myself I had most of it in my face and over my hair. You never saw anything so awful as I looked. Brushing it off left long black streaks in all directions, and the taste on my lips was filthy; the three people waiting for their medicine nearly had convulsions, and the doctor came out to see what was the matter."

"Oh, how delicious!" cried Gwen in enjoyment. "Whatever did he say?" while Doreen, laughing heartily, gasped:

"Oh, Paddy, you must have looked piebald!"

"Goodness only knows what I did look like," she said. "I thought the doctor was going to faint. I tried to explain, but I was laughing so myself, and meanwhile getting such horrid tastes of the wretched stuff, that I couldn't frame a sensible sentence. Finally, he grasped the situation for himself, and stayed to get on with the dispensing, while I went to try and get my face clean." While they were still laughing, she got up to go.

"I'm coming to call on you if I may?" said Gwen as they shook hands.

Paddy looked doubtful.

"It's rather an awful place to come to," she explained, "the ugliest part of Shepherd's Bush. You'd never find it."

"Oh, yes, I will. I'll have a taxi, and refuse to get out until he stops at your door. He'll find it after a time."

"I'm only a visitor at my uncle's now, though," she continued in the same doubtful voice, "and —well, to tell you the honest truth, my aunt is rather tedious. She's quite sure to help me entertain you, and she'll give you a detailed history of every church work in the parish, from its earliest infancy."

"I know!" cried Gwen with a sudden idea. "We'll go to the surgery, Doreen. We'll hunt up some old prescriptions, and pretend we're poor people come for medicine. Yes, that will be much better fun! I've never seen a dispensary, and I'd love to poke about in all the drawers and bottles," to which Doreen agreed readily and Paddy turned, to the door.

Lawrence followed her.

"Shall I get my head bitten off if I venture to escort you to the hall?" he asked, so that she alone could hear.

"I would not trouble you for the world," she replied frigidly, and offered her hand.

Lawrence looked into her eyes, and something like a flash of sword-play passed between them.

"All the same," he remarked, coolly, "I am going to send you home in a hansom, and see you into it myself."

Paddy saw it was useless to object there and did not want to make a scene, so went stiffly downstairs. In the hall the lordly James stood waiting.

"Call a hansom," said Lawrence briefly.

"Not for me," said Paddy, with her nose in the air. "I am going in a 'bus."

"But it is raining fast, and you will only get wet." Lawrence spoke a little urgently, while the butler waited with impassive face.

"I love getting wet," icily.

The faintest suspicion of a smile hovered over Lawrence's lips, but he only turned to the butler and said, "Go and ask Miss Doreen's maid for a cloak and umbrella."

Paddy was unpleasantly aware that she could not afford to risk getting her one smart costume spoiled, so she yielded with a bad grace.

When they were alone he turned to her again, and his thin lips compressed into a straight line.

"I see you are a good hater," he said, "but I only like you the better for it. Do you remember—I said you had given me a new interest in life, and that I would subdue you some day? I am going to begin now."

"And I replied that I despised you. I have seen no reason to change my mind. It is not of the least consequence to me what you do."

There was a gleam in his eyes that might have meant either admiration or war, but Paddy, a moment later, only flung out of the house without deigning him so much as a glance.

When she had gone, Lawrence did not return to the drawing-room. He went into his den and closed the door. On the hearthrug he stood looking silently at the floor.

"By Jove," he muttered a last, "who would have thought she would develop like this. Paddy-the-next-best-thing," with a little smile, "has become Patricia-the-Great."

Chapter Thirty Two.

Paddy Learns Her Mistake.

True to her word, Gwen called for Doreen a few days later, and the two drove in a taxi to Shepherd's Bush and found their way to the surgery, where Paddy, in a large black apron, was busy with her prescriptions. They stayed about ten minutes and then drove away again, leaving Paddy less able than ever to resist Gwen's overtures. At the same time, she felt no less incensed against Lawrence and anxious to avoid meeting him, which was the cause of her reluctance to accept an invitation to a small dance at Gwen's beautiful home in Grosvenor Place.

"I have no dress good enough," she told Doreen when they talked it over, "and I can't afford to get a new one on purpose."

"Nonsense," asserted Doreen promptly. "I know quite well you have. Why, that pretty dress you had for our coming-out dance is not two years old, and you have scarcely worn it at all. You must just send it to me, and I will get Jean to do it up for you. You simply must come. It will be such a jolly dance. Not a grand one at all, but one of Gwen's impromptu hops, as she calls them."

In the end Paddy gave in, and on the evening of the dance arrived at Cadogan Place in time to go with Doreen and Lawrence in their brougham. She knew Lawrence would be there, but was prepared for it, and chatted merrily to Doreen without ever including him if she could help it.

Lawrence took no notice, merely sitting forward, opposite to them, with his arms across his knees, casually glancing through an evening paper.

When Paddy first arrived Doreen had made her take off her cloak and show herself, and he had then, as she well knew, though he said nothing, criticised her keenly. Doreen had been enraptured.

"You look splendid!" was her verdict. "I don't know what it is about you, Paddy, but somehow you always manage to look striking nowadays. Don't you think so, Lawrence? Here am I, got up at endless expense, mentioned in the fashionable papers as 'pretty Miss Doreen Blake,' and yet, when we go into the room together, I'm sure everyone will look at you."

"If they do, it will only be my hair," laughed Paddy. "It's so difficult not to stare at carroty hair."

"Stuff!" from Doreen. "But am I not right, Lawrence?"

Lawrence was standing a little apart, lighting a cigarette, and he did not answer for a moment.

"Paddy has a lot of original ideas," he said at last, "and they somehow cling about her. The crowd is always struck with anything original."

Paddy was pulling on a long glove. "I guess I'll have this stocking in half before I've done," she remarked, with studied unconcern, "and then I shall have to pin it to my sleeve to show I possess it, which is, after all, the main thing about it."

When they reached the Hon. Grant-Carew's, however, and had got rid of their cloaks, Lawrence came up to them while chatting with Gwen and asked Paddy how many dances she would give him.

Paddy tried to prevaricate, but both Gwen and Doreen were watching, and Lawrence persisted. He had purposely chosen that moment, knowing she could hardly refuse before the other two.

"Give him three," said Gwen decisively. "I'll allow that number, as he's a lovely waltzer, and you're sure to enjoy them; but the rest of your programme I'm going to superintend myself and see that you don't get any tiresome partners at all."

Paddy bit her lip and flashed a look at Lawrence that seemed to dare him to take advantage of her position. He, however, only smiled slightly with his usual impassivity, and wrote her name three times upon his programme. He then glanced at Gwen significantly, and she, in an easy, natural fashion, possessed herself of Paddy's programme and handed it to him.

Paddy was inwardly furious, but obliged to take it with a good grace. When they had their first dance, however, she hardly spoke, and afterward insisted upon remaining in the dance-room, so that she could watch the other guests instead of keeping up a conversation. Lawrence pretended not to notice, but chatted pleasantly about the people and pointed out any one of note to her. The same thing happened at each of his dances, and whereas Paddy was brilliant with enjoyment with all her other partners, she immediately became constrained and silent with him. And each time Lawrence chatted in his pleasantest way, and pretended not to notice it.

Later, however, he suddenly dropped his pretence, and took the bull by the horns in his most resolute fashion. It had been arranged that Paddy should return home in a hansom straight from Grosvenor Place, and after saying good-by to Doreen she turned and nodded a casual good-by to Lawrence, standing near.

"I am coming with you," he said calmly.

"Oh, no, certainly not," and Paddy looked very resolute. "There is not the least necessity to drag you all that way. Besides, you must see Doreen home."

"Doreen will go home in the brougham. I am coming with you."

For one moment there was a dangerous look in Paddy's eyes; then Doreen chimed in with:

"Don't be silly, Paddy. Of course Lawrie will take you home. As if he were likely to do otherwise."

Paddy saw there was no help for it, and tripped down the steps and into the hansom without giving him a chance to offer his hand. Lawrence gave the address and stepped in after her.

"Do you mind my cigarette?" he asked, to which Paddy replied coldly, "Not in the least," and drew further back into her corner.

"You seem more angry with me than ever to-night," he began presently.

By this time Paddy had just about exhausted her none too large supply of cold hauteur, so, feeling she must vent her anger somehow, she turned upon him suddenly, which secretly pleased Lawrence because it was so much more natural to her.

"Of course I am angry with you," she exclaimed. "I think you have behaved abominably. You have simply laid traps for me, first over the dances and then over this drive. You know perfectly well I would have refused both if Doreen and Miss Carew had not been with us."

"That was strategy. They say all is fair in love and war."

"I don't care what they say; you are a paltry enemy, because you take a mean advantage."

"And supposing I weren't an enemy at all?"

"But you are; you can't help being. You only did it purely and simply to annoy me. You knew I did not want to dance with you, so you thought you would make me, just for an amusement for yourself—because it's a new experience to have an unwilling partner, or something equally silly. It was only on a par with most of your actions."

Lawrence slowly knocked some ash off his cigarette.

"I can't understand Miss Carew helping you," Paddy ran on. "If she is going to marry you, it is no reason why she should encourage you in annoying other people."

Lawrence raised his eyebrows slightly.

"What makes you think Miss Carew is going to marry me?" he asked.

"Well, when people are engaged to each other, don't they usually marry!"

There was a faint gleam of amusement in his eyes, but he managed to hide it by studying the end of his cigarette.

"And what makes you think Miss Carew and I are engaged to each other?"

Paddy shook herself with an irritable movement.

"Because you are, of course! I have known it a long time."

"Longer than we have, I suspect," with provoking calmness.

Paddy puckered her forehead into a frown, and condescended to look at him.

"Of course, I don't know whether it is announced or not yet, and I'm sure I don't care, but I heard from a mutual friend of yours and hers that it was settled when you were in India over a year ago."

"Might I ask you the mutual friend's name?"

"It was Captain O'Connor. He met you both in Calcutta. But really, except that I like Miss Carew very much, this is a most uninteresting topic."

"On the contrary, considering we have never been engaged at all, and it is very unlikely that we ever shall be, I find it extremely interesting."

"Never been engaged at all!" gasped Paddy.

"Never to my knowledge," with the same provoking calmness.

"Impossible! Captain O'Connor told me he had congratulated you both, and that he heard it from Miss Carew herself."

A sudden light broke on Lawrence. "Did he tell you it happened a year last Christmas?" he asked.

"About then. He was passing through Calcutta on his way home."

"Ah!" significantly.

"Then you were engaged," scathingly, "and with your customary changeableness have broken it off again?"

"Yes, that's about it. But this was a record in quick changes."

"Why?—how?" irritably, feeling there was something she did not understand.

"Merely that it only lasted one evening."

"One evening!" incredulously.

"Yes. But, of course, you do not care to hear about it. I quite understand that my affairs in any shape or form are not of the slightest interest to you," which was quite a long sentence for Lawrence.

For a few minutes Paddy felt squashed; then her curiosity got the better of her.

"Did Miss Carew do it?" she asked.

"She did. She asked me to be her tool for one evening, having got into a scrape with a hot-headed Irishman and a woolly-lamb Englishman. Since, almost as long as I can remember, I have been at Gwendoline's beck and call, I was perfectly willing. I presume the hot-headed Irishman was your friend Captain O'Connor."

For some minutes Paddy was struck dumb. It had never entered her head to question the engagement, and she had not mentioned it to Doreen because it was such a sore subject. Hastily reviewing the past year, however, she could not but see that, on the whole, the news, though incorrect, had been most beneficial to Eileen. Undoubtedly, from the time she learnt of Lawrence's supposed engagement, she had been better able to pull herself together and set steadily about forgetting him. Only this could not, to a girl like Paddy, in any measure abate what had gone. For every tear Lawrence's heartlessness had made her sister shed, she felt she had an undying grudge against him, and she would not forget. Presently, to break the silence, she remarked:

"I don't know how you can help falling in love with Miss Carew. Why aren't you engaged to her?"

"Well, one very good reason, perhaps, is the fact that she is practically engaged to someone else."

"Is she?" with ill-concealed eagerness. "Who is he!"

"Unfortunately he happens to be a younger son, which is a heinous and not easily-overcome offence in her mother's eyes, and hence the delay."

"What a pity! Is he nice?"

"One of the nicest chaps I ever met."

"Oh, I do hope it will come out right in the end."

"There is not much doubt. Gwen has her father on her side, and I think it is chiefly a question of time with the mother. But, for the matter of that, Gwen always gets her own way in the end. Her mother arranged for her to be a countess eighteen months ago, but at the last moment she advised the earl not to propose to her, and sent him flying."

"How splendid of her!" cried Paddy, forgetting her anger for a moment. "And she is going to marry a plain Mr Somebody now?"

"Well, he holds a captain's commission in the Guards, and considerably distinguished himself in South Africa. I'm not sure it wasn't his V.C. that took Gwen's fancy first."

"How nice! I do like her so much. I hope she'll be able to marry him soon and be awfully happy. Do you think I might mention it to her?"

"I'm surprised she hasn't already told you herself. She is not in the least reserved about it, and she is awfully in love with him. She is as good at loving as you are at hating, Paddy," and suddenly he was looking into her eyes, with an expression she had never seen on his face before, and which stirred her pulses unaccountably. She fidgeted with her hands, compressed her lips, and stared straight before her, feeling in every corner of her being that he was still looking at her with those calm, compelling eyes.

"Well!" he asked at last, and his voice was full of that winning quality which had gained him such easy conquests in the past. But it only made Paddy hotly distrustful, and she gripped the front of the hansom and called up every fighting instinct she possessed.

"Miss Carew would hate in my place." She drew a long breath, as if gathering herself together for a special thrust. "Since she loves as strongly as I hate, I am glad it is some one else, and not you, to whom she has given her love." She was unconsciously sitting rigidly upright, and from his corner, with his compelling eyes still watching her face, that gleam that might have been either love or war again passed through them.

"You hit hard," he said at last; and then, with the slightest inflection of a taunt in his voice, added: "Why don't you look at me—are you afraid?"

Paddy bit her teeth together hard, and her breath came a little fitfully. She was not afraid—that was quite certain; but, on the other hand, she had not quite the calm assurance she usually felt. She would greatly have preferred not to look at him.

"Well?" he said again.

Paddy took her courage in both hands.

"No, I am not afraid," and she turned her head a moment and looked full and deep into his eyes.

Suddenly he gave a low, harsh laugh.

"My God!" he muttered. "Patricia the Great!" And then he flung his half-smoked cigarette away and stared into the night.

Neither spoke again, and a few minutes later the cab drew up at her uncle's door. He sprang out first and offered her his aid, but she gathered up her dress with both hands and ignored him. At the door she fitted the latchkey into the lock herself. While she fumbled a little in the dim light, she felt his eyes again fixed on her, and before she managed to get the door open he said, in low, distinct tones, "The new interest you have given me is growing apace, Patricia. I see it is going to be war to the knife, but, if I'm worth my name, I'll win yet."

"Good-night," she said jauntily, as the door at last opened, then slammed it in his face.

Chapter Thirty Three.

Patricia the Great.

It would be difficult to say when the awakening first came to Lawrence. Before it came he felt it growing every day. After it came, it seemed to have been there all along. At first he blinded himself with the belief that he was only piqued. That it would on the whole be entertaining to break down her defences and subdue her. He was grateful to her for giving him even that much new interest in life.

Afterward he faced the situation with entire honesty. He admitted frankly to himself that he loved her, and he knew, without going any further, that it was the love of his life. All the past peccadilloes, entanglements, fancies, were nothing—were mere episodes—nothing seemed real any longer except that he loved Paddy Adair. He, the graceful *dilettante*, the highly eligible society man, the casual, cynical scholar—she, the harum-scarum tom-boy, the fearless Irish romp—"Paddy-the-next-best-thing."

When the awakening had come, and he faced the facts squarely, he believed he had loved her ever since the night of the Omeath dance, when, in his den, she had flung defiance at him, and marched off with her head in the air, in lofty disdain.

He reviewed what had transpired between them since, and; his thoughts were gloomy enough. Most emphatically the defiance and the disdain were still the dominant notes she was at no further pains now, than then, to hide her contempt. He knew that since the night of Gwen's dance she had resorted to strategy to avoid him. Since his mother and Kathleen returned home there had been much sight-seeing and entertaining, and Paddy was continually requisitioned. Yet she contrived to turn up on the occasions when he had another engagement, and remain absent when he made a victim of himself for the express purpose of seeing her. Even at a second dance she had outwitted him.

"Lawrence will take you home," Doreen had said in his presence, and Paddy had politely replied: "Thank you." Yet when he sought her neat the end of the evening, it was to find she had already gone—undoubtedly missing two dances rather than accept his escort.

The third time, however, he was one too many for her. He watched from a safe vantage ground until he saw her give a quiet glance round, and then surreptitiously slip away. Instantly he accosted Doreen.

"It is raining in torrents," he told her, "and I don't want the horses to wait to-night. I shall go home now, and send a taxi for you and Kathleen at one o'clock."

Doreen thought it a little odd, but was immediately claimed by a partner, and Lawrence gave her no time to reply.

When Paddy slipped cautiously out of the cloak-room and made for the door, she stopped short before a coated figure unmistakably waiting for her, and said: "Oh!"

"I'm going to take you home in the carriage," said Lawrence, with a resolution against which she felt powerless. "I've arranged with the others to be fetched in a taxi."

Paddy flashed defiance at him, bit her teeth together, and descended the steps with the air of an outraged princess. Lawrence reflected that it was a long way to Shepherd's Bush, and smiled grimly to himself—partly at the feelings of his coachman, and partly at the success of his ruse.

So they bowled along in a comfortable brougham, though Paddy disdained the padded cushions, and sat bolt upright like a terrier on guard. Lawrence sat back in his corner and watched her, feeling for the moment almost content. It was something, at least, to have captured her for a few minutes and have her all to himself. Her skirts brushed against his foot, her flowers exhaled a delicate perfume in the carriage, her cloak, falling open, slipped back a little on to his knee. Lawrence had reached the stage when a man is thankful for very small mercies, and he was vaguely thankful for these.

"Am I permitted to express an old friend's congratulations on your appearance?" he asked presently, in a voice that held no mockery.

"When I am with you I seem to do nothing but repeat myself," was the crushing reply. "How often am I to tell you that what you do, say, or think, is not of the smallest consequence to me."

"You could not please me better than by repeating yourself," a little whimsically. She stared in front of her.

"Can any one come to your surgery for medicine?" presently. "If I came with an ill, would you try to administer healing to me?"

"I should try to administer a rebuff that would prevent your ever coming again."

He smiled a little. "You couldn't hit harder than you have; and yet I still come."

"That is your colossal obstinacy. Nothing in your life has ever attracted you except the unattainable. I understand perfectly, that because I happen to have the hardihood to withstand your overtures, and the originality," with finely toned satire, "to prefer your room to your company, it amuses you to thrust your attentions upon me, just to see how soon I shall give in and bow down with the rest. You may save yourself the trouble. I shall never give in. It is only because of your mother and sisters that I assume any degree of friendliness whatever."

"And what if I say I will never give in either? I am a strong man, Paddy, when I make up my mind about anything."

"You are nothing of the kind. You are a coward, or you would not persist in taking unfair advantages of me."

He flushed, but refused to get angry.

"I have taken no unfair advantage to-night. Only yesterday you accepted my escort before Doreen."

"Only because I was cornered, and you knew it."

He was silent for a space, then returned to the charge.

"Why won't you cry a truce, Paddy?" and his voice was strangely winsome. "No one is hurt now, and you cannot choose but feel in your heart that it was a good thing I went away in time."

To any one less unsophisticated than Paddy, less direct in all her thoughts and actions, less fearlessly independent, such a tone of voice must have been dangerously alluring—coming, moreover, from such as he, with all his advantages, to such as she with all her losses. But Paddy was a soldier to the backbone. Having thrown down the glove and entered the combat, she would give and take no quarter. Personal gain was nothing—personal loss still less—Lawrence was the enemy—the enemy she had declared war against, and until the conduct that had so infuriated her was amply atoned for, she would not only stick to her guns, but was of the stuff to die uselessly beside them for a lost cause. She was her father over again at the sternest moments of his brilliant career. No parleying with the enemy—War. The old charm for once fell on heedless ears. She continued to look rigidly out into the night, with her face averted, and did not even condescend to reply.

She was thinking with no small satisfaction that he would no doubt soon be leaving London for a long time. Already arrangements were in progress for Mrs Blake and the girls to go to Mourne Lodge, and it was not in the least likely that Lawrence would accompany them. At any time he had only gone under protest, and that very evening Doreen had expressed curiosity as to where he would go when they departed. The thought that she would probably not see him again for months after to-night, further gladdened and fortified her.

When he spoke again she was ready for him.

"Well?" he asked, in that most beguiling of voices. "Is it to be a truce, Paddy—for the sake of the old days!"

She stared straight before her.

"It is only when the old days cease to exist there can be a truce between you and me," in measured tones. "On account of the old days, and because they will live to our last gasp, I shall never again be your friend."

Then a surprising thing happened—a thing that took her breath away, and left her speechless. Suddenly, from leaning back in his corner, he started up, and bent forward, and seized both her hands in his in a grip of iron.

"I don't want you to be my friend!" he exclaimed, almost roughly. "Good God! as if I should put myself out, and go to the lengths I have, just to gain a friend!" He gave a little harsh laugh. "A friend, indeed!—no, I don't want your friendship, listen, Paddy—" the hands gripping hers tightened, and she saw in the dim light that he was very white, and his eyes gleamed strangely, and masterful resolve filled his face. "It is a *wife* I want—not a friend—and a *wife* I mean to have. This feud is nonsense. It is mere obstinacy now. If I behaved wrongly to Eileen I am sorry. I can't say any more, and you can see for yourself it was a good thing we never got engaged. Are you going to let an ancient thing like that come between us—punish two people for a third one who is unhurt? I say 'two,' because I know I could make you happy, if you would drop this—this—prejudice, and be your old self again."

While he was speaking Paddy herself turned very pale and for a moment there was a bewildered expression in her eyes, as she continued to gaze fixedly before her. Then once again she rallied her forces for a final blow. She wrenched her hands from his and faced him squarely.

"You must be mad!" she said. "You can't know what you are talking about. How many times am I to tell you that I hate you?—Listen! hate you—*hate* you. I do not know what you mean by a prejudice. I know that you dared to trifle with one of my house—I know that you nearly broke my sister's heart—I know that you are heartless, and cruel, and selfish—and then you talk to me of love and marriage,"—she paused for very indignation.

"Yes, I do," he interrupted decisively, "and I shall again, in spite of your kind summing up."

"Then thank goodness you are going away, and, at least, we shall not meet any more for a long time!"

"Who told you I was going away!"

"Don't you always go away in the summer?—and besides the others are leaving for Mourne Lodge directly."

"And what if they are?"

"You must go somewhere."

"Certainly. I am going to Mourne Lodge with them."

Paddy was momentarily staggered, then she peered out of the window at the street. "We are just arriving," she said, "I can let myself in. You need not get out in the rain."

He only gave a low laugh, and took the latchkey out of her hand.

As he opened the door, he looked once more hard into her eyes:

"Good-night, Patricia the Great. We shall meet again at Omeath."

Paddy went upstairs feeling a little dazed, and then commenced throwing things about to relieve her feelings.

"How he dare!—how he dare—!" a slipper crashed into the fireplace. "Anything for novelty. I suppose he thinks he will amuse himself with me next! He talks as if he imagines I am merely playing—as if a little coaxing and cajolery—he's—he's—bother these tangles!" and the beautiful hair began to suffer badly from its owner's perturbed frame of mind. "But he'll soon find he's mistaken,"—the hairbrush missed the window by half-an-inch, and fell into the water-jug: "Oh! if only I were a man and could fight him!—But I'm a Dublin Fusilier General's daughter—and I ought to know something about fighting!" Over went a chair backward, bringing down a small table laden with photo frames. "I'll be even with him yet—the sweep!" with which she dived under the bedclothes, as if she were a whole regiment of Fusiliers storming a position.

Chapter Thirty Four.

Robert Morony on Church Restoration.

It was not until the second week in August that Paddy was able to start on her summer holiday, and then she journeyed to Omeath to pay her long-counted-on visit to the Parsonage.

Eileen and her mother and the two aunties were all at the little station awaiting her, when the train drew up soon after seven in the morning, and, like some small terrier beside itself with excitement, Paddy almost fell headlong, upon the top of them all. From the very instant she caught sight of her old friend the giant on Carlingford Mountain she threw off all cares, all recollections of London, all responsibilities, and stepped into the Omeath train almost the identical, headstrong, happy-go-lucky Paddy of eighteen months ago. Such a hand-shaking there had been at Greenore, for she knew all the railway porters and the station officials and everyone connected with the hotel, and, judging from the greetings, they were as pleased to see her as she them. At Omeath the others began to wonder what time they would manage to get her as far as the Parsonage, for every man, woman, and child had to be talked to and shaken hands with.

There was a great spread for breakfast—everything that they knew she liked best and poor Paddy had to taste something of each dish to please them, until she was obliged to impress them politely that she had reached the utmost limit of her capacity. After breakfast she and Eileen went off on an exploring expedition through the village. At the church gate they met the sexton, old Robert Morony, a sort of monument of longevity to the village.

"I've been to see the restorations, Robert," cried Paddy joyously. "Doesn't the church look lovely!"

"It do, indaid, Miss Paddy," answered the old man, shaking hands with unmistakable pleasure. "Faith! did ye iver see sich a luvely place o' warship afore? An' everythin' so compact lik'! What I mean, nothin' stunted."

"I should think not, Robert. Trust Aunt Jane and Aunt Mary to do a thing thoroughly if they undertake it. When I heard the church was to be restored by them, I said, 'Begorra! that'll be an edifice to be proud of now!'"

Robert chuckled with delight.

"But shure, an' you don't see the half," he explained eagerly. "It's all them nice things you don't see as so pleases me. Now would you belaive—there's actually twelve new dusters! positively bran' new, all folded as neat an' trim-lik' an' put away where no one can see 'em. Now that's what I call restoring a church properly—indaid, I just luve the sight of 'em."

"I quite agree with you, Robert," and Paddy's eyes twinkled rarely. "It's the things I can't see, that I love to look at."

"Egzactly," with growing excitement. "*I* ought to 'a' showed you roun', Miss Paddy, 'cos I knows where everythin' bides. Why, there's six new lamp glasses, all a-lying there case o' accidents, wrapped up in beautiful tissue paper. I'd a-lik' you to see they lamp glasses. Oh! an' the new iron safe," getting almost beside himself. "Did ye see 'im a-sittin there in the vestry, on all they hymn books, all neatly stacked underneath, looking as important like as if 'e knew 'e was livin' in one o' the foinest churches in ould Oireland?"

"When an iron safe sits on hymn books, what do you suppose hatches out?" murmured Paddy wickedly to Eileen.

"Did ye see the new bell rope?" ran on Robert, waving his stick about in a somewhat dangerous fashion to eyes and noses. "A brave wee bit o' rope that—strong 'nough to hang a man, as I says to Andrew Murphy. The blue ceiling with the yellow stars is all very well, and the new altar, and the winder with the angels playin' on real Oirish harps—but 'tis all a bit popish to my thinkin'—and I lik' that brave wee rope, and they lamp glasses in tissue paper, and they twelve bran' new dusters the best. Faith! 'tis meeself should have shown ye roun'. I'm shure ye didn't see the half. Did ye notice the new tumbler o' wather for 'is rivirence to drink from when 'is sermons is too long-winded for 'im? Faith! we did make a job of it. Ivery 'ole and corner turned out and clained. Shure, it's meeself did the back seat by the font, and to my sartin knowledge it 'adn't been cleaned out this ten or twelve year. Niver more'n about once since I've had the cue o' the edifice this forty year."

This finished Paddy, and with a hasty farewell she sped off to the beach for her first sail; later on in the day writing Jack a long epistle upon Robert Morony and the church restoration, which Jack read lying at full-length on his back on the grass a month later; and his shouts of laughter brought his colleagues round to beg a share of the fun.

Two days later Eileen and her mother left for Dublin, and Paddy became the spoiled darling of the Parsonage.

She went everywhere just as of old, and though for a little while she avoided Mourne Lodge, not wishing to meet Lawrence, she soon found her strategic position untenable, and was obliged to yield to the insistent persuasions of Kathleen and Doreen, who began to look genuinely puzzled and distressed over her extraordinary reluctance to visit them.

Then she decided to take the bull by the horns, and instead of putting their first encounter off any longer, seek it purposely, and *get* it over. With this end in view she bicycled to Mourne Lodge, in a more or less ferocious frame of mind, once more to confound the enemy. As it happened, however, the enemy had seen fit to change its tactics, and instead of the new graciously polite Lawrence, there was only the old casual, indifferent looker-on. Paddy, with all her artillery in readiness, was for once non-plussed. "How do, Paddy!" he said coolly, when he joined them at tea, and sat down as far from her as possible, and commenced playing with his dogs, taking no further notice. Of course it is one thing to have all your guns in readiness and get a few good round shots in, and quite another to be calmly and loftily ignored, and Paddy's instant impulse was to hurl every portable article within reach at his head. To make matters worse, she was furiously aware that she had blushed crimson when he first appeared, and that he had probably seen it, and drawn his own conclusions. To show him she did not care, she fired one or two shots at him at random, but the result, as she ought to have foreseen, was only a further assumption of the very indifference that irritated her. He looked at her as if she were not there, and maintained, for the most part, his habitual silence.

Neither did it prove to be for that day only, but each time she came. There was just a casual greeting, and then silence, and he declined all part in their daily excursions.

Paddy told herself she was relieved he had at last realised it was useless to try and make friends; but at the same time it was rather dull without Jack, or Eileen, as she could not always be off to friends, and she almost wished they could have just one battle-royal to liven things up a little. It was all very well to have no parleying with the enemy, but that did not mean one would be content to sit down quietly in sight of the enemy's lines, and never so much as fire a shot; certainly not for an Irish Fusilier's daughter. She was vaguely wishing for this encounter the day she paddled about alone in Jack's little skiff, because it had been too wet to bicycle to Newry, and she looked a little doleful, until another skiff, impelled by long, smooth strokes came out of the sunlight and drew near.

She watched it coming, admiring the long, even strokes, and wondering a little fitfully, who was its occupant. As it came nearer, she recognised Lawrence's thin profile, and lean, muscular figure, she felt a sudden quickening of her pulse, and a half hope that there was a chance of a skirmish. Or would he row straight past and merely throw her a casual greeting?

On and on came the skiff, and still the long even strokes—evidently he was going straight by. Two strokes away, however, he suddenly stopped pulling and leaned on his oars. The boat drifted up beside hen. Paddy got her guns ready.

"Hullo!" he said casually. "I thought you were playing in the tennis tournament this afternoon."

"I was knocked out first round," trying to speak as casually as he, but with a sudden inflection of regret she could not wholly stifle.

"Were you?" in some surprise; "that's a new experience for you!"

"I am out of practice."

"Don't you play in London?"

"No."

"Why not?" rolling himself a cigarette.

"I have no opportunity."

"You must miss it a good deal."

She was silent.

"I suppose you'll be going back soon?" going on with his cigarette with a resolutely cold, impassive air.

"Yes! I haven't much more than a week left." She fidgeted restlessly. This impassivity was too maddening.

"You won't like that?"

It was because the mere thought nearly made her cry, that she replied jauntily:

"Oh! I don't mind much. I'm getting used to London now."

Still he would not look up.

"Shepherd's Bush is hardly London," a little cruelly.

"Anything is London that is not Omeath," she retorted.

He smiled a little to himself. "I thought you had just implied that you rather liked London."

"I said I didn't mind going back. I don't; Mother and Eileen will be there." She flashed one of her old glances at him, but he was still too much occupied to look up. It made her vaguely angry. There was no necessity to treat her as if she were a wooden post. She cast about in her mind for a bone of contention, and at just that moment Lawrence finished rolling his cigarette, struck a match, and lit it.

"Well, I must be off," in the same careless tone. "See you at the picnic, I suppose,"—and almost before she could reply he had pulled away, and gone without once looking at her.

Paddy rowed to the shore, feeling that she wanted to hit some one. "He's growing as dull as ditch-water!" she exclaimed snappishly, as she tied up her boat.

Chapter Thirty Five.

The Picnic.

A few days later came the great picnic up the mountain. The Blakes gave the picnic, and the guests numbered about seventy, half of them proceeding to the climbing-place upon bicycles and the other half driving. The weather was not very promising from the first, but it was too large an undertaking to put off, and they accordingly started out.

Paddy went in the Mastermans' carriage with the two aunts. As they drove along she wished, a little unaccountably, that Ted Masterman was one of the party. "After all," she mused, "he was better than no one, and it was so very tame without Jack. Really, there was no one in the least adventuresome or enterprising."

Then she fell to wondering what line Lawrence would take, and whether, perhaps, to-day, he would rise to a quarrel. Once more she hoped he would.

It was, in consequence, more irritating than ever that Lawrence not only proved quite amenable, but appeared in a wholly new light that separated them effectually the whole day. For the first time in any one's recollection, he assumed, with his most ingratiating charm, the *rôle* of host. He was absolutely indefatigable in attending to the wants of his guests, most particularly all the elderly ladies and quiet ones. The rowdy faction, with Paddy at their head, he ignored just as far as was compatible with his new *rôle*. Paddy herself he never once addressed. She might, indeed, not have been there.

About five o'clock a slight mistiness frightened most of the older folks home out of the damp, but the younger ones, headed by Paddy, who was beginning to get desperate, started off on a climbing expedition. After a short time most of them gave in and came back again, but a few went on, Paddy still leading. Then these few gave in also, owing to the increasing dampness, and shouted to Paddy to come back.

"Don't wait—I'll soon catch you up," she called, and then she climbed on a little higher to see if she could find the wonderful earthwork entrenchments she and Jack had once thrown up for a miniature sham fight.

The others leaned against rocks and waited, chatting gayly to pass the time. After a little while, as she did not come, they concluded she had returned to the starting-place by another path, and trooped back without feeling the least concern. Lawrence and Doreen were helping people into their carriages and saying good-by to various guests, when the former heard some one ask casually:

"Isn't Paddy Adair here?"

He glanced round.

"She went with your party up the mountain," he said.

"Yes, but we missed her, and concluded she had come back here ahead of us by another route."

"She is probably with the Parsonage party," and he vent at once to find out.

Meanwhile the mistiness was fast developing into a thick fog, and to linger on the mountain in such was extremely dangerous, owing to the deep bogs in many places, so everyone hastened to depart. Lawrence, without causing any alarm, managed to find out that nothing had been seen of Paddy, and hastened to draw Doreen aside.

"I am going to look for Paddy," he said. "Don't let her absence get to mother's ears or the aunts'. She is not likely to be far away, and they would only worry unnecessarily. You had better go home and we will either follow or go to the Parsonage."

He spoke so quietly and calmly that Doreen felt no misgivings whatever, and most of the others somehow had the idea that Paddy had gone home to Omeath in the Masterman's carriage with her aunts, so that the picnic broke up quite naturally, and the young folks started off on their bicycles in haste to get through the ever-thickening fog, little dreaming that one of their number was risking his life to find another.

Lawrence thought afterward how foolish he had been to go alone, only he had not really imagined Paddy to be more than two or three hundred yards away. He knew the mountain better than most of them, and how there was but one passable path from above the spot where they had picnicked, so he kept carefully along this, picking his way step by step with difficulty in the enshrouding fog. After half an hour he stopped to consider. He was now certain Paddy had taken a wrong turn and strayed aside somewhere, but in what direction it was almost impossible to tell. Should he go back and get help, he wondered. Either course was full of danger, but it was not the danger he feared. So dense was the fog that in going back he knew there was a possibility of losing his own way, and then Paddy would be worse off than ever, the probability being that no one would think of searching for them for hours. No, he decided finally, he would go on and look for her rather than risk getting lost or losing time in returning. Again and again he stood and shouted, but the heavy atmosphere drowned his voice, and there was no answering shout. Then gradually a great fear grew up in his heart. What if harm had come to her? What if this, one of her beloved mountains, had turned upon her in pitiless treachery and swallowed her up in one of its treacherous bogs? He held his breath with horror at the thought.

Surely, surely, no harm could come to her—it could not be; even stern, inexorable Nature could surely let no hair of her head be hurt! Yet all around was unseen danger, that direst of all foes, and he knew that, even if she were alive, to struggle through that mountain mist was to hold one's life by a thread.

Yet he pressed forward, the nameless fear growing ever stronger in his heart and filling all his being with an anguish of intolerable suspense. By the help of a walking stick he carried he was enabled to find the path and keep to it, otherwise he would have been likely to stray aside into a bog himself. But the thought of personal danger found no room in his brain; he would have risked his life a hundred times for Paddy and thought nothing of it.

He must have been out nearly an hour, going further and further from home all the time, when, in answer to his call, he fancied he heard a distant reply.

"Paddy!" he shouted again. "Paddy!—Paddy! Are you there?"

He listened with painful intentness, and then with a sudden thrill of almost ungovernable joy, as he heard a faint voice call "Here!" and afterward give the cry they had used when searching for each other since childhood.

"I am coming!" he shouted. "Don't move!" and he began picking his steps in the direction from whence the voice came.

After great difficulty and many stumbles, he at last found himself in close proximity to the call that sounded from time to time to guide him, and then through the thickness he saw the wood of a little kind of shelter probably used at some time for tethering goats, and a second later he had gripped hold of Paddy herself.

And she made no effort to resist him as, carried away by a rush of feeling, he could not control, he strained her, half-fainting, to his heart.

Paddy trembled violently from weakness. Her cotton blouse was wet through, and she was perished with cold and dread, for she had passed through a terrible time trying to find her way back to the others before she came across the little shelter and sank down worn out. Without quite knowing it, she clung to Lawrence for a few moments, and under the sudden reaction broke down into a few gasping sobs.

He soothed her with the utmost tenderness, and then slipped off his coat and made her put it on, buttoning it up himself. He next arranged a kind of seat for her, where she could lean back against the framework of the hut, and then set to work at once to make a fire, cursing himself inwardly that he had not had the sense to bring a flask of brandy.

Fortunately he had plenty of matches and some old letters, so that, by pulling down pieces of the shelter, he was quickly able to light a comforting fire, and busied himself keeping it going while Paddy had time to recover herself.

When she did so, however, her first impulse was to shrink away, and there was a questioning expression in her eyes as she watched him.

He noticed it at once, and sought to give her confidence by carefully keeping his face turned away from her.

"Are you warmer now?" he asked. "I'm so vexed I came away without a flask."

"I am quite warm," she said, and then suddenly discovered he was in his shirtsleeves, and exclaimed, "Where is your coat?"

"I got so hot climbing," he replied unblushingly, "and then, after lighting the fire, I could not bear it on."

She looked down at herself.

"No, no, you have given it to me," she cried. "Oh, how could you—you will be frozen!" and she began to take it off.

"No, Paddy," and a firm hand closed over hers; "you are not to take it off."

"But I must," she cried. "I can't see you catching your death of cold. Let go, Lawrence."

The hand only held more firmly.

"Listen to me. I have got twice the hardihood that you have, and there is not the least fear of my catching cold. You are in my care until someone comes to look for us or we are able to find our way back, and I shall not allow you to take off that coat."

He smiled, and in the firelight his thin face was very winning.

"If you are obstinate, I shall just sit beside you and hold it on."

Paddy buried her face in her hands and became suddenly silent.

Lawrence stood and looked at her bent head in the firelight, and a yearning expression that made his face more attractive than ever stole over his features. He longed to fold her in his arms once more and cheer and soothe her, but, even if it were possible, he had no longer the excuse of a sudden uncontrollable rush of feeling. So, instead, he folded his arms very tightly, bit his teeth together, and, moving to the further side of the fire, stood leaning against the wall. At least there was no harm in looking at her, as long as his gaze did not embarrass her. He would play fair—a great many undesirable things he might be, but he would never have dreamed of taking any advantage of such a circumstance as this which threw them alone together in peril on the mountain. He would only look when he knew she was unaware of it. He was glad that she elected to sit thus, with her face buried on her arms. At least it made it possible for him to gaze and gaze. He forgot that he was getting chilled to the bone from the damp in spite of the fire. Why should he remember so slight a thing as that?—why, until it was necessary, remember anything but that they two were alone together, shut off from all the world, in the little hut on the mountain. And, sweetest thought of all, for the time being she was in his care, dependent on him for warmth and safety, perhaps for life itself? So he stood silently on the far side of the hut, tending the fire when it needed it, and watching, with his soul in his eyes, how the little flames shone on her beautiful hair. He was afraid to think of the moment when he had first found her and she had half-clung to him. It unmanned him. If he let his mind dwell on it, he might forget that under no circumstances must he take advantage of their position. He wondered if she had heard what he said in those first moments, and if that was why she so persistently kept her face hidden? It occurred to him that he had never really known before how beautiful her hair was. The damp had only made it wave and curl more luxuriantly, and when a specially bright flame shot up, it shone like burnished copper. He felt a sudden longing to touch it—to run his fingers through it, and let the little stray tendrils curl round them. It required all his strength to stay patiently there on the other side of the hut.

After a time he stepped across to her.

"You must be getting cramped," he said. "Let me try and make you more comfortable."

She let him help her to her feet, and afterward try to find a new position. While doing so, he paused a moment and seemed to be hesitating. Then he bent toward her and said very quietly:

"If you would lean on me, Paddy, I could keep you so warm and comfortable."

He waited for her to speak.

"I would rather not," she answered, in a low, strained voice, and he said no more about it.

Presently, however, when she seemed to be settled as comfortably as circumstances would permit, he asked: "Would you rather I left you, and tried to get down the mountain to fetch help?"

She caught her breath with a queer little gulp, and he leaned lower to catch her answer.

"I don't want to bother you, Paddy, and I'm not afraid. I will go and try, if you would rather."

Still there was no answer. Paddy was wrestling between a wish for him to stay and a feeling that, to be true to herself, she ought to tell him to go.

Lawrence stood upright and looked down at her a few moments in silence. At last he spoke again, and there was a suggestion of pain in his voice:

"I won't worry you, Paddy, if you'll let me stay. I—I would much rather not leave you here alone." He leaned down. "What shall I do, Paddy?"

"Don't go," she said in a low voice he could only just distinguish, but his face brightened all over instantly, as he turned away to busy himself again with the fire, afterward taking up his stand once more on the far side from her.

Chapter Thirty Six.

The Rescue.

Meanwhile the little ladies at the Parsonage looked anxiously out into the fog, and wondered that Paddy should have gone to Mourne Lodge on such a night.

"I suppose they will keep her until to-morrow," Miss Jane remarked; "but I am rather sorry she went. It is just the weather to take cold."

And at Mourne Lodge Mrs Blake said: "How odd of Lawrence to stay at the Parsonage so late. Did you say he went home with Paddy, Doreen?"

Doreen looked worried, but she only replied:

"Yes; he said he should not be late."

Another half-hour passed, and then Mrs Blake asked; "What made him go home with Paddy at all, Doreen?"

Doreen was now fidgeting nervously, glancing constantly at the clock, and at last she decided to tell her mother exactly what had passed. Almost before she had finished, Mrs Blake was out in the hall peremptorily ordering one of the stable-boys to be sent for at once, and she waited at the open door until he came.

"Take a bicycle," she cried, in the same decisive manner, "and ride as hard as you can to Omeath Parsonage. Go to the back door, and, without making any noise, find out from the servants if Mr Lawrence has been there this evening. If he is there it is all right! but if not, come back here as quickly as possible, and tell them not to let the Misses O'Hara know that you came. Do you understand?"

"Yes, m'm," and in two seconds the boy was gone.

Another anxious half-hour passed, during the whole of which Mrs Blake paced the drawing-room, quite unable to sit still a moment. When she heard a step on the gravel, she hurried instantly to the front door.

"Is he there?" she asked, quite unable to conceal her anxiety.

"No, m'm—he has not been there at all, and they all think Miss Adair is here. I told them not to say anything, but cook is so anxious she is coming here on foot now."

Mrs Blake blanched a death-like hue, but never for an instant lost her head.

"Rouse George at once," she exclaimed, naming the head coachman, who had been with them for years, "and tell him not to lose a second in coming here. Stay—tell him Mr Lawrence and Miss Adair are lost on the mountains, and he must get a search party at once; then come to me."

The boy rushed off, and she turned quickly to the housekeeper, now anxiously waiting near.

"Blankets, Mrs Best," with almost unnatural calmness, "and a flask of brandy, and candles for the lanterns. There is nothing else we can prepare. I think."

George had gone to bed, which made it only the more incredible how he got up and got his party together in the short space before he was at the hall door; but there they stood, four alert men, with poles and lanterns, perfectly ready to risk their lives at a moment's notice for the master and Miss Adair. Mrs Blake explained in a few short sentences what had occurred and which way they had better take, but it was only at the very last she faltered.

"Don't come back without them, George," she said, in a low, husky voice, to the faithful old servant, and, with a like huskiness in his own throat, he answered:

"I will not, m'm."

Then commenced another terrible watch for the mother and her two daughters, when each tried in vain to frame words that might help the others.

There was nothing for it but to endure in silence and continue that restless pacing to and fro. At twelve o'clock the housekeeper came in with hot cocoa and biscuits, but all turned away at once. Mrs Best was another old and privileged servant, however, so she would take no refusal.

"Shure, 'tis no good gettin' fainting," she said, trying to speak cheerily. "Indeed, m'm, it's meeself will have to give it ye if ye won't take it." And then they tried to drink the cocoa to please her.

"There's Eliza downstairs," she continued. "About as much use as a child, rocking to and fro under her apron and moaning about little Miss Paddy, and what a wonderful baby she was, as if that would do any one any good. Relating all the mischief she used to be up to in one breath, and what a sainted angel she is in the next."

"Poor Eliza," said Mrs Blake, with a smile. "She is a faithful old soul. To think of her walking all this way from Omeath upon such a night!"

Still the time crept on and no footsteps sounded on the gravel, and away up the mountain Lawrence tended his little fire and began to look round anxiously for the fuel which was fast dwindling away. From time to time he stepped out into the fog and shouted, but sound could scarcely pierce the dense air, and he knew he would not be heard any distance away. Each time when he stepped out Paddy raised her head and watched him, instead of continuing her gaze at the flickering fire, but the last time he noticed that she did not stir.

He bent down over her and said her name softly, but there was no answer, and he saw that, worn out with exhaustion, she had fallen into a troubled sleep. For a few moments he was at his wits' end to know what to do for the best. The fire could not be kept going much longer, and meanwhile the damp cold increased hourly. Should he rouse her and try to make the descent? Which course was the least dangerous?—to crouch in the cold, damp shelter, or try and pierce the black gloom of the night? He looked at the sleeping form a moment, and then made up his mind. In such a strait, all things must be disregarded except whatever might diminish the danger. Whereupon, having come to a decision, he immediately set about carrying it out to the exclusion of all else. First he hunted round for every scrap of possible fuel and made up the fire; then, very tenderly and gently, he gathered Paddy into his arms, as if she had been a child and soothed her into a deep, dreamless slumber.

How long they remained thus he did not know. Paddy never stirred after the first half-unconscious resistance, but just slept on in the calmest, childlike sleep, and rather than disturb her he kept the same position, regardless of the severe cramp that seized him first in one limb and then another.

The only movement he made was to bend occasionally and touch her hair with his lips, but, apart from this, the fire went out and they remained in absolute silence and stillness—Paddy kept warm and comfortable and soothed into a restful slumber, while he sat upright, without even a coat, numbed with the damp and cold and a martyr to cramp.

Only what of it? While she lay in his arms, and every nerve of his body was strained in serving her, could he ask more? Lawrence looked out into the awful gloom, felt the creeping cold through all his bones and the sharp, shooting pains in his limbs, and was content. Of a truth he was not a man to do his loving by halves when it was real.

But human nature is not infallible, and it is doubtful if he could have endured much longer by the time a vague sound over the mountain fell on his ear. He raised his head and listened intently.

Yes—there it was again—a shout! Good God! some one was coming to them. With the utmost gentleness he managed to disengage himself and then struggle to his feet, but only to collapse ignominiously on to the ground, overcome by cramp through his whole body. He made another effort, and dragged himself up by the wall; then, still clinging to it, shouted with all his might.

Instantly rang back an answering shout, and within five minutes the little search party stood in the tumbled-down shelter, almost too overjoyed for words.

Old George gripped his young master's hand and the tears rained down his face.

"We were losing heart," he said. "We were almost giving you up, but I'd never have gone back to face the mistress without you."

"Have you blankets?" Lawrence asked, trying not to show what he was suffering, and still quite unable to stand alone.

George took in the situation at a glance, seeing him in shirtsleeves and the deadly pallor on his face.

"The young lady won't hurt for a minute or two," he said with sudden sharpness to the others. "Come and help me chafe the master's limbs," and he almost lifted Lawrence bodily, laying him down on a blanket and setting to work with a will, after first giving him some brandy. After a little while the pain gave and the colour came back to his lips, but meanwhile Paddy had awakened, and, without making any sound, sat watching. She knew instinctively what had happened, and she would not for worlds have attracted any attention to herself until Lawrence was better, his drawn face and blue lips going straight to her heart.

After a little, with George's help, Lawrence managed to get to his feet and stand upright, and then he turned at once to Paddy.

"Give me the flask," he said, and the others waited while he poured out some brandy and held it to her lips. Then he seemed quite himself again, and prepared to start for home, arranging everything, and, as usual, compelling acquiescence. Paddy wanted to try and walk, but he would not hear of it, and finally she had to get into the litter he contrived for her with blankets and be carried down the steep and dangerous slope.

At three in the morning the sound of footsteps at last fell on the straining ears at Mourne Lodge, and Mrs Blake hastened wildly to the door, her composure fast giving way.

"Lawrence!" she called out into the night. "Lawrence!" And only a mother could have spoken the name so.

"We're all right, mother," came back the answer cheerily; but as he came up, overcome at last, Mrs Blake fainted into his arms.

Chapter Thirty Seven.

"Stay here with me."

Paddy lay on the drawing-room sofa at the Parsonage and watched the birds skimming over the loch with a strained, anxious expression in her usually laughing eyes. Her aunts had fetched her from Mourne Lodge that morning, and there had been a great scene of general weeping and embracing and exclaiming. The news had somehow got all round the neighbourhood in an incredibly short time, and when Miss Mary was watching casually for Paddy to come home on her bicycle about eleven, there came instead a boy with the news that she and Lawrence had been lost in the fog all night and carried home in the morning.

Instantly there was great consternation in the Parsonage, and the small boy sent flying off for the one conveyance available in Omeath, in which, immediately afterward, the two sisters set out for Mourne Lodge. They found Paddy still a little dazed and shaken, but otherwise none the worse for her adventure.

"Lawrence saved me," she said as soon as they gave her time to speak. "If it had not been for him, I should probably have died of cold. He risked his life for me."

That was quite enough, and away rushed Miss Jane, with Miss Mary hurrying after her, to look for Lawrence. They found him in his den, with newspapers lying round him, apparently reading calmly. Only could they have looked in unobserved a moment sooner, they would have seen the newspapers were all out of reach, and, with compressed lips and knitted forehead he was staring gloomily at the floor lost in thought. However, he heard footsteps, and snatched up a paper just as the door opened, and neither of them had good enough eyesight to see that the sheet he held before him was covered with advertisements for housemaids and cooks.

Miss Jane came up to him with an almost sublime expression of gratitude.

"Paddy says you saved her life, Lawrence," she said simply. "I feel as if I must go down on my knees to you."

"Pray don't," he answered in his usual manner. "I won't answer for the floor being particularly clean. I simply hate the room being dusted, you know."

He got up, and with a little laugh tried to change the conversation. But neither of the ladies had the least intention of being put off in this manner, and they tried his patience considerably before they had finished their outpouring of grateful thanks. Then they retired again, and Lawrence closed the door after them with a momentary relief, only to be quickly superseded by his previous gloom. It was as though he had aged since yesterday. Several times last night, and again this morning when he sat beside her a little while in her bedroom, his mother had watched him covertly, and wondered what there was in his face that seemed strange to her. Now, when left alone again, he threw the papers aside and, sitting down at his writing table, buried his face in his hands.

He had been up early in spite of his awful night, had seen George and the other three men, and sat with his mother, and sent the loveliest flowers Mourne Lodge could produce to Paddy's bedroom; and now it was only mid-day, though it seemed half a life-time since he had sat in the hut holding Paddy, regardless of all things in heaven and earth but his precious burden. He went over everything again and again, moment by moment, unable to bring his mind to anything else. The night of such horror to all others was already to him the most precious memory of his life.

Only what was to come next? It was this thought that caused that moody, unheeding stare into vacancy.

"I will not live without her—she shall come to me," he muttered half-fiercely, and dreamt of all he would say to win her when they met.

Meanwhile the aunties took Paddy back with them, insisting upon watching over her as if she were an invalid, and finally inveigling her to the drawing-room sofa to lie quietly with closed blinds.

In this Paddy was not sorry to acquiesce. She wanted to be alone, and the shaded light was soothing. Through a dim sense of confusion—a confusion that she felt incapable of unravelling as to what had, and what had not, taken place—there were certain recollections that made her cheeks burn, and caused her to hide shrinking eyes in the cushions. How, oh how, was she ever to face him with those recollections lying between them? She half knew that in the first moment she had clung to him, and she had an indistinct remembrance that he had kissed her hair, and spoken in a low, passionate voice, calling her soft, endearing names.

Afterward, certainly, they had regained their old footing, but what about that long sleep? Under what conditions had she been able to sleep thus peacefully in the midst of such discomfort? That was the question Paddy dare not face, remembering his pallid cheeks and blue lips, while the old coachman brought the circulation back into his cramped limbs. She half hoped he would come to-day, while she was lying in the darkened room. It would be easier to get through the interview in the dark. But he did not come, and she lay restlessly, puzzling out the enigma in which their adventure had placed her.

What about that hate of hers! Can one—*may* one—hate one's preserver! She half prayed he would let her thank him quietly, and then go away. For hate or no hate, she perhaps owed him her life, and gratitude was his due.

But two days passed, and Lawrence did not come, and as she recovered further from the shock, she rallied herself, and felt more equal to the interview. She believed it was consideration for her that kept him away, and was grateful. In two days more her holiday would be up and she must return to London, and once away the adventure could be put aside. If only it had not been so hard to go—

On the afternoon of the third day Paddy wandered alone to a little creek by the loch, and, sitting down on a fallen tree, sank her chin in her hands and gazed across the water with a whole world of yearning longing in her eyes at the thought of leaving it all and returning to the streets, and chimney-pots, and smuts. So rapt was she that she did not hear some one approach over the moss and stand silently beside her—some one who saw the yearning, and read it aright with mingled feelings of regret and gladness.

"I began to think I'd never find you," he said at last in his quietest way, and Paddy started violently, and flushed to the roots of her hair, while she continued gazing across the loch, quite unable to meet his eyes.

He sat down on the log beside her, and leaned forward with his arms across his knees, playing idly with a twig he had picked up.

"I went to the Parsonage first," he continued, "and they told me you had gone out directly after lunch, and they believed you were sailing. I went down to the beach and found the boat, and decided you had taken a walk instead, and came to look for you. I was lucky to find you in such an out-of-the-way corner. Are you quite all right again!"

He was still keeping his eyes from her, playing with the twig, and Paddy unconsciously clenched her hands hard in her effort to feel collected.

"Yes, thank you!" She hesitated, still looking hard at the loch. Then she gulped down a long breath and took the plunge. "I am glad you have come. I have been wanting to see you." She noticed suddenly that he looked white and ill, and his face was a little drawn. "Have you been ill?"

"No, I have not been ill, only worried. I should have come sooner—only—" he hesitated.

"I wanted to see you to thank you," she interrupted. "Of course I know you risked your life to save mine. I might easily have died up there with the cold—and you might easily have slipped into a bog looking for me. No—" as he tried to stop her, "I must go on. Don't you see how it's just strangling me to remember that you risked so much—after—after—" her voice died away, she could find no words. She knew all in a moment that the casual acquaintance of the last three weeks was once more the lover, and the further complication unnerved her.

"As if that made any difference," a little harshly. "Haven't I told you that your scorn and threats cannot in any way change me—and never will. Good God! do you suppose I care two straws about risking my twopenny-halfpenny life when it is for you?"

She shrank away visibly, and he changed his manner.

"There, I don't want to worry you—but for Heaven's sake don't thank me. I can't stand it. There can be no question of thanks between you and me."

"But how can I help it?" she cried a little piteously. "Don't you understand that I *must* thank you —that it is the one and only return I can make?"

He looked into her face a moment and decided to humour her.

"Very well, only let us consider it finished. If it eases your mind, I will accept your gratitude; but I must be allowed to add it is absolutely uncalled-for, seeing I would risk a dozen lives for you cheerfully any day."

Her eyes fell before his, and she clenched her hands yet harder. Then he quite suddenly changed the subject.

"They tell me you are going back to London in two days. Is that so?"

"Yes."

"How you must hate it?" He looked round at the gleaming, beautiful loch and the mountains beyond. "It must be desperately hard to go back." She could not trust herself to speak, and he continued in a voice that had suddenly grown dangerously sympathetic. "I always think it is harder for you than the others. Your mother and Eileen always have each other, and any one can see how much that means to both. But you, somehow—since the dear old General died—seem to have had no one to take his place."

Great tears gathered in her eyes, and fell on her clasped hands. Why, or why, did he unman her! He was playing with the twig again, and pretending not to notice. "Isn't that so?" he asked.

She caught her breath and steadied her voice with an effort.

"I have been very fortunate," she said. "I might have had to go right away from everybody as a nursery governess, instead of having so many friends, and such a nice post, and plenty of liberty."

"But it is still London, isn't it? And after all, even friends are hardly to you what the mountains, and the loch, and the country life were. Be honest, Paddy," suddenly looking into her face. "Don't you just hate to have to go away and leave it all again?—don't you just hate it like the devil?"

She threw back her head with a sudden jerk, as if from some unendurable thought.

"Oh, yes—yes," she breathed, "like the devil, there is no other word. But what of it? I am going —I must go—I am not the only one who has had to give up a country home. Why do you make it harder for me? Why do you remind me of it at all?"

He leaned toward her, and she felt his eyes looking through into her soul. "I remind you, because I don't want you to go. Do you think it doesn't hurt me too—*now*? I, with all that I have—you with nothing—not even your own special chum since the General died."

She drew her hand across her eyes hurriedly.

"And it isn't as if you were obliged to go." He was leaning nearer—nearer. "Paddy, dear little woman, don't go. Give it all up and stay here with me."

"No, no. It is impossible. Please leave off. Why won't you understand?" and she wrung her hands together.

"It is *not* impossible," resolutely, "and it must be. It has got to be, Paddy. It is you who won't understand." Then he ran on whimsically, giving her time to collect herself: "Good Lord! it seems only the other day I was carrying you round on my shoulder, when I came home from Eton for the holidays. I remember I thought, you were the ugliest little creature I had ever set eyes on. You were so ugly, you fascinated; I couldn't take my eyes off you. But even then you had a way with you. Every one always did exactly as you wanted. If they didn't, you got into no end of a fury, and hit out right and left. It was awful sport making you wild, Paddy. Sometimes, when I've got hold of you, you've kicked at me as hard as you could with your fat little legs, but I always enjoyed the fun of it. I didn't think I'd ever want to marry you, though," with a whimsical smile; "it would have seemed too much like inviting a hurricane to one's fireside. It's quite the very last thing that would ever have entered my head, until—until—" he paused. "I don't know when it began, Paddy, but now I want nothing else in heaven or earth."

"Please don't go on," she managed to say; "please don't."

"Ah, but I want to; and after all it needn't hurt you. It's so good to have you all alone like this and tell you about it. Ever since the night on the mountain, I've been talking and smiling in my usual inane fashion, and all the time there was a seething volcano underneath. It hasn't been a pleasant two days; I wouldn't care about having them over again. Hour after hour I have longed to start off to the Parsonage; sometimes I have got as far as the lodge. But I felt I ought to give you time to recover thoroughly, and so I forced myself to turn back. When I awoke this morning I knew I should come to day. I had reached the utmost limit of my patience. Did you expect me? Did you, perhaps, hope I should come to-day!" She had put her hands up to her face, and now he tried to draw one of them away. "Why won't you look at me, Paddy! Why won't you let me see your face! Come, be your own bright self again. Chuck all this cursed nonsense about being impossible. Don't you know that my arms are aching for you? Do you hear, Paddy!—*aching* for you—and you sit there so silent and distant. Are you thinking of London and that beastly dispensary! Why, it's all done with, little woman; your home is going to be here in the future. Mourne Lodge is yours, and the horses are yours, and the boats, and the shooting, and everything. Ah! I'll make you so happy—"

She got up swiftly, suddenly, and thrust her hands out before her, as if warding off something. Her face was deathly white, and she looked only at the loch.

"Oh, stop! stop! Don't you realise it is *impossible*?" He changed colour visibly.

"Perhaps I have been too sudden after all," he said. "Perhaps by and by—"

"No, *newer*," and she mustered all her powers for the final word.

He gave a queer little laugh.

"'Never' is a long time," with a touch of the old cynical manner.

"I mean it," resolutely.

"You mean you prefer London—and the dispensary—and the loneliness to Mourne Lodge, and the loch, and the mountains?"

She was silent.

"Is that what you mean, Paddy!"

She tried to evade the question, but he would not let her. He stood up close to her, his face a little stern, his lips rigid. "Look at me, Paddy," in a tone of command.

She hesitated a second, then once again summoned all her courage, and looked steadily into his eyes.

"Now, why won't you stay here and be happy, instead of going back?"

"Because I hate you," and though her voice was low it contained no shadow of faltering.

Lawrence turned away sharply, and stood looking at the loch. His face grew, if anything, a little sterner, but showed no symptoms of defeat. Paddy could only wait, feeling vaguely wretched.

When he spoke his voice had changed somewhat. "You are candid as ever, but I am not convinced. It is because I believe I can turn your hate into love, I will not give in. Tell me one thing—is it the old bone of contention that stands between us!"

Paddy was silent.

"Tell me," he reiterated.

She answered hesitatingly. "I—I—don't want to be unkind after—"

"Spare me that," with a slight sneer. "Try and pretend the mountain incident is a myth."

She looked wretched.

"Well, what were you going to say? You needn't mind about being unkind. You forget I am used to it."

"I was going to say—" She hesitated again, searching about for words. "Oh, don't you realise that I don't trust you? Why do you put me in the difficult position of having to say this, just now of all times! Can't we leave it at that? Won't you believe I am grateful for the other night, and leave it there?"

"No. By God! I won't," and there was something almost fierce about him. The very fact that she shrank from him, only seemed to madden him, and it was as though he tried to soothe his own goaded feelings by goading hers. "The other night has only made it more impossible to leave it there. Why, when I found you, I took you in my arms—you know I did." The colour flashed in her cheeks, and he ran on: "Just as if—feeling as I do—having once had you in my arms, I'm going to tamely let you go again. Why, I never took my eyes off you the whole time. When I couldn't see your face, I watched your hair. It was freezingly cold, and I never knew it. It might just as well have been overpoweringly hot. I had got you—there—all alone—in my care— dependent on me—icebergs and volcanoes themselves couldn't have crushed me." He stopped as if he could hardly trust himself to say any more, and with a desperate attempt to bring him back to a commonplace level she said, "Please don't go on. You've managed to be cold enough the last three weeks. Let us go back to that again."

"You silly little goose!"—and he laughed harshly—"cold—to you! ah, ah! I was no more cold then than I am now, of course I wasn't. When we have been together you haven't said a word that I have not heard, nor moved an inch without my knowing. It was a subterfuge to see if you noticed; and you did. Ah, ah, Paddy, that's one to me. You know you wanted me to quarrel, and I wouldn't. Now own up."

He tried to take her hand, but she drew away, and stood with them both clasped behind her. She began to feel that the whole situation was getting beyond her.

Then suddenly, with his customary variableness, Lawrence grew quiet again.

"You say you don't trust me. Well, I will show you I can be trusted. I have never cared enough before. Is that altogether my fault? I care enough now, and I will show you. Is it that alone that stands between us? If you could trust me, you would let yourself go? Paddy!"—he moved suddenly nearer, and looked squarely into her eyes—"just as if I didn't know that under ordinary circumstances I should win you easily enough. I'm not bragging. Heaven knows I've faults enough, but bragging is not among them. It's because, somehow, I know that under ordinary circumstances it would be natural for your love to surrender to mine, before anyone else you know, that I snap my fingers when you protest that you hate me, and refuse to be daunted. If I could slay the spectre between us, and show you that I was to be trusted, would you marry me?"

Paddy looked hard at the loch, and said, "No."

"Why not?"

"When I have said a thing, I have said it. I will not marry you, because I hate you."

"Now you are merely absurd. Why do you hate me?"

"Because I cannot forget the past."

He gave an impatient gesture. "Heroics! Heroics!—*you* were never hurt. I tell you it is a spectre, and you ought to have the sense to slay it. Instead, you enlarge on it—positively drape it in visionary attributes, and offer yourself as a sort of burnt offering to it. You ought to have lived a few hundred years ago. By Gad! Paddy, you'd have made a fine Joan of Arc!" and he laughed with a touch of bitterness.

Paddy stared at the loch and remained silent.

"Patricia the Great at the head of an avenging army—leading on fools and knights-errant—devastating a peaceful, harmless land for the sake of a Dream—a Prejudice—a Chimera. I see it all."

She looked helplessly unhappy, but he would not spare her.

"Listen to me, Patricia the Great. You shall keep your feud, and cling to your prejudice a little longer, but *I will not give in*. I want you. That at least is a plain, ungarnished truth. Perhaps if you knew me as well as some, you would realise that it is the sort of truth I have a little habit of making into a fact, in spite of dreams and prejudices. This thing has got to be, Paddy. I repeat what I said before. If I am worth my name, I will win you yet."

"Ah, why will you talk like this, when it is so useless," she cried. "Why will you not be friends? Lawrence, let us be friends. Let me thank you for the other night, and, for the sake of it, drop the old feud. I will try to do this to show you I am sincere in my gratitude."

His face grew suddenly whiter than ever with concentrated passion and determination. "We will do nothing of the kind. I don't want your friendship. You can take it back. Do you hear? I refuse your kindly pat on the shoulder, and your offer to be a good girl because you think you owe me thanks. You can keep your feud and your hatred—anything is better than a soppy middle course. It is my turn now, and I refuse your offer of sisterly affection, which is what it amounts to. I will have your love some day, but until then, your hate, please. As long as you go on hating I shall know at least that you are not indifferent, and that the sound of my name does not pass unheeded by your ears. And we will continue to cross swords—we will be as we were before. If you want to show this gratitude you talk of, show it that way; it is the only thing I ask of you."

She shrank from him a little bewildered. The strength of his passion stirred every fibre of her being, and the thought crossed her—would she be able to withstand him for long? But Lawrence cooled suddenly. He had said his say; for the present, there was nothing further to be gained. In two minutes his face was almost as impassive as of old, as he remarked cynically:

"Trust an old fool for being a big fool. I am ranting like a street preacher. Well, I will go home and find my level again. Good-by, Paddy." He gripped her hand with such force that she uttered a little cry.

"There, I didn't mean to hurt you, only to show you how I can grip, if I make up my mind to anything. Remember I am your enemy. Go on hating as hard as you like, until I make you love. We shall meet again soon in London."

Then he strode off through the wood, and left her by the loch alone.

Chapter Thirty Eight.

Gwen's Views on Matrimony.

When Paddy got back to London, her mother, and Eileen, and the doctor, and even Basil thought she was changed in some way, but they did not know how. She was quieter than she used to be, or at any rate given to moods, bursting out now and then into unusual spirits which had yet a ring of not being perfectly genuine.

Curiously enough, perhaps, Gwendoline Carew was the only one who actually knew what was affecting her. She had met Lawrence in the autumn at a shooting party at a mutual friend's, and quickly recognised some change in him too. Of course she had taken the first opportunity to tax him with it, and absolutely refused to be put off with cynicism or scoffing or anything else.

"Don't waste time talking to me like this, Lawrie," she had said, "as if I didn't know you too well by this time. Just have the grace to bow your superior old head for once, and own you've reached a fence you can't clear."

"Wouldn't it be better to make sure first? I wouldn't for the world tell you an untruth."

"I'll risk it. Besides, Lawrie, who knows! I might be able to help."

"I have rather a weakness for managing my own affairs."

"I know you have, and on the whole they do you credit, but it seems to me there's something on foot now, that you're just not quite so dead certain sure about as usual."

Lawrence was silent.

"Once before it was the same," said Gwen. "Don't you remember when a certain father died, and you were in doubt? Well, didn't Gwen manage you then and help to keep you from running off the track!"

"I am not in doubt now," he answered.

"No, but I strongly suspect that you are in love."

He only looked steadily before him and made no sign.

"If it's Paddy," said candid Gwen, "I'll just move heaven and earth to help you. If it isn't you can 'gang yer ain gait.'"

She waited, and presently Lawrence said quietly: "It is Paddy."

Whereupon Gwen forgot she was a young personage of importance mentioned often in the fashionable papers, and danced a little jig all round the room.

"Lovely!" she cried, "just lovely! You must get married before me so that I can be a bridesmaid, Lawrie."

"You are somewhat premature," dryly. "Paddy has refused to marry me."

Gwen came to a sudden standstill.

"Refused," she repeated, as if she were not quite sure she had heard aright.

"Yes, plain, ungarnished, unmistakable refusal."

"Little idiot!" said Gwen, "what's she dreaming of!"

"I don't know, but she was at considerable pains to impress upon me that even medicine bottles and that beastly dispensary were preferable to Mourne Lodge with me."

Gwen made a curious whistling sound with her lips—again not in the least what one would expect from a young lady mentioned in fashionable papers, and sat down beside Lawrence looking quite subdued.

"Well, don't look so blue," she said presently. "Where there's a will there's a way. What are you going to do?"

"I'm going to win."

"That's right. Never say die. I expect you've taken her rather too much by surprise. I'm quite sure when I last saw Paddy, it had never entered her head for a moment that you cared a fig about her except to tease. Give her time to come round a bit. It sounds like playing a salmon, doesn't it? I'm sure it will be heaps more interesting than if she'd said 'yes' right away, and you'll both care more in the end. That's what I tell Bob sometimes. I was much too easily won, and I want to go back and begin again, I just dropped right off the tree into his hands like an over-ripe cherry. Disgusting to think of—isn't it? I ought to have let him mope and pine a bit, and pretended I didn't care. Only I'd have been so horribly afraid he thought I meant it, and gone off, or something. I guess that sort of thing is all very fine to talk about and in story books, but when it comes to pretending you don't like a man, when you're just dying to have him all for your own—why it isn't human nature. Them's my sentiments!"

Lawrence could not help smiling, but it was poor enough comfort for him, though before they separated Gwen did really cheer him a little by her determined hopefulness and sanguinity.

With Paddy, however, she did not get on in the matter quite so well as she had expected. At the very first allusion Paddy simply drew back into herself, and refused to be coaxed or cajoled into uttering a single word. Gwen tried several times and then had to give in.

"Oh, well, if you won't, you won't," she said. "I always thought I took the biscuit for pure, downright obstinacy, but I hand it on to you now."

Lawrence himself did not come to London until the end of October, having decided it was best not to be in too great a hurry, and he had better have a turn at the pheasants first. When he came he stayed with the Grant-Carews, and it was here he met Paddy through a little subterfuge of Gwen's.

"My poppa and momma," she wrote to Paddy, "are going to a terrible, overpowering, grand-turk, political luncheon party, to which flighty young persons like myself are not admitted, but have to remain at home alone and bear the weight of the distinction of belonging to some one who has been admitted. Do be a dear girl and come and bear the weight with me. With your company and a liberal supply of De Brei's chocolates I anticipate getting through the afternoon all right. In case of accidents, however, I may just mention the fact of our loneliness to one of His Majesty's Horse Guards, but you will have no occasion to be uneasy anyway—*Comprenez*?"

Paddy accepted the invitation, but as Gwen fluttered across the drawing-room to receive her, her quick eyes instantly descried in the far window the back of a well-cut masculine coat, that was somehow familiar.

"Who is here?" she asked at once.

"Only Lawrence," said Gwen, in the most casual fashion. "He is staying with us. Didn't I tell you?"

Paddy made no reply. The plot was too apparent, but this very fact put her on her mettle, and helped her more than anything else would have done.

"How do you do?" she said to him, trying to seem perfectly at ease. "I thought you were shooting pheasants in Suffolk."

"So I was until both they and the shooting grew too tame."

"That's his way of saying his aim was either too sure, or too wide, I don't know which," put in Gwen. "Or possibly he got into one of his bear-like moods and no one could put up with him, so they sent him on to us. Have you ever seen Lawrence when he's like a bear with a sore head?" running on. "He's just lovely! I think that's my favourite of all his hundred-and-one moods. Most people are afraid of him, which is silly. If you don't care a fig, and do a little bear-baiting, you can get no end of fun out of it. I wish you would dispose of a few of your moods to Bob, Lawrie. I'm dreadfully afraid he'll turn out hopelessly tame as a husband. Still he can hardly go on worshipping for a whole life-time without a break of some kind. He's bound to turn cranky one day. Won't it be interesting to see the first symptoms! That must be one of the most entertaining parts about getting married, I think—to find out what you each get cranky about, and how you do it."

"I'm afraid you'll keep poor old Bob so busy," said Lawrence, "he'll have no time to indulge in cranks for himself."

"Oh, yes, he will. I like fair play, and I'll see that, he gets his chance. It's only cricket, you know, to let your husband have a good old round-up occasionally, and pretend you're much impressed, and all that."

She dashed off into another subject. "What a delicious hat, Patricia! Where did you get it? My! what a swell we are to-day. Is it all put on for me, or for Lawrence?—or have you designs on my poor darling Goliath? Doesn't she look charming, Lawrie?"

"Don't be silly, Gwen," a little crossly.

"Quite charming," said Lawrence quietly, and opened the door for them to go down to lunch.

At lunch Gwen plunged into a very sore subject without knowing it.

Paddy was treating Lawrence with polite affability, as if to imply that for the sake of what had happened on the mountain, she would, as a special concession, at any rate not be rude. Lawrence was lackadaisically entertaining, with his old callous air, when Gwen suddenly said:

"Why won't your sister ever come here with you, Paddy? What a funny girl she is. She seldom goes to see Kathleen and Doreen either."

Paddy looked vexed and uncomfortable, but Gwen ran heedlessly on: "Do you know I think she has one of the loveliest faces I've ever seen in my life. I'd like to sit and look at her. Doesn't she like going out?"

Now it was Paddy's most firm and invincible belief, that the reason Eileen had so persistently declined all Owen's friendly overtures and invitations, was from nothing in the world but a dread of meeting Lawrence. Of course she no longer fretted—it was easy to see that; but, judging from her own staunch heart, Paddy argued to herself that though she did not fret, she still remembered, and could not face the pain of a single meeting that could easily be avoided. Consequently a great many delightful gaieties had been sacrificed to the old wound. And when Paddy called this to mind, her anger with Lawrence's heartlessness received fresh fuel.

As a matter of fact, it was not Eileen's reason at all. When Gwen first showed her unmistakable liking for Paddy, and shortly afterward included both sisters in an invitation, Eileen had made up her mind resolutely to stand aside. She foresaw that were she once to join in their outings, it must inevitably mean fewer invitations for Paddy, as one can always be so much more easily asked than two, and as she was not particularly fond of gaiety, and would as soon remain at home with her mother, she made her decision in the beginning and stood by it, without, however, entering into explanations. Paddy probed her once or twice, and then drew her own conclusions.

"She has never been to see me once," Gwen ran on. "I think it is too bad of her."

She seemed to expect Paddy to say something, so Paddy remarked casually: "She hates leaving mother alone. It has always been the same," and then she shot a sidelong glance at Lawrence. The fact that he was calmly going on with his lunch without the very smallest symptoms of embarrassment, or consciousness, vexed her unreasonably, and she wished with all her heart he had not come. Her polite affability from being genuine took a sarcastic turn that was not lost on Lawrence, but he deviated in no measure from his unperturbed, lackadaisical serenity.

"He hasn't as much heart as a plaster cast," was Paddy's inward comment, which, had she stopped to think of it, showed a distinct lack of discernment in herself, considering what he had endured for her on the mountain.

Very shortly after lunch they were joined by the redoubtable Guardsman, who captivated Paddy at once, with the delightful boyishness that somehow mingled so irresistibly with his splendid proportions, and his almost pathetic devotion to Gwen—who dubbed him alternately, the Babe, or the Giant, or Goliath.

"We're all going for a walk in the park now," she informed her assembled guests, "and then, perhaps, we'll have tea at the 'Hyde Park Hotel,' and Paddy can go back to her precious bottles."

Paddy could only acquiesce, and of course Gwen and her giant were very quickly steaming ahead, with that expression of blissful satisfaction which is to be seen in the very backs of some amorous couples.

Paddy once more commenced to converse with affable politeness to her somewhat incommunicative companion.

At last her small stock of patience gave out.

"It's your turn now," she said a trifle witheringly. "I've thought of the last half-dozen remarks."

Lawrence gave a low laugh. "I hope you don't want me to think they were any strain," he said.

Of course no self-respecting daughter of an Irish Fusilier could stand that. "I wished to be polite," she retorted, "so I tried to suit my remarks to my company."

"Then I wonder you don't discourse on villains, and ogres, and blood-thirsty monsters, and that sort of thing."

"I am quite sorry I couldn't," with a little snort. "Only inane platitudes seemed adaptable."

Again Lawrence laughed.

"You're a stunner at repartee, Paddy. I never knew such a fighter in my life. First it was fists, then feet, and now it's tongue."

"I am Irish," with naïve simplicity.

"So am I, but it doesn't make me want to lay every one out in about half-an-hour."

"Of course not," scornfully. "You are the sort of Irishman who goes about the world getting your countrymen a bad name. You only shine when you are doing what you ought not."

"Another injustice to Ireland," with mock pathos—adding: "and when you shoot barbed arrows, and fiery glances broadcast, with a reckless indifference to inflicting hurt, you are shining at doing what you ought—is that it?"

"Oh, don't be an idiot!" with impatience. "You make an effort at being polite now, and talk sense."

"But if being polite rests in suiting one's conversation to one's companion?" significantly.

"Then we won't be polite," laughing in spite of herself. "You can be natural and talk drivel, and I'll be warlike." She glanced round the park with a sudden expression, half-longing, and half-humorous—"Heaven! how I wish we could go ratting!" she said.

But before they parted they had one of their old tussles. Lawrence suddenly taxed her with looking pale and tired: "Are you ill?" he asked. "Is it that beastly dispensary?"

"I was never so well in my life before," obstinately.

"I know better. You see, I've known you every single bit of your life, so I'm in a position to judge."

"You have not," with flat contradiction. She felt instinctively he was getting lover-like, and felt she must repress him at any cost.

"How have I not? I certainly knew you when you were a month old. I was offered the supreme privilege of carrying you round the garden, but you were so like a black-beetle I funked it."

"There were the three years when you were abroad," with a show of indifference.

"Ah, to be sure, I didn't know you then." He smiled a little—that old whimsical smile. "Had I done so there would probably have been no second trip abroad, and no deadly feud, and Mourne Lodge might have had a second Boadicea rampaging through its stately rooms as mistress."

She quickened her steps. "I must get my 'bus now, or I shall be late. It is no use attempting to attract the attention of Gwen and her giant."

"You bring me down to earth with such thuds," with a plaintive air. "I dream of stately halls, and modern heroines gracing ancient shrines, and you annihilate both the vision and the poetry in one merciless blow, metaphorically flinging a Shepherd's Bush 'bus at my head. As it is quite out of the question for me to inflict myself upon the lovers, I must take you home in a taxi."

"I am going in a 'bus," willfully. "If you want a cab drive, go to your club," and she turned her steps resolutely toward the road.

"I see you mean to be unmanageable—but I can wait—my time will come. If I see you getting pale and ill-looking, it will come sooner than you think."

"I don't think at all. I haven't time—at least not to think of you. My bottles and prescriptions interest me far more."

"Liar," he murmured humorously—looking hard into her face—and her mobile mouth twitched irresistibly as she crossed the road to her 'bus.

She climbed on the top to get the air, in spite of the moist November atmosphere, and though she had been spirited to the last with Lawrence, her heart grew heavy as they trundled down Notting Hill toward the enveloping greyness of Shepherd's Bush, and she wondered if she had been wise to go. It was not the first time that Paddy had had misgivings about the wisdom of seeing much of Gwen. She always hated the commonplace, middle-class streets so afterward, the stuffy little dispensary, with its rows of foolish, inane-looking jars, and monotonous medicine bottles; the hopeless mediocrity of her whole surroundings. At moments she longed passionately to be with Jack galloping over the grass plains of the Argentine; and her heart was sore at the fate which had condemned her of all people to mixing medicines in a dingy suburb. She even ruminated a little wistfully, if only Lawrence had not been Lawrence. If some other man had lived at Mourne Lodge, and wanted her to make her home there, what a heaven on earth she might have had! Or if even Lawrence had been different—and there had been no dividing memory. How strange it seemed that he should combine such charm with such heartlessness. She understood better now, how it was Eileen had become a victim. It was natural enough, since it had pleased him to please her. But she knew more of the other side, had known it all along, through her greater friendship with his sisters. Only that morning, in a letter from home, Doreen had written: "Lawrence has been shooting pheasants in Suffolk. Long may he stay there. Before he went, and just after you left the Parsonage he was in one of his most bearish moods. If he wasn't sullen he was cutting. He either sulked or sneered till we were sick of him in the house. Of course Kathleen quarrelled with him about the way he spoke to mother, which is so silly of her, as mother understands him, and doesn't really take any notice; whereas Kathleen ends in making us all miserable. However, he had the goodness to take himself off after the 12th, and it's been peaceful ever since."

Paddy stared into the greyness. Of course Eileen had been spared; such a nature must surely have broken her heart—but that was no excuse whatever—merely a reflection.

Chapter Thirty Nine.

A Christmas Surprise.

The few weeks to Christmas passed uneventfully. The Blakes came to London and Lawrence joined them, and they all seemed to slip back into their old groove for the time being. Paddy came and went much the same as before, and Lawrence strove to possess his soul in patience. Once more he resorted to subterfuge to find out when she was likely to be coming, and in general she succeeded in outwitting him. If she was half expected he would sit in his smoke-room with the door ajar, and listen to hear if the stately James opened the door to a familiar voice. If she came he would casually join them all at tea. If she did not he went to his club. Once he inveigled her into the sanctum itself. That was a red-letter day. He went downstairs to see her out, and in the hall told her in a voice of most disarming naturalness, that he had a beautiful little setter pup in his room—wouldn't she like to see it?

Paddy hesitated, and was lost.

She could never resist dogs. The little creature was in a basket near the fireplace, and she took it up in undisguised delight, going eagerly over its points with him. Then she put it back and turned to the door.

"Don't hurry," in that same disarming voice. "There are a good many things that will interest you here, if you will only look at them."

Paddy murmured something about the dispensary, with one eye on the door, and the other on a model yacht. With great diplomacy Lawrence turned his head away, and said simply, "Oh, well, another time perhaps."

Paddy said: "Is that a model of the *Shamrock*? What a little beauty it is!"

They went over the points of the yacht, and she became engrossed in it. Then she suddenly made an unaccountable movement for the door. It had dawned on her that she was parleying with the enemy. That the enemy was dangerously alluring. Feeling a little mad with herself, she made her exit ungracefully. A jerky good-by—a feeble explanation of her sudden haste—and she was gone.

Then Lawrence smiled. His extremely wide and varied experience with the opposite sex had made him correspondingly wise. In that moment he saw victory in sight. Far enough away still, perhaps, but yet there. It was becoming a duel of wills. To him it was his strength of will and personality, against her fanaticism. He had chosen a strong word, but fallen short in grasping all it involved. How many a strong will has been worsted even by a weak fanatic! How many a weak will, under the influence of fanaticism has achieved the deeds of the strong!

He knew that day that in some way she was not wholly indifferent to him. He believed she was just a little bit afraid, and that, to him, was the sweetest thought of all.

Paddy hurried home, and wondered why she had been so stupidly weak as to go and see the puppy. She was genuinely vexed, and the incident had the present result of making her absent herself longer than usual, and be more difficult, when at last she came.

Lawrence went to his store of understanding, and said: "She has discovered that she is afraid."

Then Christmas approached. It had been arranged for Mrs Adair, and Eileen, and Paddy to cross to Omeath for a week, somewhat to the latter's surprise, for it seemed to her extremely rash for Eileen and her mother to take such a journey at that time of the year. However, her remonstrances were quickly swept aside, and the plans made. Then came a letter from Aunt Jane begging Mrs Adair and Eileen to start a week before Christmas, and if Paddy could not come with them, for her to follow on Christmas eve. To Paddy's amazement Mrs Adair immediately showed signs of consenting. For one moment it was almost a shock to her—it seemed so strange that they should go off like that without her, when they knew she could not possibly go before Christmas eve. Seeing her mute surprise, her mother hastened to explain that the aunties had a very special reason for wishing it, and then Paddy decided there was something in the air of which she was entirely ignorant. A year ago she would have promptly asked innumerable questions, but somehow a secret in her own life had raised a dim barrier between her and her mother and sister, and she felt, with a vague sense of loneliness, that, perhaps, they likewise had a secret they kept from her. She made no demur about their hurried departure, but kissed them good-by with a bright face, though something in her eyes made Eileen remark as the train steamed out of Euston:

"It's rather too bad, mother, isn't it?"

"She will understand all right on Christmas Day," Mrs Adair answered, and a beautiful colour stole over Eileen's face.

Beyond doubt, as Paddy had conjectured, there was something in the wind. There were two others, however, who were much pleased by the arrangement, namely, Gwendoline and Lawrence.

"It's just capital, isn't it?" Gwen exclaimed. "Now you'll have to take Paddy over on Christmas eve."

Lawrence said little, but Gwen saw a light come into his eyes that he could not altogether hide. Paddy at first was vexed, and showed it.

"Don't be an idiot," quoth Gwen. "Why, it stands to reason it's pleasanter to have an escort for a long, cold, dark journey like that, and Lawrence is splendid to travel with. He just looks after you all the time and doesn't bother to talk. I shall come and fetch you in the brougham in the afternoon and go to Euston, and see you both off myself."

She did so, and Paddy's good aunt was immensely impressed by the magnificence of the livery and horses of the equipage, that drew up in the dingy Shepherd's Bush street that December afternoon, outside the doctor's highly coloured front door. Gwen herself she only saw dimly through the drawing-room curtains, inside the brougham, but even that glimpse so impressed her that for several days the church guilds and things had a rest, in favour of this vision from the far-off fashionable world.

Paddy took it all very coolly. She did not even wear her best hat, which greatly scandalised her aunt, but as Paddy explained, it was too heavy on her forehead to travel in and the other would do quite as well.

When they reached Euston, Lawrence was waiting, having artfully reached the station first in order to procure not only their tickets, but, by a substantial tip, the first-class compartment for themselves.

"What! here already!" cried Gwen. "Ye gods and fishes, is the world coming to an end! Mark it down on your cuff, Lawrence, that you once caught a train with five minutes to spare, instead of leisurely strolling up after it was already on the move, and having to scramble into the guard's van."

Lawrence took no notice.

"Do you prefer the dining-car or dinner baskets?" he asked Paddy.

"I don't need either, thanks. I never feel hungry on a journey."

"Have the baskets, Lawrie," said Gwen. "Then you are not tied to any time, and you don't have the bother of going to the restaurant car."

Paddy turned away. "I must get my ticket," said she.

Gwen looked highly amused. Indeed the whole performance was tickling her so, she could hardly refrain from bursting out laughing at the two of them.

"I took the liberty of getting your ticket when I got my own," said Lawrence. "I thought it would save you the trouble."

Paddy murmured a word of thanks, and opened her purse.

"How much do I owe you!" she asked.

Lawrence caught the gleam in Gwen's eyes, and could not help an answering gleam.

"I'm not quite sure," he said. "May we leave it for the present?"

A little demon possessed Gwen. "Don't forget the tips for the porters when you're settling-up," she said.

Paddy looked rather black, and Lawrence had to turn away to buy some papers.

"You are a wretch, Gwen," said Paddy. "You know perfectly well you wouldn't let anyone pay for you."

"Oh! wouldn't I!" with emphasis. "I'd just think how jolly lucky I was to be all that much to the good."

Lawrence came back with his arm full of illustrated magazines.

"Nothing like plenty of literature to keep one from getting dull," said Gwen wickedly. "But my! won't it complicate the settling-up!"

A guard came along and told Lawrence they would be starting in two minutes, and so obsequious and marked was his deference that Gwen was again taken with an unaccountable spasm of amusement.

"You scoundrel, Lawrence," she murmured, in an aside, "that cost you nothing short of a sovereign."

Lawrence pretended not to hear, but led the way to their compartment and placed the magazines on the seat. Paddy was thoughtful a moment, and again a little black.

"I don't want to travel first," she said. "I can't afford it. Let us meet at Holyhead and cross on the steamer together."

"It's a pity to waste the ticket," said Lawrence, "and the thirds are so crowded. Besides there is no time now."

"No, they're just off," put in Gwen quickly. "Good-by, Paddy. Sorry I can't be in for that settling-up. I'm so afraid Lawrence will cheat you. Have a good time. See you on Thursday," and a few seconds later the train was steaming out of the station.

Gwen's last remark with reference to Thursday was an allusion to a visit she and her adoring Goliath were paying to the Blakes in a few days. They were to have gone over with Lawrence, but at the last her parents refused to part with her for Christmas Day, and they were not starting till the twenty-seventh.

"It will be lovely to have Gwen in Ireland," Paddy said, as they settled themselves, "but she ought to have paid her first visit in the summer."

Lawrence gave a little laugh.

"I don't suppose the seasons make much difference to people in her and Bob's happy state of mind. It's just likely she will hardly know whether it is December or July,"—then he proceeded to shake out his big, warm rug and tuck it all round Paddy.

She tried to remonstrate, but she might as well have talked to the rug.

"I won't worry you the whole way if you're good, Paddy," he said, with a smile, in which there was a touch of wistfulness; "but you'll just have to let me take care of you; it would be any man's right who had known you as long as I have."

She coloured and lowered her eyes, but made no further demur. When he was satisfied he had done everything possible, and again sat down, she opened one of the papers, and buried her face in it, pretending to be carefully studying the illustrations. But in reality something of a tumult was stirring in her heart. It was so good to be taken care of—poor Paddy. The way her mother and Eileen had gone on ahead had hurt her more than any one knew, and Lawrence's careful attentions only made her feel the contrast. If it had only been Jack—or indeed anyone but Lawrence.

He had opened a paper also and now sat quietly reading opposite to her, not attempting to worry her with conversation. Once or twice Paddy ventured to glance covertly into his thin, keen face after discovering she could do so without his knowledge.

She was wondering a little why, occasionally of late, she had experienced a wholly new and unaccountable sensation, something like dread. How could she be afraid?... she the fearless! Was it the subtle suggestion of strength? Hardly so, for Ted Masterman was no less strong, and she had never had any anxious qualms with him, nor remotest suggestion of loss of self-confidence. Was it the thin, cynical lips! Was it the something indescribable that suggested unscrupulousness? In repose it was not a reassuring face. The mouth was a little cruel, the jaw had an obstinate set, and there were fine lines of irritability round the keen eyes. Only when he smiled was there real charm, and even then it depended on the measure of his wish to please; though, because his smile was rare, it was invariably attractive.

Paddy watched him covertly, feeling interested. She realised that he had the look of a man who could not be thwarted with impunity. A man strong enough to be patient up to a certain point, and then capable of being unscrupulous rather than give in. She wished vaguely that he had been different, and at that moment, before she had time to lower her gaze, Lawrence looked up suddenly from his paper straight into her eyes.

There was no time for subterfuge, and a sudden flood of colour in her cheeks told its own tale.

Lawrence smiled his sudden, fascinating smile, and resting his arms across his knees, leaned toward her.

"What were you thinking about, Patricia!"

"Nothing," said Paddy, and shut her mouth with a little snap.

"Come!" coaxingly, "you may as well tell me."

But she would not be inveigled, and picked up her papers again, saying that she had forgotten. Lawrence, however, was not so easily put off.

"Do you know you have such a funny mouth, Paddy," he said. "It doesn't shut properly, and when you want to be very firm you have to use great pressure. It almost looks as if it had a spring that didn't work quite properly, and sometimes, although you are very determined to be severe, it persists in getting unmanageable and twitching. It's quite the most fascinating, irresistible mouth I ever saw in my life."

"Don't be silly," trying not to see how altogether engaging his manner had become. "In about two seconds I shall put up my umbrella."

"Don't do that," he laughed. "It would be too unkind. I don't mind your firing bombs at me in your conversation, but I should mind very much if you hid yourself."

"That is the reason that would have more weight with me than any other for doing so," promptly.

Lawrence sat back and laughed outright.

"Clean bowled!" he said. "'Pon my word, Paddy, there's no getting in edgeways with you."

"Give up trying," dryly. "Read a book and improve your mind instead."

"Does it need it so badly?"

"Never too old to learn," without looking up.

"You needn't say it as if I were your grandfather. I'm only thirty-five, and what are you? Let me see, Doreen is twenty-five, and you are eighteen months younger, therefore you must be either twenty-three or twenty-four. Time you were growing wiser, Paddy, and suiting yourself to your world, and its exigencies."

"I suppose you mean *your* world!"

"Mine and yours. It's got to come some day, Patricia. Why not now?"

She shut her lips more tightly, and pretended to be buried in her paper.

"You can't possibly know what you are reading about. Put the paper down and talk for a little. You will only damage your eyesight."

Still no answer.

He ventured further. "Do you remember the last time we were alone in a small space between four walls at this hour!"

She put the paper down suddenly, and looked straight into his eyes. "You are not playing fair," she said.

He sat up quickly, and drew his hand across his face, and then said quite simply: "You are right. I apologise."

Paddy was instantly mollified, and he saw it, and took the opportunity to get up and rearrange her rug.

"It is all right," she urged, but he only smiled, and persisted in tucking her up more cozily. Once again Paddy had that fleeting sense of the satisfaction of masculine protection, and looked a little wistfully down at her book.

"If I promise to play fair, will you talk?" he asked. "It is so tiring to read."

She could not but agree with him, and they spent the rest of the journey talking about Lawrence's travels, and the wonders of far-off lands. When he would take the trouble he was a delightful conversationalist, and Paddy gave an exclamation of astonishment when she found they were nearing Holyhead.

Lawrence smiled inwardly, but was far too clever to mar his momentary triumph by seeming to notice it, and they remained good friends until the train steamed into Omeath station.

Paddy, of course, was hanging out of the window, watching for each familiar landmark, but when the train drew up, she uttered an exclamation of such boundless amazement, incredulity, and delight mingled, that Lawrence was quite startled.

Coming running down the platform was Jack O'Hara.

Chapter Forty.

A Budget of News.

Paddy was out on the platform in half a twinkling, and with a little cry of "Jack!" darted to meet him with hands outstretched. Jack caught hold of both, and shook them until she was quite exhausted, and cried for mercy. Lawrence stood looking on, and his brow grew black as thunder. If Jack had only known it, in that one minute he had practically all the revenge he need wish, for any fancied contempt in the past.

"Can I give you a lift?" Lawrence said, when they would listen. "My motor is here. How do, O'Hara! You look as if South America suited you."

"It did A1," answered Jack, not even noticing Lawrence's ill-concealed anger—as indeed he had small occasion to. "What shall we do, Paddy, walk or drive?"

"Oh, ride on the back of the train, of course!" she cried, "and home through the garden, just like we did as children. Oh, Jack, I've had to be so grown-up for two years. I absolutely refuse to be grown-up this Christmas holiday—we will—we *must* be children."

"Anything you like," he cried, with the utmost readiness. "Come along," as the train moved. "Send up Miss Paddy's portmanteau. Good-by, Lawrence!" and they sprang on to the step of the guard's van and rode the short distance of railway to the Parsonage garden, leaving Lawrence to go home in the most unenviable frame of mind imaginable, which he later vented upon the household generally in his cold and cutting fashion, regardless of the fact that he was damping every one's Christmas.

But what cared Jack and Paddy?—least of all Paddy—for whom a joy seemed to have dropped straight from, the skies. What a noise there was, to be sure! and how Jack and Paddy *would* talk at once, and make it impossible for any single sentence to be coherent.

At last, in desperation, Paddy picked up the little table-bell and rang it lustily. "If I can't be heard, you shan't, Jack," she said, and, the moment he opened his mouth, started ringing it again. Jack immediately flew round the table to get the bell, and behold! if the two little ladies weren't collecting the breakables again, and casting agonising glances at the cups and saucers and plates on the breakfast-table—just for all the world as if two long years of separation had not rolled by since the last scrimmage, and these two mad things were not a day older. If Paddy had not been in such a state of eager excitement, she must certainly have noticed sooner than she did an air of portent that still prevailed, as of some momentous event not yet revealed.

As it was, they all went to the little church as usual, Jack and the aunties sitting one side, and the Adairs on the other side, for the sake of old times; and came home again, and had their Christmas dinner, before Paddy got an inkling that further news was in the air. Up to then the whole conversation nearly had run upon Jack's adventures in the Argentine, and she had plied him with such an endless string of questions that there had really not been much opportunity for any other subject.

After dinner, however, they collected round a big log fire for a cozy afternoon, and a few minutes later a letter and parcel arrived by hand for Paddy. Both were from Doreen Blake, the parcel containing a handsome Christmas present, and the letter a piece of news that made her give a little exclamation of pleased surprise.

"Only fancy!" she cried. "Doreen Blake is engaged. What fun! How I wonder what he is like!"

The others looked up with interest.

"Evidently he has come over for Christmas, and it is only just settled," Paddy ran on. "I am pleased. Dear old Dorrie. He is a barrister, and they met last September, in Scotland. Really, engagements seem to be in the air. First Gwen Carew, then Doreen—and now I wonder who will be the third."

A kind of subdued murmur made her look up quickly, and something about Jack and Eileen caught her attention for the first time. In spite of herself, it sent a little chill to her heart. She folded her letter and sat down on the floor, leaning against Aunt Jane's lap.

"Now," she remarked, "I'm ready to be told why Jack has come home in this unexpected manner. You don't any of you seem to have been very communicative so far."

"I like that!" exclaimed Jack, "when you haven't given anybody a chance to get a word in edgeways all day—but there! you always did monopolise the whole conversation."

"You've come back more uppish than ever, Jack," she retorted. "Anybody would think you had come in; for a fortune at least."

This seemed to tickle them all quite unnecessarily, and Jack burst into a hearty laugh.

"You all seem rather easily amused," said Paddy, "or else I am getting very dense. What is the joke?"

"Only that you fired a shot at random and made a bull's-eye," laughed Jack.

Paddy looked more puzzled than ever, but suddenly she leaned forward and exclaimed:

"You don't mean that you have come in for a fortune, Jack?"

"Not exactly," he answered, "only a trifle of 20,000 pounds."

"*You've* got 20,000 pounds?" incredulously.

"Yes. An obliging relative of my mother's, I had scarcely heard of, died a little while ago and left no other heirs but me."

For a moment Paddy was too astonished to speak, and they all watched her with eager happiness in their eyes. Undoubtedly there was more to come. At last she looked up with a twinkle.

"My! if you'd only had it a bit sooner, Jack," she said, "we might have bought up all the chocolate in Mrs White's shop, and all the bull's-eyes, and all the licorice. Goodness! what a feast we would have had."

"We'll do lots better than that," he cried. "We'll have new boats, and new rifles, and new fishing-rods."

"I'm thinking that isn't quite what brought Jack home after all," remarked Miss Jane.

"Ask Eileen," said Jack, in a way that made Eileen blush.

"What, more secrets!" cried Paddy. "It seems to me you'd better just start at the beginning, and tell me everything that has been going on behind my back in this barefaced fashion."

"Yes, only unfortunately we don't quite know where the beginning is, do we, Eileen?"

"It's too bad, Paddy, to tease you so," put in Eileen quickly. "The real truth is that last summer, when you didn't happen to be at home to see, letters from the Argentine began to come much oftener, and were not handed round for public perusal as usual. And then—You go on Jack," smiling at him.

"And then," said Jack readily enough, "some one wanted desperately to go along with the letters, and for some time could not find a way. At last, some one wrote and asked if he might come if he could find ways and means, and all unbeknown to every one but themselves, letter-writer and recipient arranged a little plan, if they could only manage to bring it off. While still in doubt as to ways and means, distant relative most obligingly dies, and then it is hey presto! and catch the next boat."

Paddy crossed the fireside circle in a flash, and flung herself upon Eileen.

"Oh, Eily, Eily," she cried, "you are engaged?—are you really engaged to Jack?"

"Yes, Paddy," and her voice and eyes spoke all she could not say.

"Oh, I'm so glad, I'm so glad, I feel as if I must just hug you both! and the aunties too, and every one. What a lovely Christmas present, a new brother."

"But that isn't really all," cried Jack. "We're going to live at The Ghan House. Only think of it! and you and your mother are to have the west wing all to yourselves, and live there with us just as long as ever you will."

After that every one joined in, and the rest of the afternoon was spent in discussing numerous projects, interesting to all alike. Paddy joined in likewise with seeming eagerness, but deep down in her heart, minute by minute, a certain dragging weight made itself more and more apparent. She would not for worlds have said so yet, for fear she might damp their happiness, but she knew quite well she would not go and live at The Ghan House with Jack and Eileen. An indefinable something, she hardly knew what, made her shrink instinctively and very certainly from such an arrangement. No, she would prefer to go back to her dispensing, and be independent, even if it was London, and she had to go alone.

There were tears on Paddy's eyelashes that night when she fell asleep. It seemed to her as if a sudden, most unlooked-for weight of loneliness were crushing her, and her whole soul longed and longed for the father sleeping quietly in the churchyard close beside her. She did not for one moment grudge Jack and Eileen their happiness—only just at first, just until she had got used to the new order and readjusted her own feelings a little—it was not easy to rejoice without one single qualm of painful remembrance.

The following day a lively call from Doreen and her *fiancé* on horseback cheered her considerably and helped her still better to hide everything from the rest; and the day after there was a little teasing and good-humoured raillery about a parcel from South Africa which had been forwarded from England. It contained a beautiful white ostrich-feather boa, and there was a delightful letter with it, begging her to accept it as a Christmas token, all of which told its own tale of constancy and steady persistence on the part of the lonely Englishman exiled there, and still dreaming of her when he had time to dream at all. Jack made most of such an opportunity and gave her little peace, and Paddy took it in excellent part, because she was glad of anything that would help to blind them to a certain circumstance nearer home.

In the evening they had one of their wild "scrimmage" parties, for the sake of old times, and to every one's astonishment, Lawrence arrived with the Mourne Lodge party. He had, of course, heard the news, and professed to have accepted his invitation for the express purpose of congratulating the happy pair. This certainly was open to doubt, though the genuineness of his congratulations was equally certainly not so.

Paddy fought shy of him from the first moment, and as she was naturally the ringleader of the scrimmage party, whereas he played Bridge in the study, it was perfectly easy to avoid an encounter. Only, as it happened, for that evening at least, Fortune was on Lawrence's side. The scrimmage party were playing a game in which one of their number had to go out of the room, and it chanced to be Paddy's turn just when Lawrence, being "dummy," strolled into the hall for a smoke.

Before she knew of his presence, he had walked up to her and said: "Paddy, do you know you are sitting under the mistletoe?"

Paddy gave a start, blushed in a way that made her inwardly furious, and moved to the other end of the oak chest upon which she had been seated.

"You needn't be so haughty," he laughed. "You know perfectly well I've kissed you lots of times, only unfortunately it was when I didn't want to. I remember once the master scolding me because I made such a point of kissing Eileen, and ignoring you. I argued that you were such an ugly little brute, and invented the fable that you hated kissing."

"It was no fable."

"Wasn't it?" humorously. "Nature never gave a mouth like that to a woman who hated kissing. Some day I'll remind you of that, Paddy."

"I loathed you," she remarked, refusing to be drawn. "You were the most objectionable, bad-tempered, conceited little beast that ever wore a silly little top hat and Eton suit."

He laughed with a relish.

"That's better!" approvingly. "It's impossible not to think there is something the matter with you, when you are not dealing out bombs of some sort. Why were you looking so woebegone when I came from the study, out here all alone in the hall?"

"I was not looking woebegone."

"Oh, yes, you were—just as if I shouldn't know." There was a pause, then he said with unexpected gentleness: "You were thinking about Eileen and O'Hara getting engaged, and you being left out in the cold." He put his hand on hers suddenly: "Mavourneen," he said in a voice of enthralling softness, "you were lonesome."

For one moment she left her hand in his, and then sprang to her feet with a bound: "An objectionable, bad-tempered, conceited little beast, that's what you were," and she slipped past him back to the drawing-room.

Lawrence remained a few seconds longer, and in his face was a strange mingling of yearning and satisfaction. That one moment had been passing sweet, the very most he had had to encourage him all through—yet how it made him hunger for more! And she had looked sad when he found her, he had seen it distinctly—the little droop about the lips—the little air of unwonted thoughtfulness.

Ah! she must come now—there must be no more delay—surely with Eileen's engagement a recognised fact he could make headway at last. Surely this was the moment to strike hard. He would take his opportunity.

There were again tears on Paddy's lashes that night, and she tossed restlessly. She shut her eyes, and shut her ears, and tried to shut her mind—but nothing would wholly drown those few words, coming as they did in her first hours of loneliness—nor the ravishing sweetness of the tones: "Mavourneen, you were lonesome."

It was like a spell upon her. Some unreal enchantment that possessed her spirit. Of course it must be broken. Things could not go as they were. Once for all she must *make* him see the uselessness of his quest, and it must be soon. That Eileen was healed and comforted did not make the smallest difference. The past was still the past. The handwriting still glowed on the wall. Over his coveted happiness—over any happiness for them together—was writ large the sentence of old: "Tekel—Found Wanting."

In this mood, and feeling very resolute, Paddy started out two days later, to deliver judgment.

Chapter Forty One.

In Lawrence's Den.

It was to a small luncheon party, given especially for the three pairs of lovers at Mourne Lodge, that Eileen and Paddy and Jack set out that bright, crisp morning. Gwen and her giant, Doreen and her barrister, Eileen and her stalwart rancher—these were the three amorous couples whom Lawrence, Kathleen and Paddy had to severally and together keep within the bounds of rational dinner-table conversation for a whole hour. After that they were prepared to wash their hands of them and let them hide away and discuss delightful nothings to their own delectation until tea-time. Doreen and the pump-handle court representative announced their intention of playing billiards, which no one thought it worth while to contradict, however sceptical he felt, and anyhow they bent their steps in the direction of the billiard-room. Eileen and Jack decided upon a quick walk, and the giant, of course, merely waited orders. At first they seemed to hang fire. Gwen was manoeuvring in a way that certainly meant something, but it was very difficult to tell exactly what. As a matter of fact, she was waiting on the off chance of Kathleen being called away. Directly the hoped-for call came she was prompt to act.

"Come along, Paddy," she said, putting her arm through hers; "let's go and rummage round in Lawrence's den. I think it's just the loveliest spot in the whole house! Did you ever see such a rag-tag and bobtail of odds and ends before? I just love poking round there." And she led the way at once, Lawrence and the giant following.

For several minutes she really did poke round, and then she discovered she had lost her handkerchief, and promptly dispatched the giant in search. As he was naturally as close to her as he could be she had no difficulty in adding in a tone that he only could hear, "Don't come back." After three minutes she looked up in the most natural way imaginable and remarked, "Whatever can Goliath be doing? My handkerchief must be in the dining-room. Perhaps he can't see so far as the floor."

Paddy had seated herself in a large easy-chair, and, scenting nothing of the plot, was idly watching the fire. She had, in consequence, no time to realise what was on foot until it was too late.

"I shall have to go and help him search," said Gwen with a pretence at annoyance. "He is a terrible muff at finding any thing."

Whereupon she calmly departed and closed the door behind her, leaving Paddy sitting in the big arm-chair, and Lawrence leaning against the mantelpiece, looking down at her with an odd little twinkle in his eyes.

In the dining-room Gwen found Kathleen, but she was quite prepared for the emergency.

"Where has everybody gone?" Kathleen asked wonderingly.

"All gone out, I think," Gwen replied unblushingly, and then went off with her Giant to the drawing-room, knowing perfectly well Lawrence's sisters never went into his den, and that therefore her strategy was quite successful.

Meanwhile, when Paddy saw that Gwen had closed the door after her, she leaned forward with a doubtful expression and appeared about to follow.

"Don't run away," said Lawrence, "or I shall think you are afraid of me."

"I am not afraid of anyone," stoutly, still looking toward the door.

"No, I know you are not. Still, the others most certainly don't want us; we should only be in the way."

It was too true. Paddy leaned back and stared into the fire, and that little droop hovered round her lips again. Kathleen was sure to be with her mother, and the others all dispersed.

"Not even anyone to go ratting with," he said, with a tender little smile.

The lips twitched and then settled again to the droop, while she tried to reinforce herself for the struggle that loomed ahead. No use to run away now. The time had come for a final understanding, and it must be faced.

Lawrence watched her a little while in silence, and there was absolute stillness in the room except for the cheery crackling of the fresh log he had just thrown on the fire.

"You look, somehow, as if you were prepared for the worst," he told her, smiling. "Am I such a terrible ogre?"

She did not speak, and he pulled up a chair beside her and sat down, holding his thin white hands out to the blaze.

"Do you remember the last time you were in my den?" running on. "It was the night of the girls' 'coming-out' dance—the ultimatum, so to speak, when you declared war. I remember it perfectly—I always shall. You were all in white, Paddy—a fluffy kind of dress that suited you, admirably. I remember being surprised to see how pretty you *could* look. But, of course, it was your hair—you had always treated it so abominably before. I sometimes think it is the loveliest hair I have ever seen in my life—and I've seen a good deal," with a humorous little shrug. "And then, of course, your eyes are good, and there's the fascinating mouth."

Paddy could not resist a smile. "When you've done going over my points?"

"Your points are A1, Patricia," with admiration in his eyes. "You are a thoroughbred to your finger-tips."

"Well, don't be personal, or I shall go. You know I don't like it."

"No, don't go. I'll try to be good."

He was silent a moment, and slowly that same air of the previous evening, suggestive of sadness, crept over her face again, and there was a weariness in her attitude as she sat back watching the flames and clasping each arm of the chair with delicate, tapering fingers.

"Paddy," he said simply, "chuck all those foolish doubts and fancies of yours, and give in. I can't bear to see you looking forlorn."

"I will not: I will never give in."

He squared his shoulders unconsciously, and her fingers gripped the arms of her chair more tightly.

"You can't help yourself in the end. Why prolong my suspense? Everything is against you. Even Fate is pairing off the others and leaving you and me alone. I know quite well you are lonely—desperately lonely—but it is your own fault. If you would only be sensible and let yourself follow the dictates of your heart, instead of a warped conscience, you could be happy with the rest. I say your heart, because somewhere, hidden away, there's a soft corner for me you are afraid of. Isn't that so, Paddy!" and he looked searchingly into her face.

She made no reply, staring into the fire with a perplexed, unhappy expression.

He put one hand over the fingers nearest him and held them fast. She attempted to draw them away, but he retained his hold, and for the moment she went with the flood.

"You have not answered me, mavourneen."

"I have only one answer—I will not give in."

"And I say you will. This new loneliness has come to help me. Already you are nearer to me than ever before."

She drew a long breath.

"It is only because I see we must come to a real understanding once for all. We can't just go on as we have. That's chiefly why I remained here now. I want to make you understand."

She sat up and drew her hand away. "Lawrence, you must leave me in peace. A man cannot honestly want to marry a girl who—who—" Ah! why did she falter?

"Well, little woman! Who—who—!"

"Doesn't love him," a trifle lamely.

"Ah, Paddy! you were going to say 'hate,' and the lie died on your lips."

She flushed in the firelight, but continued bravely:

"It makes very little difference. The fact remains that I do not love you and I will not marry you."

"Marry me first, and I will soon teach you to love."

She felt her breath coming fitfully and her pulses leaping strangely, and she bit her teeth together to steady herself as she still stared into the fire. Oh! why did he give her that unnerved feeling! What in the world was the matter with her! She felt as if she only waited to hide her face in the cushion. He seemed to understand, for he turned his eyes away, and, leaning forward, softly kissed her hand. "It would be difficult, little woman—you were made for love, and I—well, I somehow seem to just worship you, and that's all about it."

Once more she tried to rally herself, pressing her hands to her eyes as if to shut out everything that distracted her from her one purpose.

"It is no use," resolutely. "Of course, I understand you have a certain power when you like, and that you are so confident because sooner or later you have always won. But that is just what fortifies me now. I don't want to go into the old arguments. I want you to understand once for all that I *am* fortified, and I *do* mean what I say, and not all the loneliness in the world will change me. It is no use talking as you do, and hoping as you do, because there are barriers which neither of us could move, even if we were both agreed. Be sensible and be kind. It would be kind to leave me alone in future, and sensible to be content that you have, to a certain extent, broken down my hate."

"Content!—*content*!" and there was a low, vibrating passion in his voice that stirred her to her depths. "Content to give in when I have come within sight of my goal! Content to lose my wife for a whim—a prejudice—a quixotic idea of righting a wrong that, has long since been wiped out in the most satisfactory way in the world! Do you hear, Paddy?—*my wife*?—no, by God, because I choose to think of you like that now, I will not be content and I will not give in."

His violence frightened her, and she shivered a little. He saw it, and, with one of his swift changes, became suddenly penitent.

"There—I didn't mean to frighten you. You look quite bewildered, and so pale. I am a brute. Poor little woman. Don't take any notice—don't remember anything except that I won't give in, because I know you are not as indifferent to me as you pretend, and also because you are lonely and forlorn." His voice grew entrancingly gentle, "Patricia the Brave, Patricia the Independent, left out in the cold, and no one to realise that she feels it except the Mourne Lodge Bear. Mavourneen—mavourneen—bears have understanding when they love as I love you."

Big tears gathered in her eyes and splashed down unheeded on her hands. He leaned nearer, and a tremor passed through her. When he spoke in that enthralling, wholly gentle cadence, it was as though her thoughts and faculties became numb. It was as though solid ground were slipping away beneath her feet—branches breaking to which she was clinging for safety. She could only clutch with a spasmodic grasp at the grim spectre of her old resolve. She hid her face in her hands, staggered at the growing feebleness of her own resistance.

"Paddy—dear little girl—my arms are still aching—*come*."

She sprang up, white and trembling.

"Oh, Lawrence, please stop—I am not quite myself to-day. Let us go and look for the others."

He hesitated a moment, then said:

"They don't want us, and you look too tired to walk. I expect you've been lying awake instead of going to sleep the last two or three nights, worrying about future plans. Perhaps it isn't quite fair to press you any more now. Anyhow, I've had more to-day than ever before, and I feel I can afford to wait. If I don't say any more about the future, dear, will you just sit quietly there and rest until tea-time? See, I'll give you two more days to get thoroughly readjusted to the new order of events, then I shall come to the Parsonage and claim you. Will you agree to stay here quietly, Paddy, if I promise not to worry you?"

She murmured an assent.

"That's a sensible little woman. I'll clean my gun—do you see? I like doing it myself occasionally, and I've often thought how I'd love to do those sorts of things in here with you—I fiddling round with my hobbies and you sitting there—no need to say anything, but just to see your skirts, and your little feet, and your hair, and feel in every breath of me, not only that you are there, but that you *belong* there." He moved away. "I suppose we're all family men at heart, directly we pass the frivolous stage and have wearied of banal excitements. I never meant to be anything but a bachelor, but now I want a home and a fireside that is the real thing the same as all the rest of them. I want you—*belonging* there.

"But I'm trespassing already. If I don't mind you'll fly yet—you're such a wild little bird. Don't take any notice; you can go to sleep if you like. There's just half an hour before tea-time. No one will know you are here; they are all too taken up with each other to think of anything else."

Paddy closed her eyes gratefully, wondering why she felt so deathly tired.

Chapter Forty Two.

"What would an Irish Fusilier do?"

They thought her a little strange at home that evening, but after a time Jack and Eileen vanished, and making a tremendous effort, she contrived to chatter to the aunties about her dispensing in a fairly brisk fashion. She did not, however, altogether blind them, and she was glad enough when the need ceased, and she could go to bed.

Eileen was sleeping with her mother, and Jack at the inn, so that she had his little room all to herself, and as soon as she was alone she flung herself down on the bed and burst into tears, overstrained nature finding no other mode of relief.

When she had had her cry out, she lay quite still and tried to think—tried to understand how it was that the question she had meant to settle once for all in the afternoon was more unsettled than ever. Why was it more unsettled? There could not possibly be any temptation of giving in. Giving in meant only one solution. It meant that she, Patricia Adair, would marry Lawrence Blake.

Oh! it was impossible—impossible!—the man she had over and over again asserted that she hated, and declared she would kill.

Then why was there any difficulty? Why this growing sense of a problem she could not solve?

Supposing Patricia Adair did marry Lawrence Blake. What of it?

But she tore the thought out of her mind. She would not suppose it.

It came back in another form—a series of mental pictures cruelly contrasting Shepherd's Bush and the dispensary with Mourne Lodge. For Paddy knew well enough that under no circumstances would she accept a home from Jack and her sister—under no circumstances give up her work and her independence, to be dependent on any one's bounty. No, she would go back to her work alone, and they would live at The Ghan House without her.

But how it hurt to think of it!

The dingy suburb, the grey street, her aunt's everlasting platitudes, for of course she would live again at the doctor's house—just grey, lifeless monotony, instead of the lake and the mountains.

And how he had understood!

"*Mavourneen, mavourneen, bears have understanding when they love as I love you.*"

She tried to crush out the recollection, conscious that her soul was sounding indefinable warnings as a far-off accompaniment. Oh, of course, he was fascinating—had she not always known it—known all her life that there were two Lawrence Blakes, and one as alluring as the other was repellant. Resolutely, she turned her thoughts to the unpleasing one; she who had somehow had special opportunities of clear sight. She remembered the old rumours of excess and extravagance. Had not her own father shaken his head gravely long ago, and said things he imagined she would not understand. Perhaps she did not then—but now! Unprincipled, unscrupulous, fast, wild, a gambler. "Wild oats," she told herself—"Wild oats." It was not that that built the barrier—this barrier that was as a grim spectre, waving ghostly arms between them. Could anything, even mercifully, write "wild oats" over his heartlessness? When she thought of those locked hands in the boat on the loch, her blood still boiled—of how very nearly Eileen's delicate constitution had broken down altogether under her silent fretting—of how her mother had grieved and fretted likewise. She thought of his moods at home. How often—oh, how often

—she had longed to strike him for the tone in which he sometimes spoke to his mother and sisters. For his selfishness, his coldness, his sneers. How often she had gone home pitying the girls such a brother, hating him with all her young enthusiasm. And then, further complicating everything, flashed again the recollection, even in those days, of his charm, if he happened to be in the right mood. Why, even Doreen and Kathleen were influenced by it; every one was. If Lawrence were in his charming mood, the whole house was sunny and gay, and Paddy had quickly enough forgotten old feuds, and immensely enjoyed a good-natured, wordy battle with him. When she hated him most, he had still had a lurking attraction for her, or she would not have bothered to cross swords. Only a lurking attraction is not love. The old spectre still stood firm, waving ghostly arms between them. And even if it were love, the feud still stood. Eileen might have forgiven and found other happiness. She might have trampled down all bitterness, but did that make the wrong less wrong—did it affect her, Paddy's, view of the case? A personal wrong may be forgiven by the sufferer without in any way affecting an outside judgment. There is still the wrong in the abstract. True, vengeance is unchristian—but it was not vengeance she wanted any longer; could she—dare she—fly in the face of her own passionate sense of Loyalty? It seemed to Paddy that if she yielded to the wave that seemed like to sweep her off her feet, she not only let go her watchword of Loyalty, but she compromised with her half-formed, dimly seen ideal of Love. Always before her mind, if she thought of love in the future, had been the image of such men as the grand old General—the gentle, kindly doctor—the simple, manly, open-hearted Jack. Among such as these, how could she give such as Lawrence the place of honour? It was incredible that she should think of it. To do so, she must surely be disloyal to the past and disloyal to herself. But how resist him? Who could help her? She got up at last and went to the window. In the light of the stars, glimmering faintly across the garden, were the headstones—"where the dead people wait till God calls."

Feeling suffocated by the four walls of the little room, she hastily threw a shawl round her head, slipped into a big coat, and crept noiselessly out of the house, down the little path, and through the wicket-gate into the churchyard, where a beautiful Maltese cross marked the spot where the brave old soldier was taking his well-earned rest.

"Daddy," she whispered, "daddy, try and help me now. There isn't any one else who would understand."

She leaned her face against the cold granite. It was comforting to be there. "What shall I do, daddy? I know you understand all about it, and how it is so difficult. Daddy—darling old daddy —what would an Irish Fusilier do?"

She clung against the cross yearningly, and in the night air, with the calm stars looking down, the waves whispering on the beach, and her beloved mountains all around, she grew calmer and stronger. It pleased her to whisper her thoughts to the night, as if the unseen spirit of her beloved dead listened near.

"Ought I to run away, daddy? I remember how often you have said only a selfish, vain-glorious officer will risk his men against desperate odds, rather than retreat. 'Retreat, if wiser, and take up a better position—never mind the dispatches home—save your men and win the glory as well; it is sometimes nobler to retreat than to go on.' Is that what I must do, daddy? I feel there are desperate odds against me. Would it be braver to retreat? Is that what an Irish Fusilier would do? You, at least, will understand that I was not a coward."

She pressed her lips against the granite for love of the grand and simple soul it stood to commemorate.

"Daddy," she whispered, and there was a tiny, wistful smile on the fascinating mouth. "I'm not an Irish Fusilier, but, perhaps, I'm the-next-best-thing."

Then she went quietly back to bed, with her mind made up.

But the next morning, it was only by a great physical and mental effort that she was able to appear at all like herself at the breakfast-table, and when the meal was finished she was glad to slip away unobserved.

Eileen's suspicions, however, had been previously roused in the night by a light step in the passage, and, afterward, a dim figure crossing the garden. She was tactful enough to say nothing of this, but at the same time determined to try and find out if anything was wrong, and how she could help. In this Paddy had cause to be grateful, because her plans could scarcely he carried out without Eileen's help.

When her sister sought her upstairs, and asked in a quiet, firm way, "What is the matter, Paddy? Something has happened to you," she only hesitated a second, and then replied with as much calmness as she could muster:

"Yes, Eily, I'm in rather a difficulty. I was going to ask you and Jack to help me."

"Paddy, we will do anything—anything," Eileen cried earnestly.

"I know you will, but it isn't much I want—only that I am going back to London to-night, and I want you to help me manage it without any more questions and explanations than can possibly be helped."

At first, Eileen was dumbfounded and greatly distressed, but Paddy was evidently desperately in earnest and meant to go.

"Don't ask me anything, Eily, if you really want to help," she said wearily. "Just break it to mother and the aunties a little while before I start and help to arrange some excuse for me to any others who ask questions."

In the end it was all managed so, and Jack prepared to go to Greenore with her and see her safely on the boat for Holyhead, from whence she would go straight back to her uncle's.

At the last moment Aunt Jane stole softly into her bedroom—Aunt Jane, whose heart had always leaned to Paddy, just as Aunt Mary's had leaned to Eileen.

"My child," she said very tenderly, "I can see that you are in some great trouble, and I shall not know how to keep from fretting about you, because you have always been as my own child to me, and I would rather suffer myself than see you suffer. Only we may not choose who shall be glad and who sad, and no doubt if we could, things would only be worse in the end. But you won't forget your 'old maid' auntie by the loch, darling, whose heart will ache silently, thinking of you day and night."

The tears gushed from Paddy's eyes, and for a moment she seemed about to break down altogether, but in a few minutes she had managed to pull herself together again.

"Are you sure you must go away alone like this?" Aunt Jane asked yearningly.

"Yes, auntie, quite sure. I love you so much for coming to me now, but you mustn't make me break down. Please help me to keep up, auntie, just until I get away."

And Miss Jane did—having her own cry out later by herself—while the steamer started into the black, wintry night, and Jack stood watching it from Greenore pier, with a mist before his eyes and a queer huskiness in his throat. Just when life was opening for him with all its sweetest and best, it seemed hard, indeed, that Paddy—his old chum and playmate—should be assailed with this trouble of which she would not speak, and in which apparently none of them could help her. Jack cared just as much as his present happiness made it possible for him to care about anything. Long ago, though he only remembered it with a smile, the sole problem of his life had been which of the sisters he loved the best. Fate had tipped the balance to the elder's side, without in any measure depreciating the other; but Jack never knew, and never would know, what a difference that final choice had made to Paddy.

Chapter Forty Three.

A Man's Pain.

Lawrence received his first intimation of what had happened through Gwen; as Paddy had foreseen.

He had been sitting most of the morning in his den, with the London newspapers, the lovers having all taken themselves off, with an air that forbade any one to follow on their peril, but he had not done much reading. Small wonder, indeed! Why read of stocks and shares, of wars and rumours of Wars, of the vagaries of Cabinet Ministers, and the sweet, childlike levity of Irish members—when the happiness for which your whole life seems to have been waiting is coming to you to-day?

No, Lawrence did not read, he sat instead, gazing into the fire, making delightful plans for the future, in which Paddy was all in all. The chair she had sat in was pulled up to the hearth, but he had not used it since; he felt it was her chair now, and his fancy loved to see her sitting there still, with her two little hands clasping the two arms, and her head leaning back with that slight air of weariness which somehow made her only the more enchanting.

He was strangely happy that one morning, there had never been anything in all his life before in the least like it. In the afternoon he meant to go and look for her by the loch; he believed she would be waiting for him—and if not, well he would go to the Parsonage and claim her.

He went over the interview in his fancy, detail by detail, as it might be, as he would like it to be.

Paddy would be shy, that was a delicious thought to him. He had known too many of the women who meet a man half-way without the slightest qualm, and practically thrust his first kiss upon him, thinking of it only as one of many to follow. How different it would be with Paddy! He even wondered, with a little inward smile, whether she would let him kiss her at all this first interview, or at any rate before they were just parting. He did not mean to press her or hurry her in any way. Once having her promise, he could afford to wait.

Still it was deliriously sweet to think of, and he sat forward with his arms across his knees picturing the sacred moment. He thought how he would coax her, and how she would yield gradually, and then he would fold her in his arms and hold her tight against his heart while their lips met.

He was roused by a step coming along the passage to his door, a hurried step, that had a suggestion of being agitated in some way. Then the door opened, and Gwen put her head in to see if he was there. Finding he was, she came in and shut the door quietly behind her, and something in the quiet of her usually radiant face was ominous.

"What has happened between you and Paddy, Lawrence?" she asked, coming close up to him. "I thought everything was all right; that it was practically settled." He clenched his hands suddenly.

"It is. Why?"

Gwen looked at him, and a wave of painful feeling passed over her face.

"She has run away," she said; "she went back to London alone last night."

Instantly, as in a flash, he understood. He did not speak, he did not utter a sound, but sat there in a silence that became terrible, his hands clenched and his mouth rigid. Gwen gave a little shiver.

At last to break the awful tension she continued:

"We called to see her this morning—Bob and I, and they told us she had crossed last night. They told us some sort of a tale about her uncle wanting her, but of course I didn't believe it. I just pretended to, and then came back here feeling as if I'd had a shock."

Still he did not speak nor move, only staring with that fixed gaze into vacancy. If there was any difference at all, he was grinding his teeth together, to hold in check some inner tumult, rising momentarily higher.

Gwen grew a little frightened. She had never seen him like this, never seen any man, in the first deadly throes of an anguish that was as life and death to him.

"What are you going to do, Lawrie?" she said. "Perhaps, she has not really run away from you."

Still no word or sign.

She put her hand on his shoulder to rouse him.

"What are you going to do, Lawrie?" she asked again.

"Go to the devil!" in a low, bitter voice of unmistakable meaning, and without raising his eyes.

She slipped down on her knees beside him and clasped her hands round his arm.

"Don't, Lawrie—don't," she prayed, all her long affection for him crystallising, and grasping just all that his bitter words might mean. "I can't bear you to take it like this. Oh! it is terrible, and just when I am so happy. I will go to Paddy, she will listen to me—I will make her see things differently. Lawrie, don't look like that—she shall be yours, I promise you she shall. You shall have your happiness."

But he only shook her off roughly.

"Leave me alone. You! you have got your happiness, what do you know about mine?"

It was the first time in her life that he had spoken roughly to her, and Gwen shrank back almost as if she had been struck.

"You can't—you can't—mean to speak to me like that, Lawrie—"

"I think you had better go away," was all he said. "I might do you an injury."

For a moment she was transfixed, then she rose to her feet, and turned slowly to the door. Here she paused a moment.

"I will tell them you are not well, and do not want any lunch," she said. "Later on I will come back."

After lunch Mrs Blake rose quickly from the table, and went toward the door. Gwen was immediately in a fever of anxiety. What should she do? In desperation she put a detaining hand upon the mother's arm:

"You—you—are not going to Lawrence?" she stammered.

"My dear," answered Mrs Blake, "didn't you say he was not well?"

"I know—I know—but—indeed, it would be better to leave him alone for a little." Mrs Blake regarded her with surprise. "I don't understand you," she said a little haughtily. "I only wish to see if I can do anything for him."

"He said he did not want to be disturbed," murmured poor Gwen distractedly.

"My dear, I am his mother," and Mrs Blake passed out of the room.

Gwen stood a moment watching her cross the hall with a fascinated gaze, and then suddenly darted across to the drawing-room, and burying her face in a sofa-cushion burst into tears, to the unutterable consternation of her faithful giant, who followed immediately, and had much ado to soothe her. They were startled presently by the sound of a door being violently slammed, as only a man could slam it, and then halting footsteps approached the hall. Gwen went to the door, but drew back horror-struck. Mrs Blake was going toward the stairs, and her face was the colour of a corpse. She looked as if she were dazed and petrified. Then Kathleen, who had been waiting nervously in the dining-room, crossed quickly to her with open arms, and a little cry of, "Mother! Mother! what is it?—are you ill?"

Her mother looked at her as if she could hardly understand, and then dropped senseless. A second later Bob Russell carried her upstairs, and laid her on her bed. Gwen stayed with Kathleen until she had come round, and then slipped away to the drawing-room again, feeling utterly unstrung. Doreen and her *fiancé* were fortunately out to lunch.

"It was Lawrence," she said, in reply to Bob's anxious questions; "he must have been terrible, and to her, his own mother! Oh, it is awful, Bob," and the tears streamed down her face again. Bob sprang to his feet.

"Shall I go and throttle him!—the worm! A man who can behave like that to his mother, isn't fit to live. I'll go and tell him so—I'll—I'll—"

"Oh, no, no, no," cried Gwen, "you don't understand. It is dreadful of him, but he is mad about something. I knew it, and I tried to stop her."

The giant went on muttering imprecations, however, and Owen had hard work to hold him when presently that distant door slammed again. She crossed to the window quickly, and was just in time to see Lawrence stride down the drive, with that terrible fixed look still on his face.

No one sat down to dinner that night, except Kathleen, and Gwen, and Bob Russell. Mrs Blake was too ill, and Lawrence did not come back. Doreen and her barrister were still away.

Kathleen was in a state of pent-up fury, which now and then burst its bounds in passionate indictment against her brother. "Why can't he stay away," she said, "if he can't behave like a gentleman? I'm sure we don't want him here, he is always a wet blanket, and upsets mother about something or other every day. It has been the same ever since he went to college. He doesn't care for anything in heaven or earth except himself; I'm sick of it. If he doesn't go away and stay away, I'll just take mother to live somewhere else altogether."

Gwen was much too fond of Lawrence and much too staunch to her friends not to speak a word for him in spite of her own inward anger.

"There is a reason for it, Kit," she said. "Don't judge him to-day. He'll be all right again presently."

"Until the next time," with an angry sneer, very like her brother's. "I tell you it isn't good enough, Owen. He's not going to behave like this to mother again, I'll get between them if he kills me for it. What has he ever been to her but a curse?—drinking, and gambling, and idling about the world. Oh, I dare say he's charming enough to you always! we all know there isn't a man could be more fascinating when he likes, but how much does that go for beside scenes like this?"

Gwen set her teeth.

"You are not fair," she said. "Lawrence has behaved like a brute to-day, and I dare say it isn't the first time, but he has neither gambled nor drunk for years, and there have been times when he was goodness itself to his mother."

"And few and far enough between too," sneered Kathleen. "I'm only thankful that he hasn't got engaged to any friend of mine; for if I cared for her very much, I'd sooner see her in her grave than married to Lawrence."

"Nonsense!" exclaimed Gwen sharply, and then stopped short, suddenly remembering she was a guest, and the dinner finished in a constrained silence.

"Bob and I will go on to Dublin to-morrow," she told Kathleen later, "and don't bother about us this evening. We will look after each other, and you stay with Mrs Blake."

When Doreen and her *fiancé* returned, she made up some sort of a tale to them, and then persuaded every one to go to bed early, that Lawrence, if he returned, might come in and go to his room unnoticed.

She did not go to bed herself, however, but sat up with her door open, waiting for him. At two o'clock in the morning she heard his latchkey in the front door, and went down bravely to meet him.

When Lawrence saw her he glared at her angrily, but she took no notice, though inwardly shocked at the unspeakable change on his face since the morning. He was deathly white, with an almost tigerish expression, and she knew he had been drinking.

"I couldn't rest until I knew you had come in," she said, trying to speak naturally.

"What did you suppose I should do?" with a bitter sneer. "Go and drown myself, or cross to England with a pistol! No, thank you! I'm not that sort. I shall not oblige any *Police News* with a paragraph."

"What are you going to do, Lawrie?" unheeding him. "Bob and I are going on to Dublin to-morrow—you come too—"

He strode into the dining-room without answering—and she followed him. On the sideboard stood the spirit decanters as usual, and she saw his eye instantly turn to them, and a second later he had his hand upon the whisky.

Quickly she was at his side:

"Don't have any more, Lawrie," pleadingly. "You have had quite enough," and she placed her hand over his. For one moment he glared at her again, then let go, and sinking into a chair by the table, buried his face in his hands.

"Have you been playing billiards?" she asked, resting her hand on his shoulder.

"Yes."

"For high sums, I suppose?"

"Yes."

"I hope there isn't misery in some other house in Newry to-night, through you."

"On the contrary, some of them must feel quite rich."

"Then you lost?"

"Yes."

"I'm very glad."

"Thank you," dryly.

Gwen stood looking at him, noting vaguely the lines that had deepened in his face, and wondering what to do.

"Lawrie."

"Yes."

"Your mother is ill. She fainted, and Bob carried her upstairs."

He winced, but his face did not soften.

"You must have behaved like a blackguard to her," and there was a tremor of intense feeling in Gwen's voice.

"It's quite likely. But I warned her—why did she come in? I told her not to, and she has known me long enough."

"I wonder what Paddy would think of it?"

He ground his teeth.

"What does it matter?—what does anything matter? I used not to care, and I will be the same again. I have been a fool to let myself get set upon anything—" He got up, and pushed his chair aside roughly. "I am going away to-morrow! I don't know where, except that I shall go to London first—afterward, to the devil, as I said before."

He turned to the door, and she could not but follow.

"You needn't worry any more to-night. I won't touch the whisky again, and I won't shoot myself," and without waiting for her, he strode off up the stairs.

Chapter Forty Four.

"I Cannot Come."

For a whole week Lawrence knocked about London, and it was just as well for their peace of mind that none of those who cared for him saw him.

One Sunday afternoon he suddenly called a taxi and drove off to Shepherd's Bush.

On asking for Miss Adair he was ushered in and led to the dingy, old-fashioned drawing-room. It was some time before a step approached, and then the doctor, with a keen look in his kindly eyes, entered alone.

Lawrence was watching the door with a fixed intentness that scarcely gave when the unexpected comer entered.

"My niece has a very bad headache," the doctor said simply, as he shook hands. "She does not feel equal to seeing any one to-day. I am sorry you should have had this long drive for nothing."

"Is she ill?" Lawrence asked bluntly.

"Oh, no, only ailing a little. The weather has been very trying the last week."

The doctor studied the visitor carefully. Paddy's hurried return had caused him much food for anxious thought, coupled with her evident low spirits and loss of appetite. He shot a bow at a venture.

"I think you come from Omeath?" he said.

Lawrence assented, but seemed lost in thought.

"Wouldn't she see me just for a few minutes?" he asked. "I don't want to worry her, but I have come from Omeath, and she might like to hear about them all at home."

The doctor went away, but came back again alone.

"She is not well enough to-day," he repeated. "She thanks you for calling and is sorry she cannot see you."

And Lawrence was obliged to call a cab again and drive away. As he went down the steps he met a slim youth who regarded him somewhat fixedly, but Lawrence never even saw him. He would have been a little amused, perhaps, had he known that the same youth shook his fist threateningly after him from behind the safe shelter of the doctor's front door.

"If you're the cuss who's worrying Paddy's life out of her," he mentally apostrophised Lawrence's back, "I'd uncommonly like to have you in the dissecting-room," which blood-curdling threat Basil was fortunately quite unable to carry out.

Lawrence went back to his club and wrote a letter to Paddy.

It was a beautiful letter. Nature had, of a truth, been erratic with this one of her children, for it seemed impossible that the writer of this letter and the man who could speak to his mother in a way that made her really ill for days could be one and the same.

It distressed Paddy beyond words. In spite of everything she might say, his suffering tore her heart. Yet her will held firm, and she would not tell him to come. She wrote him a little letter, however, in which he perceived that she no longer pretended to be repulsed by him, and that absence might be serving him better than a meeting just then. He held the letter long in his hand, and was conscious of a sudden swift regret. "If there were more girls like her," was his thought, "how much better it would be for us men and for all the world. If I had only loved her sooner, or some one like her, I should have been a different man to-day."

Ah, that eternal "if—if." And meanwhile all things march on the same. The girls will not see, so the men do not heed, and there is folly and wrong and weakness where there might be strength and rich content. Where there is a great man there was a great woman before; and so it would seem Nature is always trying to point out to us that, though the Men have the strength, the Women have the power, and where they are strong and true all things are possible—for the fireside, the household, the sphere of influence at hand, the greatness of the nation itself. Be smart, be comely, be gay—why not?—only ring true also, and the men who admire you for your comeliness, will worship you for your goodness.

Lawrence kept his letter and read it often, but he did not go away. He liked feeling that he was there in the same city, breathing the same air, although she remained inexorable about seeing him. Often, in fits of despair, he thought he would go away, but always in the end he decided to remain.

He bought a racing motor, and seemed to find some relief in flying madly over the county at a terrible pace. Three times he was had up for furious driving, and the third time his fine was the heaviest ever exacted for a like cause, and he received a strong reprimand as well and a threat that a fourth offence would be even more strenuously dealt with.

He left the court laughing, and his friends began to wonder anxiously where his recklessness would end.

Gwen returned to town about the time of the third offence, and remonstrated forcibly with him, but made no visible effect.

"Have you seen Paddy again?" she asked him.

"She will not see me."

Gwen knit her forehead in perplexity.

"I have written, and she has not answered," she said. "I don't know what to make of her. I must go and see her."

"Not yet," he said, and she looked up in surprise. His face, however, expressed nothing.

"I wrote to her, and she answered it," he continued, "and I do not want her to be worried about me for the present. Stay away for a little while, Gwen. I think she would rather you did."

So Gwen possessed her soul in patience for three weeks, to please Lawrence, and then went upon an unexpected errand.

Paddy was roaming about restlessly that dreary winter afternoon at the beginning of February when Gwen came. She had been out in the morning, and she kept trying to make up her mind to go out again for something to do, but instead she continued to roam about with that odd feeling of unrest, quite unable to settle down to anything.

Eileen and her mother had come back to London again now, but only until the spring quarter, when, the lease of their house was up, and they hoped to have done with London for good.

The wedding was to take place in April, there was nothing to wait for, and several hearts eager enough to see it happily become a fact.

The Ghan House was being renovated throughout, and Eileen was busy with her trousseau—no time to spare between January and April.

Paddy helped a great deal. She did not like plain sewing—indeed, she very much disliked it, always contriving to prick herself badly and leave little danger signals, so to speak, where she had stitched. She might have been said to be preparing Eileen's trousseau with her heart's blood, only not with the meaning this phrase, beloved of serial writers, is generally intended to convey.

She had her own views as to quantities, which, however, as they did not at all fit in with her mother's and Eileen's, she wisely kept to herself. No use warring against the majority, and little matter either way. If the others thought dozens of everything necessary Paddy supposed it was all right, but, for her part, she wondered how so many clothes could possibly ever get worn, and where Eileen was going to keep them all when she was not wearing them.

"We might be making clothes for Jack as well," she remarked once, surveying the growing piles; and when they told her laughingly Jack was getting his own dozens and half-dozens, she fairly gasped.

Nothing much had been said about that speedy flight of hers at Christmas. Both Eileen and the mother had attempted to win her confidence, but Paddy would not speak. Eileen had finally guessed.

"It is Lawrence, Paddy, isn't it?" she asked.

Paddy, driven in a corner, consented, but would not go on.

Eileen had then fidgeted a little, and, blushing painfully, stammered:

"You would not let anything in reference to me two years ago influence you, I hope, Paddy."

Paddy made no reply.

"Because, as it happened, you see, it was such a good thing. I could never have been as happy with any one else as I am with Jack. Tell me, Paddy?" looking hard into her sister's eyes.

Paddy shook her head.

"I can't tell you anything, Eily," she answered. "Please don't ask me." And Eileen had to give in.

Jack tried when he came for a flying visit about wall-papers and paint and things, and it was then for the first time that they learnt of Paddy's unlooked-for decision.

"What colour is your room to be, Paddy?" he asked. "I am waiting your orders."

"You are very good," a little uncomfortably, "but I'm not coming to live at The Ghan House."

"Not coming to live at The Ghan House!" as if he could not believe his own ears, while Eileen and her mother looked up in amazement.

Paddy had to brace herself with the utmost determination.

"I have thought it all over carefully," she said, "and I have decided to stay in London. I have developed a very independent spirit of late, somehow," with a little smile, "and I mean to stick to my post."

"But, my dear child—" began Mrs Adair in great distress, while Jack threw a newspaper at her head and said:

"Don't talk rubbish, Paddy."

Eileen looked dumbfounded.

"It is not rubbish," Paddy went on bravely, "and nothing you can say will alter me. I have spoken to uncle about it, and he is going to let me live with them and pay something." She paused a moment, drawing a pattern on the tablecloth. "He does not want me to pay," she went on, "he says he will be only too glad to have me, but I would like to feel perfectly independent. He is lonely sometimes, and he always wanted a daughter."

A mistiness crossed her eyes, and she smiled a little crooked smile as she added:

"Daddy always wanted a son, and I did my best. He is daddy's brother, and he wants a daughter —I am going to do my best again. I never seem to quite 'get there,' do If—I am evidently destined only to shine as a substitute—to be only the-next-best-thing."

"But, Paddy," coming behind her and leaning over the table with his arm across her shoulders, "you hate London so," coaxed Jack. "How are Eileen and I to be perfectly happy, thinking of you pining for fresh air here?"

"You must not think—it would only be silly—you will have each other and,"—there was a little catch in her voice—"mother."

Mrs Adair looked up quickly; hitherto she had not spoken.

"No, Paddy," she said, "I shall stay with you. I do not mind London at all now I have got used to it, and I could not leave you behind alone. I should not be happy at Omeath without you."

But Paddy would not hear of it, and after a long discussion it was finally decided that she should remain with her uncle for six months. Having gained her point, she quickly drew their attention back to the wall-papers, which were eagerly discussed in their turn, amid the usual amount of nonsense and twitting on her part and Jack's.

The next day she told her uncle that she had won her point, and was coming to them, at any rate for the present. Something like tears instantly dimmed the kindly doctor's eyes; he had grown more than fond of his young dispenser and niece.

"It will be as good as having a daughter," he said, a little huskily.

Paddy laughed. "It is my particular *forte*," she said, "to be the-next-best-thing."

Her aunt was no less pleased.

"Really, my dear," she remarked, folding her hands contentedly upon her ample front, "I shall be very pleased to have you. I don't like girls, as a rule—they're all so flighty and flirty, and fond of gew-gaws and things, but you are somehow different. You are not as interested in the church guilds and parish meetings as I could wish, and you are a little wanting in respect to poor Mr

Dickinson," naming the meek young curate; "but you are young yet, and by and by you will see how empty and shallow and vain are all amusements compared with church work and the beautiful church services."

Paddy had her doubts, but she kept them to herself, and just then Basil came in to give his opinion.

"The guv'nor says you're going to stay here after March," he exclaimed. "How beastly, jolly, thundering nice!"

"My dear boy!" gasped his mother, horror-struck; "what an extraordinary way of expressing yourself."

"Says what I mean pretty straight, anyhow. I guess I'll have a key of the dispensary and only allow Paddy in at her proper hours. If we don't mind she'll go messing about with those silly old medicines half the day."

So it was all arranged, and Paddy was somewhat relieved, but her heart was unusually heavy on that February afternoon, with the weight of a longing that, in its steady insistence, was beginning to undermine those strong defences of hers, built up by that spirit of fanaticism so strangely blended with her open, generous nature.

It had been there for some time now, this creeping, growing longing, but until the Christmas holiday it had been given such short shrift, it scarcely dared to hold up its head. Whenever it did, seizing advantage of some soft moment, it was almost immediately stamped on by the warrior-like, fanatical Paddy, nursing her sense of injury, and armour-plating herself against a softness her heart clamoured more and more strongly to yield to.

But during the Christmas holiday the longing had developed an ache, which gave it a new power. The ache of an incredible loneliness, which seemed to come down suddenly out of nowhere. And always when the ache was strongest, it seemed to sound insistently in her ears and in her soul just one sentence: "Mavourneen, mavourneen, bears have understanding when they love as I love you..."

And with the sentence came other thoughts. Thoughts that thrilled and frightened her both at once, setting her heart beating to a strange new measure. It was a measure she had experienced for the first time that afternoon in his den, when all the others were paired off, and they two left alone together. When, sitting quietly at his fireside, she had felt as if her little world were entirely changed, and she left in a position that required much readjusting all round. And it was so difficult to readjust herself. With Eileen and Jack married and living at The Ghan House, and her mother with them, what was to be her place in the general scheme? Was there, indeed, nothing for her but that independent spirit, and the dispensary, and this fighting against an ache that threatened to overpower her heart? And then would come the thought, suppose she gave up fighting?... suppose... suppose... But there Paddy usually stopped short—a strange new world she was shyly afraid of lay beyond that word, and the fanatical spirit was promptly re-enforced.

Of course she could not give up fighting. It was monstrous to think it; and for a little while the old flash would be in her eyes, and the old resolute set of the lips.

And then, at the first "letting go," back would come the same engrossing memory: "Mavourneen, mavourneen, bears have understanding when they love as I love you."

Ah, what understanding he had, what wild allurement!

Fancy played with her then, laughing at the fanatic, snapping light fingers at the warrior-spirit. "Supposing you were to let yourself go," said Fancy, "and to swim out into the comforting warmth of that understanding, shutting away the loneliness with it, and letting all the readjusting solve itself into just sitting by a fireside that was all your own for ever...!"

How the ache and the longing grew when Fancy triumphed, how alluringly the voice sounded.

So it came to a day when Paddy the Fearless asked herself a question, and left it unanswered because she was afraid. But though she spoke no reply, perhaps it was given just as poignantly in a bright head buried in a pillow, and a little reluctant whisper, breathed to the feathers: "Oh, Lawrence, I can't help it. I want you. I want you."

And the next afternoon, that sombre February day, she stood in the window still remembering, still vainly wrestling and puzzling, when a taxi drew up at the door, and Gwen stepped out.

"Wait," she said to the driver and ran up the steps with a haste that was somewhat startling.

Paddy went out into the hall and opened the door herself, and immediately Gwen exclaimed: "Oh, I'm so glad you're in, Paddy. Lawrence has been hurt in a motor smash. He wants to see you badly, and I said I would take you. Be quick, won't you? I don't like leaving him. He is in great pain, and one never knows..."

Chapter Forty Five.

The Invalid.

Paddy hesitated a moment, looking straight into Gwen's eyes, almost with a challenge.

"How much is he hurt?"

"I don't know. It happened three days ago, and he was taken to a hospital, but father had him brought in an ambulance to our house to-day. Surely you are not going to refuse to come...!"

"No," said Paddy slowly, "I am coming;" but her instinct told her he would not have been moved if he had been very badly hurt, and she believed that Gwen knew it. Still, when she saw him, her heart smote her indefinably; for Lawrence lying on a sofa with his arm in a splint, and a white, exhausted air of endurance, was something she could not steel herself against. She wished vaguely that Gwen had not left them alone so quickly, and moved away a little further, uncertain of herself.

"I'm not much hurt," he told her carelessly, though even as he spoke she saw that a spasm of sharp pain made him clench his hands and teeth. "But I expect I'm in for a bad time with my arm, and may have to have it off in the end. Serves me right, I suppose." Then he added: "I don't want the mater to know anything about it yet. She would only worry herself ill. How are you? It was nice of you to come." He was looking at her as if he could read her soul, and Paddy felt her colour rising, and was unable to meet his eyes. She longed suddenly to go to him in his pain-wrung helplessness and touch his bandaged arm, and the fear that she would show it held her silent and constrained and aloof. With his quick intuition Lawrence noted everything.

"Why, I believe you're quite sorry about this stupid smash!" with a little callous laugh; "sorry in spite of yourself, eh, Paddy?" She did not answer, feeling vaguely hurt, and he ran on: "You're allowed to pity me, then, and to come and see me out of charity as the poor invalid! Well, I don't know that there's anything in the world I hate more than charity, but I seem to be with the beggars every time now, and called upon to be thankful for anything I can get."

"You know it is not charity," she blurted out. "It is unkind of you to say so. I hate to see you lying there, looking so ill. I—I—" She stopped short suddenly—pitfalls lay ahead that might engulf her.

"Let it be charity if it brings you nearer. I can't afford pride any longer. Charity should bring you close beside my couch of suffering, laying your hand on my fevered brow, and all that stuff. You are not a very good district visitor, Paddy." There was a taunt in his voice, and he saw that he was hurting her more and more, and because in some way it gave him pleasure, he drove the barbs in. "Don't look so resentful. Do you feel you've been trapped here under false pretences? Did Gwen tell you I was dying or something? How wicked of her! And now you find I've only a smashed-up arm, and all that beautiful Christian spirit of pity is like to be wasted on an unworthy object. Well, the arm hurts pretty badly, if that is any help to you. They give me morphia now and then, but I wouldn't have it to-day."

But that was a little too much, and a flash of the old Paddy came back. "You have no right to speak to me like this," she declared hotly; "it is ungenerous of you. I have done nothing to deserve it. Gwen told me that you were hurt, and that you wanted me; that was all."

"And haven't I wanted you for weeks and months!... Yet you only ran away. Paddy, why did you run away from Omeath! It wasn't quite fair. You made me behave like a brute; and to mother. I'm expiating it in my mind every hour, but, thank heaven, a mother like mine always understands. I wrote afterward and told her how it happened. I'd have gone across if I hadn't had this smash." His voice changed suddenly, as with a quick, keen expression he leaned toward her and asked: "Paddy, why did you run away?... Why do you treat me like this, *when you love me?*"

Again the tell-tale colour flooded her face, and she could not meet his eyes; but pulling herself together quickly, she answered in a voice that had borrowed some of the taunt from his: "I thought you said it was just charity."

He smiled as if the taunt pleased him. "It is certainly about the same temperature just now. But there, I won't tease you any more. You were a dear thing to come. I'll get you a cozy, inviting chair if I can, then perhaps you'll stay." He attempted to rise, but the effort brought on a sharp spasm that turned him faint, and Paddy sprang forward.

"Oh, you mustn't move, you mustn't move," she cried. "Why did you try to?... Can I get you anything...!"

His rigid lips broke into the ghost of a smile, and a great tenderness came into his eyes. "Sit where I can see you, mavourneen; it is all the healing I need."

Paddy pulled up a footstool, and sat beside him, and quietly began to run her fingers with a light touch up and down his uninjured arm. She had seen his mother do it, and knew he found it soothing. Thus for some time neither spoke, and gradually the drawn, blue look left his face. At last, from gazing into the fire, she looked up suddenly into his face, and found he was watching her intently.

"Mavourneen," he said very quietly, "I suspected that you were beginning to care at Christmas. I know it now. What are you going to do about it?"

She hid her face against his hand, and did not reply.

"What is your own idea, anyway?" he asked, in a winsome, humorous voice.

"Oh, if you could only run away with me by force," she murmured intensely. "If only I needn't decide at all. I'm just a lump of obstinacy, and I don't want to climb down and meekly give in; don't you see how I hate that part of it? You could always say 'I told you so,'" and she smiled a little.

"Bravo, Patricia! I like that spirit in you. Curse it all, a few hundred years ago, I'd just have brought along my men-at-arms and captured you. What good old days they must have been. And here we are hemmed in all round by barriers, and I haven't even got a couple of good arms to drag you onto my horse. But anyhow, the gods are evidently relenting, so I'll take heart and think out a plan." He saw her glance at the clock.

"Must you go now? Are the beastly medicine bottles squirming on the shelf? Well, I won't keep you. It isn't good enough with a crocked-up arm. In fact, it isn't good at all; it's merely maddening. You see, I want to kiss you, Paddy, and I dare say if I asked very appealingly and pathetically, you would lean over and give me a sort of benevolent, motherly salute." He gave a low laugh with a note of masterfulness in it. "But I'll have none of it. To dream as I have dreamed, and then begin with a mild caress! *Never*. I forbid you to come near me again until I'm on my feet with, at any rate, one strong arm. Then I'll show you. I had always a weakness for the best."

She stood up, a little non-plussed and uncertain, but he only smiled into her eyes with something of the old mocking light.

"Good-by, mavourneen, I'll let you know when you must come again. I've had enough healing for a little—and I'm sure the bottles are clamouring."

"Good-by," she answered, and went slowly out of the room.

But as she trundled back to Shepherd's Bush on a motor 'bus, she saw no greyness and shabbiness and desolation any more—saw nothing at all—only knew that in her heart there was a sort of shy, fierce, bewildering gladness.

Chapter Forty Six.

The Solution.

A week passed, and no message of any sort reached Paddy, so that, finally, in desperation she rang up Gwen on the telephone to ask for news. Gwen's voice sounded a little cold and constrained, and Paddy learned nothing beyond the fact that Lawrence was progressing very well. Gwen said that she would tell him Paddy had inquired, but he was sleeping now.

Paddy hung up the receiver, feeling as if a weight had come down upon her. What did it mean? Evidently he had no message for her, and Gwen no longer dreamt of coming to fetch her. She went out for a walk, and found herself in a 'bus going toward Gwen's home. She walked down Grosvenor Place, and saw Gwen come out, looking very gay and lovely with her giant, and the two of them sped away together in a motor. So Lawrence was alone. Yet she could not go to him. The situation seemed impossible, almost absurd. Surely he had not suddenly ceased to want her! Yet not for the world would she cross the road and present herself unasked. So there was nothing for it but to go back to the bottles and prescriptions, and to the making of that endless trousseau for Eileen. They—Eileen and her mother—had heard about Lawrence's accident at last, and told her of it as a piece of news. It seemed Mrs Blake had come over, and was established at Gwen's home with him. So, of course, he did not particularly want her now. When the pain was bad, his mother would soothe him with that running touch; and when he felt better, Gwen was there to make him laugh. She told herself she did not mind. That fortunately she had known him too well to let herself go in any real sense. He was just fickle as ever, that was all.

Nevertheless, a yet duller ache began to be her portion. An ache that was akin to sheer misery. The future began to frighten her a little. Was it possible the making up of medicines was to be her portion indefinitely? Perhaps for many more of the glad, joyous, youthful years now speeding by. One day a letter came from Ted Masterman, and when Paddy had read it, she stood long and silently gazing at the blank, uninteresting windows opposite. He was prospering now, and seemed full of content with his surroundings. Too full of content. In her present mood Paddy resented it. She resented it a little because she knew he possessed those traits which make for happiness which Lawrence lacked. If there had been no Lawrence, she might have grown to care for Ted. As it was, she could not care for either. At least, so she told herself, waiting day after day for the message which did not come. Sometimes she told herself she had disappointed him in some way, and he had decided to withdraw while he could. Another time, she remembered what he had said about the kiss, and her cheeks burned, and her eyes fell. Was it possible he was really waiting until he could stand with ease, and was himself again! And if so...

She wondered a little whether she would have the courage to go, supposing the message came in the end. Something in her seemed to have lost confidence. She was the same—yet different. She wanted again to run away, only now she also wanted still more to stay. She read Ted Masterman's letter again, and told herself he was a man to make any woman happy, and that if she said the word, he would come back at once, whereas Lawrence...

The uncertainty made her moody and restless, and her mother and Eileen looked at her a little perplexedly. Eileen asked her about the letter from Ted, but she only said he was prosperous and happy. "Is he coming home?" Eileen suggested, and she answered: "Not that I know of," in a way that had a final ring. Mrs Blake called one day, and told them Lawrence had made a remarkable recovery, and she was returning to Ireland at once. "Of course his arm will be practically useless for some time," she said, "but it will not have to come off. So fortunate it was his left, and not his right. I want him to come back with me, but he won't just at present. He insists he has some business to attend to in town." She laughed a little. She seemed wonderfully happy about him. Evidently, as ever, the very memory of that black afternoon had been wiped out by his later charm. Paddy thought about it lingeringly. How strong he was when he chose. How he compelled love and forgiveness if it pleased him to do so. Was it possible, she asked again, that he only wanted to break her will, and bend her as he bent all others?

The ache grew, and with it a manufactured anger against him. Surely he might have spared her. What did it profit him to make other men seem tame and colourless in her life?

It was March before the message came. Eileen's trousseau was finished and wedding day fixed, and Paddy had a growing dread of what lay ahead. Of course she was to be chief bridesmaid, and all the countryside would be there—and among them, Lawrence.

How was she to meet him on that day, after the manner of their parting? See perhaps the mocking light in his eyes, and hear his veiled taunts. But the message dropped like a shaft from the skies, suddenly, unpreparedly, and for the moment dispelled all else. It came in a note from Gwen. "Lawrence is taking motor drives every day now, but hates going alone. He wants you to go to-morrow morning, as I have many engagements. He will call for you at the surgery at half-past eleven. Do be a dear about it. I know you will—and have arranged accordingly."

There was not much sleep for Paddy that night—mostly a troubled, tossing restlessness, and in the morning she looked eagerly at the weather. It was a lovely early spring day, when the little birds were chirping lustily, and the little buds swelling to bursting point.

And something about Lawrence seemed to match them, when at last he came. A veiled light in his eyes, as of some hidden joy swelling to bursting point. A light gaiety of manner. He walked into the dispensary, and laughed at the bottles, telling her it was the untidiest dispensary in London, and he was quite sure all her prescriptions included an appalling supply of microbes. She tried to laugh lightly back, but she could not meet his eyes. Something in his manner— something quite new—unnerved her. He seemed perfectly well again, except for the slung arm, and when she inquired after that, he only said: "Oh, it will soon be equal to its work, and, anyhow, the other is strong enough now for two." And then he looked into her eyes and laughed a humorous, teasing, tender little laugh, adding: "Come along. I've an appointment I mustn't miss."

She was conscious of a sudden dampening. Then he was going to see some one else. Her company was not sufficient in itself. He said something to the chauffeur, and they sped away, out through Acton and Ealing into the country, and made a wide circuit, and came back to Richmond.

At half-past twelve they drew up before a quaint old-fashioned church, and the chauffeur got out to open the door.

"Is your appointment at a church?" Paddy asked, looking amused. "I hope you won't be long, because we lunch at one."

"Come in with me," he said; "I want to show you a curious old chained Bible here. One of the oldest known."

She alighted, still looking amused, and followed him through the big old door.

On the threshold he was greeted by the sexton with the astonishing words: "Mr Elkins has just come, sir. He is in the vestry;" and almost at the same moment a clergyman appeared in the chancel.

Lawrence turned and looked into Paddy's eyes—and immediately she understood.

For a breathless moment neither spoke, and she seemed to sway a little with the suddenness of it. The sexton moved away and they stood together alone, but Paddy, was still speechless. Then Lawrence's hand closed firmly over hers with a clasp that seemed to claim her for all eternity. "It was the best way I could think of, mavourneen," he said; then he added humorously: "but it took me all my time to get the special licence necessary."

She tried to speak, but no words would frame themselves, and her lips twisted queerly.

"Mavourneen, are you ready?... The one strong arm is growing impatient." It was the old voice of ineffable tenderness, and it swept her unresistingly into his keeping.

A mistiness in her eyes blotted out everything for a moment, and then she turned to him with a sudden uplifting of her head and squaring of her shoulders that gave him great joy in seeing the old dauntless Paddy equal to the moment.

"Yes," she said simply, "I'm quite ready."

Finis.

Lightning Source UK Ltd.
Milton Keynes UK
UKHW051158090119
335233UK00010B/619/P